LifeWay
LEGACY

LifeWay
LEGACY

*A Personal History of LifeWay Christian Resources and
the Sunday School Board of the Southern Baptist Convention*

JAMES T. DRAPER JR.

WITH JOHN PERRY

PUBLISHING GROUP

NASHVILLE, TENNESSEE

Ten-digit ISBN: 0-8054-3170-5

Thirteen-digit ISBN: 978-0-8054-3170-4

Published by B&H Publishing Group,

Nashville, Tennessee

Dewey Decimal Classification: 286

Subject Heading: LIFEWAY CHRISTIAN
RESOURCES—HISTORY \ BAPTIST SUNDAY SCHOOL
BOARD—HISTORY \ PUBLISHERS—HISTORY

1 2 3 4 5 6 7 8 9 10   10 09 08 07 06

Dedication

To the tireless, dedicated, and inspired employees and leaders who for over 115 years have served the Sunday School Board and LifeWay Christian Resources with integrity and vision.

Acknowledgments

This is a very big book covering a very big subject, and I could never have completed the task of writing it without help from some very patient, skilled, and knowledgeable people.

Thanks to Bill Sumners, director of the Southern Baptist Historical Library and Archives, and to the team at the E. C. Dargan Research Library: Pat Brown, library director; Steve Gateley, research librarian; and Miriam Evans, circulation technical librarian. Steve was particularly helpful in running down photos for me.

At B&H Publishing Group the project was under the expert eyes of Ken Stephens, president of B&H and a long-serving member of the LifeWay Executive Committee; David Shepherd, senior vice president and publisher;

Len Goss, senior acquisitions editor; and Kim Overcash, managing editor. It was Len who kept things moving along and encouraged us during the times when finishing this book seemed like a very tall order.

My past conversations with Dr. James Sullivan have been a great source of information and inspiration to this work. I only wish he could have lived to see its completion. I also appreciate the letter and other information from my friend Bill Anderson and the interview granted by Lloyd Elder.

I'm grateful as well to P. E. Burroughs, Robert A. Baker, and Leon McBeth for their previous research and writing on the history of LifeWay, and to John Perry for his collaboration in the present.

Thanks also to the thousands of men and women, some of whose names, innovations, and sacrifices we'll never know, who have built and sustained LifeWay through the years, and whose lives form the tapestry of this story. God has done great things through them; above all let us give thanks to Him for the *LifeWay Legacy.*

Table of Contents

Foreword

My first day on the job at LifeWay Christian Resources was October 17, 2005. I actually found my office a day earlier so I wouldn't get lost on my first day on the job. I had been warned about the early-to-rise work ethic of LifeWay employees, especially the president and CEO, Jimmy Draper. I had to match my predecessor's hours, so I arrived at 6:30 a.m. on the seventeenth. But Dr. Draper was already at work in his office.

With greater determination for my second day of work, I arrived at 6:00 a.m. but, once again, Dr. Draper was working hard in his office upon my arrival.

I gave up.

I now come in between 8:00 and 8:30 a.m. without apology.

Who is that man with the early-to-rise work ethic? Who is that person who has been called "the statesman of the Southern Baptist Convention"? Who exactly is Dr. James T. Draper Jr.?

I would learn much about this man over the next one hundred days.

The Board of Trustees of LifeWay approved a plan for the new president-elect to overlap with Dr. Draper from October 17, 2005, to January 31, 2006. Though I had my original misgivings about two presidents in one organization, I quickly learned that Jimmy Draper was one of the most gracious and Christlike men I have ever known. I could write my own book about what I learned from him, but, for the sake of brevity, let me share just a few thoughts.

Jimmy Draper is a man who loves people. He writes letters and e-mails of encouragement. He never meets a stranger. He is kind. "Always be kind to people," he once told me, "because everyone has problems."

Dr. Draper is a man of integrity. Under his leadership, LifeWay Christian Resources has become one of the most respected and ethical companies in America. I am proud to be the president of LifeWay because of the high standards Jimmy Draper set for the company and for all the employees.

You will soon discover as you read this book that Dr. James T. Draper Jr. loves LifeWay. While I learned much from this man, it was that one truth that was clear in all of his conversations. He simply loves LifeWay.

From the early pages of this book that deal with the visionary leadership of LifeWay's founder, James Marion Frost, to the closing pages that poignantly describe Dr. Draper's departure and my arrival, you will read more than just a history of one of the world's largest Christian resource providers. Indeed, you will read this history from the perspective of one who sat in the CEO chair, who prayed for this company, who poured out his life for LifeWay, and who studied its history with a passionate eye for detail and understanding. While objectivity has not been lost, you will still read this book from a man who loves this ministry.

I have been blessed to serve by James T. Draper Jr. for one hundred days. I am still blessed to receive his calls and e-mails of encouragement. And I am blessed to read this incredible book of the miracle called LifeWay Christian Resources. I can only pray that I will be as faithful to this task as the one who went before me.

—Thom S. Rainer
President and CEO
LifeWay Christian Resources

CHAPTER 1

The Road
to Birmingham

Among the row of respectable houses up and down Libby Hill on Twenty-ninth Street, a single window shown with light. It was the deepest, coldest hour of the evening, well past midnight but before the weak midwinter sun showed any sign of returning to the skies over Richmond. Even the milkman would scarcely be awake at this hour, much less one of the city folk living in these sturdy Victorian homes not far from the Virginia capitol. Yet through a curtain at number 5, the soft glow of electric light—still a novelty anywhere outside the city—diffused out onto the frozen lawn and the frozen street beyond.

Number 5 had seen more than its share of nighttime vigils and early morning rousings over the years. It was the parsonage of Leigh Street Baptist Church and as such had an ample sampling of both great joys and great sorrows as successive pastors there shared in the blessings and tribulations of their flocks. This predawn light, though, didn't represent a baby on the way, a death watch, a wounded marriage, a troubled heart, or any of the other responsibilities that often kept the Leigh Street pastor out of his warm bed on one of the chilliest nights of the year.

This time the pastor was all alone. And it wasn't responsibility that had stirred him from his bed; it was excitement. He'd had a matter on his mind for months, an issue he considered critical to the continued growth and success of his Southern Baptist denomination. Now he had awakened suddenly with a plan of action fully formed and rushed downstairs through the dark and quiet house to his study to write it down while it was still fresh. It was entirely original, as far as he knew, and came so suddenly and completely that there was no doubt in his mind he was divinely inspired. As he recalled that night years later, "God touched me, and I thought of it."

James Marion Frost was a Kentuckian, a graduate of Georgetown College in Lexington who pastored at First Baptist Church in Selma, Alabama, before his call to the pulpit in Richmond. He had surrendered to preach when he was eighteen, following his father into the ministry. Four years later he was ordained and took his first pulpit at First Baptist

Church, Maysville, Kentucky. Serving pastorates in Lexington, Kentucky, then in Staunton, Virginia, and Selma before coming to Richmond, he saw what a valuable tool Sunday school could be in building Southern Baptist churches. But building a Sunday school program in the denomination was an uphill climb.

What tradition of support there was for Sunday school was somewhat offset by the fact that most churches had no convenient place for Sunday school to meet, and most were rural congregations that met only once or twice a month anyway. Plenty of literature was available for Sunday school programs, but little of it was written from a Southern Baptist point of view. There had been discussions about setting up a denominational organization of some sort to promote Sunday schools and supply them with Southern Baptist lessons; Frost was convinced that expanding the Sunday school program was an essential step in strengthening the church. But there were a host of challenges to expansion—operational, political, and financial—that Frost and other like-minded Southern Baptist leaders had discussed for nearly five years. They'd assigned the limited Sunday school publications work there was to an existing group with some success, but Frost believed there was a better solution.

Now that solution had roused him in the middle of the night and sent him to his desk. He began writing by lamplight and wrote straight on through sunrise. Finishing his first draft, he dressed and set out for his study at Leigh Street.

Within a few days Frost returned to his inspired draft and refined it as an article for the *Religious Herald*. The handful of colleagues and church leaders he showed it to universally praised his proposal and encouraged him to present it to the denomination at large.

He stated his intentions for the next meeting of the Southern Baptist Convention, which would be that spring in Fort Worth: "It is my purpose to offer at the next Convention the following resolutions, and request their reference to a special committee: 1. *Resolved*: That to the Boards already existing we add another to be elected at this session of the Convention, and to be called the Board of Publication of the Southern Baptist Convention."

Moving on to the heart of his proposal, Frost explained:

> The Sunday school lies at the base of all mission-
> ary enterprises—indeed, is almost the basis of the
> future church at home and abroad. Its opportunities
> and possibilities are simply immense. But in the min-
> utes of the last Convention [in Memphis, 1889], this
> department of Christian endeavor is most conspicu-
> ous by its absence—even in the statistical tables. It
> is of sufficient importance to deserve, and has grown
> to sufficient magnitude to require, a separate
> management—a Board of Managers charged with
> supplying proper literature, and by wise methods
> increasing the number and power of Sunday schools,

and bringing them in contact with the Convention by
annual reports. . . .

There are several lines along which a Publication
Board can operate for the greater development of
even the best Sunday schools, and others in propor-
tion. The supplying of periodical literature as helps,
while of immense importance, is only one feature of
the work, only one factor of the plan. There are other
things to be done, all looking to the advancement
of the Sunday school interests. The present and the
future demand a new agency charged with this
special enterprise.

After explaining his proposal in detail, he concluded,
"I therefore offer these resolutions with profound conviction
in the rightfulness and wisdom of the measure as meeting a
radical necessity and solving a severe problem." He signed his
work and wrote the date: February 10, 1890. It was his forty-
first birthday. Seventeen days later the *Religious Herald* ran
the article on page 1, and an issue that had simmered hot and
cold for years once more became a prime topic of conversation and conjecture for Baptists throughout the South.

The matter that disturbed J. M. Frost in his sleep that
cold January night was one Baptists had prayed, stewed, pon-
dered, and argued about in its current form since the 1885
Convention meeting in Augusta, Georgia. That year Dr. I. T.
Tichenor, who had reenergized the Home Mission Board

following its move from Marion to Atlanta, proposed that the Board publish a series of Sunday school helps, "provided no indebtedness should be incurred," in order to develop new products and take control of existing ones.

The next year the Convention, meeting in Montgomery, Alabama, agreed to the proposal and signed a five-year contract with an Atlanta printer to supply some popular materials including *Kind Words*, a profitable and widely circulated Sunday school publication in print since 1866. "However," as J. M. Frost later recalled, "the new movement met with prompt, vigorous, and increasing opposition. Honored men among us thought it unnecessary, unwise, and from the first doomed to failure."

To be frank, they also feared crossing swords with the American Baptist Publication Society, which had supplied the bulk of Southern Baptist printed materials for two generations. Established in Washington, DC, as the Baptist General Tract Society in 1824, the organization moved to Philadelphia two years later, becoming the American Baptist Publication and Sunday School Society in 1840. In 1844 the Sunday school reference was dropped, though the group's purpose remained "to publish such books as are needed by the Baptist Denomination, and to promote Sunday-schools by such measures as experience may prove expedient."

When it first took over the Sunday school program in 1873, the Home Mission Board evidently anticipated an ambitious program of publishing. But by the next year the

Convention redefined that group's responsibilities, instructing it "not to be concerned with Sunday school promotion." That directive preserved the American Baptist Publication Society's role as principal supplier to Baptists both North and South. J. M. Frost observed that the Society,

> with its immense assets and resources, was in the
> field, and had many earnest friends in the South;
> it was offering credible periodicals and employ-
> ing many Southern writers; it had large patronage
> among our churches, and gathered large harvests in
> return from its business; it did no little benevolent
> work among our people, and came to hold a high and
> strong place with many. From this vantage ground
> which can hardly be stated too strongly, the Society
> through its friends, and by all the forces at its com-
> mand, withstood the Home Board movement, even
> claimed to have pre-empted the field and challenged
> the right of the Convention to publish Sunday school
> periodicals.

Through the latter half of the 1880s, Frost kept his opinions to himself, making no public statements and in fact publishing a tract with the Society. But every year the matter came up during the Convention meeting, and every year the rhetoric grew stronger, the lines more sharply drawn. One side believed Southern Baptists should control the content and reap the financial rewards of their printed material while the other believed a good system was already in place with the American Baptists in Philadelphia and getting into the book business would only distract Southern Baptists from their evangelical, missionary, and teaching work.

This division among brethren, plus the American Society's swift and powerful criticism of the Home Mission Board's new mandate, produced what Frost called "almost a war on the Home Mission Board in every department of its work." By the 1889 Convention in Memphis, this "momentous issue" had become to Frost almost "a threatening crisis in the affairs of our people." It was the winter after this contentious meeting that Frost had his inspired dream; and the next spring in Fort Worth, he presented his resolutions as written to the annual gathering. Along with the key resolution to establish a Board of Publication and the enabling legislation, he proposed specifically taking charge of *Kind Words* and related publications and appropriating any future profits "as the Convention may order from time to time."

He also addressed the question of waiting until the contract between the Home Mission Board and their Atlanta printer ended in 1891 before instituting any changes. The new Sunday school board could take over the contract immediately, he said; this step should be taken in 1890 without delay.

Frost cut a distinguished figure on the platform that May morning at the First Baptist Church of Fort Worth. Slender, balding, with a long flowing beard that made him look older than he was—an impression heightened by his somber three-piece suit and detachable collar that were the standard of the day—he was far more a thinker and bridge builder than firebrand. Yet he knew his idea of a Sunday school board was volatile and potentially divisive. En route from Richmond to Fort Worth, he had met his friend Dr. James A. Kirtley in the Louisville railroad station. "I had decided not to go to Fort Worth," Frost remembered Kirtley explaining, " but my wife urged me, saying, 'Brother Jimmie Frost may need you.'" Frost later remarked, "His kindly word was reassuring, but also intensified the feeling of uncertainty as to what the final issue might be—certain and courageous as to my own convictions, but wondering as to the outcome, not knowing what the people would say."

Supporters of the American Baptist Publication Society wasted no time defending their position. As P. E. Burroughs reported in his early history of the Sunday School Board (SSB), *Fifty Fruitful Years*:

> The Publication Society and its friends were especially active, exerting every possible influence to defeat the resolutions which Dr. Frost had announced he would offer at Fort Worth. Extensive advertising space was taken by the Society in the denominational papers. Every paper in the South . . . [with a few exceptions] lined up against the suggestion of a new board. The Baptist papers and apparently

the denominational leaders in general favored the
Publication Society, and it was generally thought that
the Society would win a signal victory in Fort Worth.

In spite of all the evident opposition and the long history of disagreement, no one objected to the resolution when
Frost read it or to his motion that followed proposing his
resolution be referred to "a committee of one from each state
represented in the Convention and that the report of this
committee be made the special order for Monday [May 12]
at ten o'clock." Frost himself was appointed chairman; and
a dozen other men, one from each state in the Convention
as proposed, filled out the number.

Frost soon realized the committee would never agree
on a plan so radical as forming a new board. Some members
agreed with him that a Sunday school board was wise and
prudent; others strongly favored keeping or increasing ties
with the Publication Society, even to the point of restoring
their responsibility for *Kind Words.*

Committee members in favor of the new board had
no particular quarrel with the Society but felt moved to
bring Southern Baptist Sunday school publications directly
under Southern Baptist control. Opponents were more diver-
sified: some pointed to similar efforts that had failed in the
past; others cherished friendships or business relations with
Society employees and applauded the collaboration currently
in place; still others saw that collaboration as one of the last

points of contact and cooperation between Northern and Southern Baptists; and then there were the undecideds, who thought a new board was too big a step to take without further study.

In the end the committee released a majority report suggesting the Convention appoint a standing Sunday school committee of nine to "gather statistical information as to the condition of our Sunday schools, and to see what can be done toward increasing their number and efficiency." Committee members J. B. Gambrell of Mississippi and W. S. Penick of Louisiana submitted a minority report recommending a seven-member committee to consider the question of publications and report back to the Convention next year.

Hearing rumors of a divided committee, attendees packed the First Baptist Church for the report. Gambrell outlined the minority report, then Frost presented the majority conclusion. Dr. J. B. Hawthorne delivered a long and passionate speech supporting the majority recommendation. Contemporary accounts described Hawthorne as "an orator typical of the old South" and compared him favorably with Henry Clay, the Kentucky politician and US presidential candidate famous for his florid, expansive, and entertaining style on the stump. The traditional decorum of the meeting was broken by laughter and applause as Hawthorne made his case. When the vote came, the majority recommendation carried resoundingly by 419 to 176.

Established in Louisville, the Sunday School Committee bought time for both sides of the controversy, preserved the *Kind Words* series as a Convention enterprise, and took over publication of the series from the Home Mission Board, where it had been an operational burden that distracted that group and drained its resources away from other work.

Over the next year the American Baptist Publication Society pressed its case as a capable and proven supplier of publications for the Southern Baptists. P. E. Burroughs describes how during that time the Philadelphia-based society "marshaled its vast resources and exerted the utmost of its power to retain and control the field," while proponents of a distinctively Southern source for Sunday school materials staked their counterclaims with equal passion. As time came for the next annual convention, the Southern Baptists expected a crowd even bigger than at the 1890 gathering.

Clearly no church in Birmingham could handle the event. Chartered as a city scarcely twenty years before, the settlement of one thousand people had grown to more than twenty-six thousand, but no congregation had a building big enough to hold all the messengers coming for the promised showdown on the Sunday school controversy. And so in May 1891, for the first time ever, the Southern Baptists held their annual convention outside a church building. They met in O'Brien's Opera House on First Avenue, a sturdy brick building at the corner of Nineteenth Street, four stories high with stores and a café on the sidewalk level.

The opening session on Friday began with a long day of routine denominational business followed at 8:00 p.m. by a sermon from Carter Helm Jones. Then at last the secretary of the Convention read the long awaited Sunday School Committee report. With no real authority, and with the Southern Baptist publishing contract still between the Home Mission Board and its outside supplier, there hadn't been much the group could do. Their unanimous conclusion was that "the needs of the denomination require either a considerable enlargement of the powers of the committee, or what is much better, the appointment of a Board to whom these great interests can be trusted."

In a replay of the year before, Dr. Frost moved that the report be referred to a special committee of one man from each state represented and that the committee make a recommendation the next Monday. Of the eleven men appointed, Frost (again serving as chairman) and three others had also been on the 1890 special committee. Of these four repeaters, J. B. Gambrell was one of two who had opposed the 1890 majority report.

The committee's first meeting began with a season of fervent prayer for unity and divine guidance. Then the group appointed Frost and Gambrell as a subcommittee to work out the differences among committee members and produce a unified recommendation. Neither man ever divulged details of their daylong session together a block from the opera house in the Florence Hotel. In memoirs written near the end of his life, Dr. Frost recalled: "It was a serious task. We represented opposing sides of the issue, but realizing the mighty moment into which the denomination had come, and what would be the far reach of our action in the settlement of the impending question, we set ourselves to the task with the best that was in us. We both cherish in sacred memory the experiences of those days in working to that end. I make no effort to set on record an account of what went on between us, though it is fresh in memory after all these years."

At the end of a long day, Gambrell proposed that Frost write the report if he himself could write the last paragraph. Frost agreed on the condition that Frost be allowed to add a final sentence. Gambrell in turn gave his approval. The end result followed for the most part Frost's dream-inspired resolutions published in the *Religious Herald* a year earlier strongly supporting establishment of a Sunday school board to publish books and teaching materials specifically for Southern Baptists. Dr. Gambrell's last paragraph called for freedom of choice in selecting publications and fairly considering both the new board and the established Publication Society:

> In conclusion, your committee, in its long and
> earnest consideration of this whole matter in all its
> environments, have been compelled to take account
> of the well-known fact, that there are widely divergent
> views held among us by brethren equally earnest,

consecrated, and devoted to the best interest of the Master's Kingdom. It is therefore, recommended that the fullest freedom of choice be accorded to everyone as to what literature he will use or support, and that no brother be disparaged in the slightest degree on account of what he may do in the exercise of his right as Christ's freeman.

To this appeal Dr. Frost added: "But we would earnestly urge all brethren to give to this Board a fair consideration, and in no case to obstruct it in the great work assigned it by this Convention."

Frost and Gambrell submitted their work to the full committee early Monday morning, where it was approved without changes. Frost then walked the block up Nineteenth Street to O'Brien's to present the report to the Convention. There he found the crowd "packed to suffocation" according to one account. A reporter inside claimed two thousand people were wedged into the theater, sitting and standing in every available aisle and vestibule, with three hundred more jammed onto the stage. Frost found it impossible to penetrate the crush in the doorway and make his way to the platform. He flagged down some passersby on the sidewalk and had them lift him through the window, then wormed his way up front, reaching the president's desk just as he was called as committee chairman to make his report.

He read it to the packed house. When he finished, there was a surreal calm in the room. Messengers and reporters expected a wild debate on the issue; that's why so many of them were there. By tradition, Frost would be first to comment on his committee's proposal, followed by a host of others eager to be heard and go on record regarding this watershed issue. But before he could pull a copy of his prepared remarks out of his coat, someone unexpectedly stepped between him and the convention president, Judge Jonathan Haralson, standing at the lectern unbidden and unrecognized by the chair.

He was a distinguished man in his sixty-fourth year, his elegantly flowing beard and distinctive profile instantly recognized by everyone familiar with denominational history: Dr. John A. Broadus, cofounder and president of the Southern Baptist Theological Seminary and proponent of an independent Sunday school board since before the Civil War. He had no official position in the Convention but was one of the most widely known and respected men in the room. Only he could have taken the platform as he did.

"I have seen for twenty years that we were divided in our preference as to where we should get our Sunday school literature," he began.

> We have not been agreed and we are not going
> to be. And now, if a majority favor a Sunday School
> Board to take in charge our Sunday school literature,
> let it be done. Let us not say that anyone is disloyal to

the Southern Baptist Convention when he buys his literature where he pleases. People have come here feeling that there is to be excitement and a heated debate. I hope they will be disappointed. Orders have been issued for full reports of the discussion. I hope there will be nothing to report. I shall be happy if no hot words are said. If anyone says anything about sectionalism he will regret it and, after he has said it, he will wish that he had not done so.

Never in my life did I so much wish to make a speech, but I will not speak.

What followed was the last thing any of the attendees expected from the jam-packed crowd in the largest room in town: complete silence. In Frost's words, Broadus had "put a lid on a volcano," doing "what few men do once, but perhaps no man would try a second time" in "a sublime moment of heroism and faith. It was masterful in the noblest sense."

From the crowd came the call, "Question!" taken up and repeated. They were prepared to call the question and vote on the committee report with no debate at all. President Haralson called for the vote. Of the many hundreds who responded, thirteen voted no. Simultaneously relieved and overcome, Dr. Broadus slumped back in his chair, crying unashamed.

J. H. Farmer, a Canadian professor visiting the proceedings, captured the moment: "Every word throbbed with emotion; it was a brief but passionate appeal for peace. The great throng bowed to his will. Not another word was spoken; the report was adopted in silence. And even as I write the tears come unbidden as I think of the old veteran sitting there, his head buried in his hands, and his whole frame heaving with emotion, which, if I mistake not, found relief in sobs."

Dr. Gambrell, Frost's former foe and current fellow sub-committeeman, proposed Frost as the corresponding secretary of the new board. The convention heartily agreed; but before they could vote, Frost declined the position, explaining that he had "an old-fashioned call to preach the gospel. I believe before the Lord my place is in the pulpit."

At Frost's suggestion the new organization would be headquartered in Nashville, the most important printing center in the South. Forty men were appointed to the Board by the 1891 Convention, including W. R. L. Smith as president, who was pastor of Nashville's First Baptist Church. The position of corresponding secretary was left open for the time being.

The first meeting of the Baptist Sunday School Board (SSB) took place at 8:00 p.m., Tuesday, May 26, 1891, in the pastor's study of the First Baptist Church on Broadway in Nashville. After years of debate and discord, the Southern Baptists finally had a chance to control their own publications for their own theological and financial benefit. This night marked a new era in the growth, development, and maturity of the denomination, a chance to begin speaking with a distinctively Southern voice. It was a night that Dr. Broadus and others had waited a generation for.

But it was a night of disappointment. Of the forty men summoned to the meeting, only ten came. Dr. Lansing Burrows of Augusta was elected corresponding secretary at a salary of $2,500 a year; he turned it down as soon as he got the news. After the years of struggle and the promise of Birmingham, this inaugural meeting seemed to signal rough going ahead. It was only the latest in a long series of challenges going back almost to the turn of the century.

CHAPTER 2

In the Beginning

The first Baptist congregation in the American South opened its doors in Charleston, South Carolina, in May 1696. Actually two different churches—one from Kittery, Maine, and the other from Boston—had joined together and moved to Charleston where the city leaders promoted religious tolerance in order to attract new residents. There was a financial incentive too: some prominent members of the Kittery church were shipbuilders drawn to the cheap and plentiful land and timber in a place where they wouldn't encounter hostile Indians.

Ancestors of these New England congregations had come originally from England and Holland. Most historians agree that the world's first recognizably Baptist church was founded by John Smyth in Amsterdam in 1609. Smyth was ordained an Anglican priest after completing his studies at Cambridge but believed the Church of England had stopped short of the full separation and purification from Catholicism he and others thought it should achieve. He became a Puritan and then later a Separatist. Attracted to the Netherlands by a promise of religious freedom (very rare in seventeenth-century Europe), freedom of the press, and a tradition of public education, Smyth and his followers moved there around the beginning of 1608.

The same year Smyth published *The Differences of the Churches of the Separation*, explaining his view that Christian doctrine is revealed only by Scripture, "and not any church, council, prince, or potentate, nor any mortal man whatsoever," and that the ability to understand and interpret Scripture was bestowed upon a priesthood of believers, "given to all and every particular person that fear and obey God, of what degree soever they be." These statements of faith held early seeds of Baptist denominational beliefs. At the same time they laid the groundwork for the fractures and splits that would recur throughout Baptist history. With no official hierarchy or codified expression of doctrine, all that held the church together was the shared spiritual interests and divine leadings of a host of individual congregations, members, and consciences.

Several foundational issues further divided the Separatists from other early Protestant faiths and sometimes from each other. One was the position of Dutch theologian Jacobus

Arminius that anyone could make the decision to accept Christ: a belief in general atonement as opposed to John Calvin's position that only the elect would be saved. Another issue was establishing a congregational form of church leadership rather than a body of bishops, elders, or some other type of ordained hierarchy. A third point was Smyth's belief, after further study, that only believers should be baptized. As church historian Jesse C. Fletcher observed, "A church, therefore, was to be formed not by covenant but by baptism." Smyth baptized himself, for which some people harshly criticized him later. In his book *The Southern Baptist Convention*, Fletcher adds, "Consensus thinking among historians points to this baptism by pouring or affusion." Smyth likely baptized his followers the same way.

Churches holding Smyth's theology came to be called General Baptists; among numerous other types were the Particular Baptists, also established in Holland and England. Founded by an Anglican clergyman named Henry Jacob who was at Oxford while John Smyth was at Cambridge, Particular Baptists held onto Calvinist theology and practiced immersion baptism, which they got from a group of Dutch Mennonites called Collegiants. While General Baptists stood fast with Arminius, they soon switched to baptism by immersion as well.

The first association of Baptist churches in America was formed among five Philadelphia-area churches in 1707 for the purpose of consulting with each other and supporting missionaries. The group's tendency toward the Particular Baptist model became clear a generation later in 1742 when they issued a confession of faith generally following the Second London Confession endorsed by the first national council of Particular Baptists in London in 1677.

Baptist congregations grew in size and number throughout the colonial period, but the Great Awakening of the mid-1700s brought growth in the denomination to a new level. It also caused another split, this time between the older, pre-Awakening churches organized along the Philadelphia model and Separate or "New Light" churches organized amid the religious fervor of the times. The Separate churches were originally offshoots of Congregational groups; when their evangelical approach met opposition from church leaders, they became Separate Baptists. As evangelist George Whitefield observed, his chicks had become ducks.

Moving from Warminster, Pennsylvania, to Charleston in 1749 near the height of the Great Awakening, a young clergyman named Oliver Hart accepted a pastorate there and founded the Charleston Baptist Association based on the Philadelphia model. In 1767 the Charleston Baptists adopted a confession of faith also in the Philadelphia association style. Hart was twenty-six at the time he took the pulpit and remained for thirty years, at which time he fled for his life because his support of American independence from Great Britain angered the local authorities. He later resumed his ministry in New Jersey.

In 1787 another product of the Great Awakening assumed the pulpit in Charleston. Richard Furman knew both the Philadelphia and Separate Baptist traditions and, according to Fletcher, "would become the spiritual father of the Southern Baptist Convention" and "the ardent advocate for an educated ministry."

Because they were so wary of church hierarchy and formal professions of faith, Baptist communities tended to develop more in isolation than other Protestant groups, especially in colonial America with its sparse population and vast tracts of wilderness. The one common interest that did pull them together was missionary support.

William Carey, a cobbler by trade, was baptized in Kettering, Maine, in 1783. Both Carey and his pastor, Andrew Fuller, believed that Christians had a responsibility to share their faith with people everywhere. Carey kept a map on the wall in front of his cobbler's bench to remind him constantly of the need, and reading *The Voyages of Captain Cook* further whetted his appetite to reach out to the world in the name of Christ.

Carey took up preaching along with making shoes, and in 1792 wrote a pamphlet titled "An Enquiry into the Obligations of Christians to Use Means for the Conversion of the Heathen" promoting overseas missionary work. For years his fellow clergymen opposed and even belittled his idea, but with his tract in print, Carey gained a following. He told Andrew Fuller he'd go into the field if Fuller could provide the means: he would "go down if Fuller would hold the rope."

Out of their efforts came the English Particular Baptist Society for the Propagation of the Gospel among the Heathen, soon known as the Baptist Missionary Society. A year later Carey and his wife sailed for India where Dorothy Carey soon died, but William Carey spent forty years in ministry.

During the Second Great Awakening, Adoniram Judson and Luther Rice, leaders of a group of Congregationalist students, became convicted, according to Fletcher, "that they shouldbemissionariesandjoinCareyinIndia."Congregationalists formed the American Board of Commissioners for Foreign Missions in order to support them.

Judson and Rice, along with Judson's wife, Ann, soon converted from Congregational to Baptist, had Carey baptize them by immersion in India, and wrote to their American supporters about their change of heart. Luther Rice returned to America to try to drum up other support, where he received some of his greatest encouragement from Richard Furman in Charleston and Furman's disciple W. B. Johnson in Savannah, Georgia.

It was evidently Johnson who organized the first national organization of Baptists with any staying power. As early as 1771 Philadelphia Baptists had tried to start a nationwide association to support missionary outreach after a pastor named Morgan Edwards declared such an organization would introduce "into the visible church what are called joints and bands whereby the whole body is knit together and compacted for increase by that which every part supplieth." In 1776 a Virginia group called the Continental Association met in support of the same goal. But neither of these produced any lasting effect. It was the widely recognized need to fund missionary activity that finally overcame the Baptists' natural aversion to associational connections.

In *The Baptist Annual Register* of 1800, the Philadelphia Association published the following notice:

Apprehensive of the advantages likely to result from a GENERAL CONFERENCE composed of one member, or more, from each Association, to be held every *one, two,* or *three* years, as might seem most subservient to the general interests of Christ's kingdom, this Association, in 1799, respectfully invited the different Associations in the United States to favor them with their views on the subject. At this meeting (that is, 1800), having received approving resolutions from three of their sister Associations, they recommended that next year a committee be appointed to digest a plan, which may tend to accelerate this *beneficial design.*

This Association think also, that it would be advisable to invite the general committee of Virginia, and different associations on the Continent, to unite with their own body, in forming a Missionary Society, and for employing Missionaries among the natives on the American Continent.

It took more than a dozen long years to convert this "beneficial design" into action. Boston Baptists formed a local society to fund Rice's organizational work in America and sustain Judson's outreach in India. Rice gathered such enthusiastic support in Massachusetts, Rhode Island, and other Northern states that the Pennsylvania Association sent him on a journey south to reach more churches there.

Despite endorsing this nationwide tour, Dr. Daniel Sharp, the pastor who started the missionary society in Boston, never saw the Southern contributors as equal partners. As he explained many years later, "It never entered into the expectations of those who started the foreign missionary enterprise that they should obtain missionaries from the South, but simply monies from the South to aid them in the noble object of sending the gospel to the heathen." This view of the relationship between North and South simmered beneath the surface for now, but it helped set the stage for the great division that would one day split the Baptists yet again.

The first truly national Baptist convocation in America convened in Philadelphia in May 1814 as the General Missionary Convention of the Baptist Denomination in the United States of America for Foreign Missions, soon known as the Triennial Convention because it met every three years. Richard Furman was appointed the body's first president, and

William B. Johnson was assigned to head the constitution committee.

At the second convention in 1817, Furman pointed out how Baptists needed to reach out to the unsaved in places besides the mission field. Though the association started in order to fund foreign missionaries, there was much more to do closer to home: "[We] cannot forget that there are thousands of our youth in the United States that need similar instructions. Sunday schools are multiplying in America—it is most solemnly wished that you may feel the importance of such institutions, and that you may endeavor to originate and support them to the utmost extent of your ability."

This was one of the earliest premonitions of how the Convention would change and expand and also of the variety of Baptist goals and objectives. In 1817 the Convention changed its constitution to include home missions and education in its purview. However by the time of the next meeting in 1820, pro-foreign missions interests, along with delegates (evidently called "messengers" from the very first) who opposed anything that looked like a representational body with power to establish and enforce policy, succeeded in reining in the focus back to foreign missions alone.

Also in 1817 several denominations, including German Baptists and Congregationalists, formed the Sunday and Adult School Union to send missionaries to the American frontier specifically to start Sunday schools. In 1824 the name was changed to the American Sunday School Union. That same year the Baptist General Tract Society began operating in Washington, DC, claiming its "sole object" was "to disseminate evangelical truth, and to inculcate sound morals, by the distribution of tracts."

Though only about one Baptist church in four had Sunday schools at the time, the Triennial Convention formed a committee on Sunday schools, which reported at the 1826 meeting that Sunday schools, "interesting institutions" that they were,

> destined to preserve many an unwary youth from the snares of vice, to dispel the shades of ignorance, enrich the mind with useful knowledge, and as fertilizing streams to irrigate future generations, are now extending and increasing in every state in the Union, and in every part of the Christian world. While your Committee regrets that hitherto so little has been done in the world for the religious instruction of children, they rejoice in the opportunity of giving their unqualified approbation to a system that is calculated to "Gather the people together."

At the same time pressure built to do more for Sunday schools, the Convention heard from Baptists who still longed for the perceived power and organizational benefits of a national denominational body. An editorial in the *Christian Watchman* of June 27, 1827, held that a general purpose convention "would have many advantages. It would not be among the least, that a large number of brethren from different States, united in the doctrine of Christ, and in their views of gospel ordinances, would see each other on the most friendly terms, and for mutual consultation on the best means of concentrating their energies in promoting the common interest of the Redeemer's Kingdom. . . . To diffuse a conviction of this duty, let us have the wisdom and strength of the whole denomination in a phalanx."

The story of Judson, Carey, and the Philadelphia Association that focused on foreign missions paralleled another sequence of events on the home front. In 1817, during the window of time when the Triennial Convention broadened its scope to include domestic evangelism, J. M. Peck and J. E. Welch went out West as missionaries to the hinterlands. When the Convention withdrew its funding three years later, the Massachusetts Domestic Missionary Society supported Peck until April 1832, when the American Baptist Home Missionary Society finally began in New York.

By the time the Baptist General Tract Society changed its name to the American Baptist Publication and Sunday School Society in 1840, it had moved to Philadelphia, where the General Convention had started, and the Convention had moved in turn to Boston. Both the American Home Mission Society and the American and Foreign Bible Society were headquartered in New York. Whether it was a matter of mere geography, accidental oversight, or sectional prejudice, Baptist leaders and church members in the South began to detect a bias toward Northern areas regarding where these organizations recruited their missionaries and also where they sent them.

In his centennial history of the Southern Baptist Convention, W. W. Barnes quoted a letter in the *Baptist Banner* of September 12, 1837 (published in Nashville) bearing down on the Northern-based organizations and their motives:

> It appears from the last report of the Executive Committee of the American Baptist Home Mission Society that they have not a single missionary in all of Kentucky, Alabama, Louisiana and Florida, and that they partially or entirely sustain one missionary in Mississippi, three in Tennessee and three in Arkansas, making in all seven missionaries for these six states and one Territory . . . only one missionary to every 428,581 souls, while in the state of Michigan . . . they have sixteen missionaries . . . one missionary to every 4,000 souls. . . . Why are these states (Illinois and Indiana) so liberally supplied? Are they more needy? Are they more destitute? They are more liberally supplied because of Northern contributions, and because Northern preachers refuse to come to the south. . . . It is, therefore, apparent, that the only way to produce effort in the south must be brought about by the formation of a Southern Baptist Home Mission Society.

A gathering of church representatives that year in Paris, Tennessee, discussed forming a separate board. Though they concluded that the Home Mission Society "had treated the south and southwest with almost total neglect," they hesitated to start any rival organization. As the *Baptist Banner and Western Pioneer* reported on March 21, 1839, "The brethren . . . were reluctant to act on the subject; not because they regarded the measure as unimportant, but from a fear that their motives and feelings would be misunderstood by our northern brethren, and their efforts to help themselves be attributed rather to what really did not, and does not now exist toward the north, than pure zeal for the advancement of the common cause of our blessed Redeemer."

Despite so conciliatory a tone, the fabric of Baptist faith would be stretched to the breaking point over the next half-dozen years on two fronts. On one, support mounted for a separate Southern organization; on the other, the church continued to debate the wisdom of a Sunday school program and how best to promote it.

CHAPTER 3

Southern Baptists

A sampling of Baptist thought in 1835 shows an unsettled state of affairs. That year the eighth meeting of the Triennial Convention heartily endorsed the American Sunday School Union and proposed that American churches raise $12,000 to help distribute Bibles and tracts overseas. The same year a Baptist association in Tennessee passed the following resolution: "We hereby declare Bible, Tract, Missionary Societies and the Sunday School Union, are inimical to the peace and harmony of the churches—Therefore, we will not tolerate any member in membership, in any of the above named Societies."

Meanwhile, Southern Baptists continued calling for more missionaries and more representation in their region. Barnes points out that, in all fairness, the Boston-, Philadelphia-, and New York-based institutions were doing their best to supply missionaries south of the Ohio Valley but had a hard time finding qualified men willing to make the trip. They offered one man a thousand dollars a year—a fantastic sum in the 1830s—to serve in New Orleans. "He agreed to go," Barnes reports, "but circumstances seem to have arisen that prevented him."

Possibly the first formal meeting of a Southern-oriented group was on May 16, 1839, when the Southern Baptist Home Mission Society met in Columbus, Mississippi. Never widely recognized, it sputtered to a halt within three years without any significant accomplishment.

While the South looked for ways to increase its influence in missionary and Sunday school work, the Western states also had their proponents and agendas. Some saw an East-West split as more obvious and important than a North-South one. North tended to be divided from South by commercial interests versus agricultural ones. They were also separated by deep cultural roots: Northern forebearers were largely Puritans; the most successful of them were merchants. Southern aristocrats traced their ancestry to Renaissance gentlemen cast in the mold of Sir Walter Raleigh and prized land, agriculture, and the pursuit of knowledge for its own sake above banking and trade.

The split between East and West divided hearty, adventurous individualists on the western frontier from settled, established residents of the former colonies. There were also the stark geographic markers—the Appalachians, the Mississippi River, and others less dramatic—that separated one area from the other and challenged any settler or missionary who headed west, whether from Massachusetts or Virginia.

What South and West had in common was their relatively scant populations, which meant congregations seldom met every week. When they did, it was usually for a preaching service only and not anything resembling Sunday school. Where the roads were impassable during extended periods of rainy, cold weather, churches stayed closed all winter.

Before 1825 Sunday school classes in the countryside were rare, and thirty years later only about one-fourth of Baptist churches in the South hosted them. Some pastors disdained Sunday school because they thought it usurped their role or threatened Bible teaching in the home. Pastors also sometimes resented the questionable credentials and denominational orientation of visiting Sunday school teachers. Reminiscing years later, a writer in the *Religious Herald* recalled a Virginia pastor who in 1821 refused to let a Sunday school class meet in the church building, "considering it a desecration of the holy day, and of the house of God . . . [to] commit to strangers the work which none can perform so well as enlightened and Christian parents." Eventually the class met under a cluster of trees nearby. Stories abound of classes meeting in homes and barns. One alert and opportunistic teacher reportedly convened a Sunday school session at the end of a square dance.

In 1844 the American Baptist Publication and Sunday School Society shortened its name to simply the American Baptist Publication Society. By then a crisis that had been simmering for the previous fifteen years or more boiled over, turning denominational attention from the question of Sunday school to something vastly more fundamental and far reaching.

Slavery was a controversial practice in colonial America and remained a contentious issue as the United States grew through the first decades of the nineteenth century. As practiced throughout the British Empire and across the world, chattel slavery was different from other types of slavery in history. Christians knew stories of slavery in the Bible. What many of them didn't know was that in the ancient Middle East slaves were most often prisoners of war, people kidnapped for ransom, or indentured servants. Their position was usually temporary and, more important, though they had to do their masters' bidding and worked without pay, these slaves generally had rights as human beings. Some owned property and even had slaves of their own. Typically they earned their freedom over time or were eventually ransomed or paroled.

Chattel slavery was different in that slaves themselves were property. Not only did their masters command them

and receive any wages they might earn, they owned them outright, owning their person the way they owned a horse or a
chair. If a female slave delivered a child, her owner also owned
the child; often the owner named it. Slaves could marry, but
families were routinely split up when spouses or children with
different owners were sold out of the community. Barring
special circumstances, slaves were on call any time, every day
of the year except for three days at Christmas. Owners held
over them the power of life and death. They were counted as
half a person each in the official census.

Only about 10 percent of white Southerners owned slaves,
and most of them were in the "cotton South"—Louisiana,
Mississippi, Alabama, Georgia, Florida, the Carolinas, and
Virginia. They understood the position of slavery opponents
but stood on well-rehearsed arguments to defend the practice.
First was the assumption that cotton and other plantation
crops such as indigo could not be economically grown without slave labor (though later studies suggested paying farm
labor would have been cheaper overall than buying, feeding,
clothing, and housing slaves). Another was the investment in
slaves themselves: an average worker might be worth two or
three hundred dollars, where a strong young man could bring
a thousand. Yet another concern was what would happen if
hundreds of thousands of black slaves were to be freed. They
had no land, no home, no education, and bleak prospects for
survival. They would flood the market for menial jobs; there
were warnings of a ruinous nationwide revolt.

In spite of these arguments and the deep-seated tradition, Great Britain eventually did away with slavery. Thanks largely to the lifelong work of William Wilberforce, a great Christian layman and member of Parliament, the slave trade was halted throughout the Empire in 1807 and slavery outlawed completely in 1830. Slaveholders were compensated by the government, slavery was abolished, the national economy survived, and Britannia continued to rule the waves around the globe.

Many Christians both in Britain and America believed churches should stay out of the slavery debate. In 1833, soon after Baptist missionaries had played a key role in emancipating the slaves in Jamaica, a group of churches in London wrote to the Baptist General Convention in Boston asking them to promote emancipation in America. After a season of heartfelt debate, the Convention passed a resolution stating in part that they could not "interfere with a subject that is not among the objects for which the Convention and the board were formed."

In a letter explaining their position, corresponding secretary Lusius Bolles wrote that Southern people, including ministers, were slaveholders "not because they think slavery is right, but because it was firmly rooted long before they were born and because they believe that slavery cannot be instantly abolished." He continued:

> We are confident that a great portion of our
> brethren at the south would rejoice to see any

practicable scheme devised for relieving the country from slavery.

We have the best evidence that our slave-holding brethren are Christians, sincere followers of the Lord Jesus. . . . We cannot, therefore, feel that it is right to use language or adopt measures which might tend to break the ties that unite them to us in our General Convention and in numerous other benevolent societies.

We have presented these considerations, dear brethren, as among the reasons which compel us to believe, that it is not the duty of the Baptist General Convention, or of the Board of Missions, to interfere with the subject of slavery.

As long as one side simply accepted slavery and the other opposed it, the two could coexist in brotherly harmony and mutual respect. What strained the national fabric to the breaking point was the rise of abolitionists dedicated to mounting an offensive against slaveholders and actively working to end slavery for good. This split soon showed itself in the division of the Baptist church into Northern and Southern camps.

The first abolitionist publication in America was *The Emancipator*, an obscure newspaper published in Jonesborough, Tennessee, in 1820. The movement gained momentum over the next two decades as the nation expanded westward and the country struggled with whether to allow slavery in the new regions. Also in 1820 Congress enacted the Missouri Compromise to try to settle this divisive issue. As a territory, Missouri allowed slavery. New York Congressman James Tallmadge proposed legislation requiring Missouri gradually to do away with slavery as a condition of statehood. His bill passed in the House but failed in the Senate. The powerful Speaker of the House, Kentuckian Henry Clay, then engineered a compromise that allowed Maine into the Union as a free state and Missouri as a slave state. Senator Jesse Thomas of Illinois attached a proviso that all future states formed from the northern part of the Louisiana Purchase be free states while those south of 36°30′ could be slave states. The Missouri Compromise kept the lid on the slavery debate for more than thirty years.

Andrew Jackson, the first president born outside the original thirteen colonies, took office in 1829. Though his native Tennessee was a slave state, it was tenuously so. (It would be the last state to join the Confederacy and the first to leave.) His election showed the country's interest in expansion and the growing political power of Southern and Western interests. But North or South, urban or rural, manufacturing or agriculture, the slavery issue lurked under every sectional difference and debate.

Baptist publications in both regions tried to hold the flock together. The General Convention in Boston had already claimed slavery was beyond their purview. The *Cross and Journal* called the subject "irrelevant to the single and

grand purpose" of the Convention, which was "the publication of the gospel to the heathen world." By 1841 abolitionist sentiment persuaded several state Baptist organizations
to break fellowship with slaveholding Southerners. After
extensively touring New York State in 1842, missionary J. M.
Peck reported that "probably a majority" of state associations
there officially opposed slavery. Yet a "very large majority" of
Northern Baptists "regard the declaration of non-fellowship
and exclusion of whole bodies, *en masse*, a thousand miles
distant, as exceedingly preposterous and subversive of all
general discipline upon the New Testament principles."

The pressure continued. The American Baptist Anti-
slavery Association began in 1840, and by 1843 some foreign
mission societies rejected any involvement by slave owners.
A group of local church organizations left the Boston-based
Mission Board to form mission support operations that
excluded slaveholders. Others hoped that by remaining in the
Convention, they could move it from a neutral position on
slavery to a negative one. The controversy ultimately centered
around appointing slaveholders as missionaries—men like
Reverend Jesse Bushyhead, a stalwart Convention member,
slave owner, chief justice of the Cherokee Nation, and missionary to his own people. Some accused the home secretary
of the Boston board, Dr. R. E. Pattison, of trying to force
Bushyhead out. Though the Cherokee leader died before the
matter came to a head, other slaveholders in the field kept
the controversy stirred up.

In 1840 members of the Alabama state convention studied the matter and concluded that abolitionism was unscrip-
tural, unconstitutional, "against the peace and prosperity of
the churches, and dangerous to the permanency of the union,"
and that they would withhold contributions to the Northern
missionary societies until it was clear they did not endorse the
antislavery movement.

In April 1844 the Society reinforced its neutrality with a
resolution approved by a two-to-one margin, declaring, "Our
co-operation in this does not imply sympathy with slavery
or anti-slavery, as to which subjects societies and individuals are left as free and uncommitted as if there were no such
co-operation." But at the same meeting, the body began
exploring the prospect of dissolving the Society, presumably
to reform as an antislavery organization. To get a clear picture of the Society's position on slavery, the Georgia Baptist
Convention asked the Society's executive board to appoint
Reverend J. E. Reeve as a missionary to the Indians. Reeve,
a slaveholder, had his support in place and his assignment in
the field; all he needed was a formal appointment.

The Society felt unfairly pressured and under the circumstances refused to give what should have been a routine
approval. Then Dr. Pattison, who so recently had Reverend
Bushyhead in his sights, declared to a Massachusetts convention that he would never vote to send a slaveholder into
the mission field and didn't think the board would appoint
any more. In November 1844, in a resolution proposed by

Dr. Basil Manly, president of the University of Alabama, the Alabama Convention asked point-blank whether the board would appoint a slaveholder to the mission field. The board said they would not. This was scarcely a year after they had declared the issue was not within their scope and that "societies and individuals" alike were free to make their own choices.

The Georgia and Alabama challenges marked the beginning of the end for a united Baptist fellowship. In April 1845 the *New York Baptist Register* wrote, "For ourselves we deplore the necessity of division, but when things reach such a crisis as they appear to have done, deplore it as we may, there is no prospect of peace or comfort in the continuance."

The Virginia Baptists took the lead in making the next move. In the *Religious Herald* of April 10, 1845, the Virginia Baptist Foreign Mission Society called for a convention of representatives from every state in the South,

> not because we reside in the South, but because [the Boston Board] have adopted an unconstitutional and unscriptural principle to govern their future course. The principle is this—That holding slaves is, under all circumstances, incompatible with the office of the Christian ministry. . . . For ourselves we cordially invite all our brethren, North and South, East and West, who are "aggrieved by the recent decision of the Board in Boston," and believe that their

usefulness may be increased by cooperating with us, to attend the proposed meeting.

There were slaveholders, nonslaveholders, and abolitionists in every section of the country. Society president James B. Taylor, who signed the article, owned no slaves, nor did some other Society leaders.

Another goal for the meeting was to determine whether "it will be better to organize a separate Bible Society, and Publication Society, or to continue our connexion with the existing institutions." Though this issue had been overshadowed for years by the slavery debate, it was still very much a question in need of an answer.

Two hundred ninety-three men, some of them representing more than one constituency, met in Augusta, Georgia, on May 8, 1845. One of their first acts was to appoint a committee to draft a constitution, and as chairman they chose Dr. W. B. Johnson, president of the South Carolina Convention, the only one present who had also been at the organizational session of the General Convention in 1814.

Until the very last, some Southern Baptists searched for a way to prevent a split. The Tennessee Baptist Foreign Mission Society reminded their brethren that the Boston Board, representing the Triennial Convention, had passed a resolution "repudiating all connection with both slavery and anti-slavery." Another group of leaders in Kentucky, Tennessee, and Mississippi agreed: "We hope our brethren in the South will pause and seek to God for wisdom before they take the step, in this matter, which cannot be retracted."

On May 10 the constitution was presented and approved, and Dr. Johnson, who had been the first president of the 1814 General Convention, was elected to the same office in the Southern Baptist Convention. The new Convention included members who were for slavery and others who were against; what it left out were antislavery abolitionists who, these messengers believed, had caused discord and broken fellowship with the North.

Even so, there were Northerners who wished the new Southern Convention every good hope for success. Writing to Dr. J. B. Jeter, Dr. Francis Wayland observed: "You will separate of course. I could not ask otherwise. Your rights have been infringed. I will take the liberty of offering one or two suggestions. We have shown how Christians *ought not* to act, it remains for you to show us how they *ought* to act. Put away all violence, act with dignity and firmness, and the world will approve your course."

Southern Baptists took up the question of establishing a publication board, which was permitted according to the just-ratified constitution, and decided not to pursue it for the present. As Barnes succinctly reports in his centennial history, "In consideration of the general circumstances, the fact that the American Baptist Publication Society had not become involved in the question of slavery, the expense involved in establishing a publishing agency, and special problems connected with establishing and supporting a theological school for the South, only two boards were then formed: Foreign Missions at Richmond, Virginia, and Domestic Missions at Marion, Alabama."

The Southern Baptist Convention was chartered by the State of Georgia on December 27, 1845, and its first official meeting set for Richmond in June of the following year. One historic chapter had ended, and another was about to begin.

CHAPTER 4

Starts and Stops

In his often quoted but never commercially printed 1972 dissertation, "The Development of a Sunday School Strategy in the Southern Baptist Convention, 1896–1926," William Preston Clemmons examined the almost half century of unrest among Southern Baptists over whether to organize a separate board to publish Sunday school materials.

He points out that when the Southern Baptist Convention was established, there were fewer Sunday schools in the South than in the North, where they were already scarce. Most Southern churches were in rural communities where even simple preaching services were intermittent and many who attended were illiterate. Publishing opponents insisted that

books and tracts wouldn't help people who seldom worshipped and couldn't read and that money spent on printing
was better spent on the missionary field. Furthermore, some
Baptists insisted that Christianity was essentially experiential,
which meant Christians had to connect personally and individually with God. Sunday school, they said, was more or less
useless, and Sunday school publications were a waste.

Then there were others, Clemmons continues, who, even
after the Southern Baptist Convention was born, felt that the
American Baptist Publication Society in Philadelphia had
done an admirable job supplying printed materials to all
Baptists since 1824 and should continue to do so. They promoted the status quo—letting the Publication Society print
for Southern Baptists—simply because it worked.

The Publication Society remained resolutely on the
fence in the slavery debate even as the Triennial Convention
wavered, then fell on the side of abolition. Dr. J. L. Burrows
had represented both the Society and the Pennsylvania
Baptists at the SBC organizational meeting in Augusta. He
was recognized as a messenger and participated in the discussions even though he did not claim membership in the new
body. The early Southern Baptists didn't see the Publication
Society to be as partisan as the Boston Board had been. With
all the various issues before them, they turned their attention
and resources to matters other than tracts and lessons.

But it wasn't long before the publication debate resur-
faced, and it moved in and out of the limelight repeatedly

over the next forty-five years. Under the circumstances it's surprising to learn that when James Marion Frost dreamed of a Sunday school board for Southern Baptists late one January night, he had no idea that the concept had been discussed by Southern Baptists almost as long as there had been any such denomination.

In his own memoir, *The Sunday School Board, Its History and Work*, Frost wrote, "I did not know there had been the former Sunday School Board." A generation later, in 1941, P. E. Burroughs elaborated: "Dr. Frost . . . was unaware of the fact that there had been an earlier Sunday School Board. As a young man in the Convention he had not known about those earlier ventures. No history of the Convention had been published."

Though its founders in Augusta launched the SBC without a publications arm, various denominational leaders and state conventions repeatedly proposed some sort of publication, tract, or Bible society. At the first Southern Baptist Convention, held in Richmond in May 1846, messengers discussed the idea at length. In the end they assigned Bible distribution to the missions boards (home and foreign) and encouraged those boards to work with the American and Foreign Bible Society in the North to help them with their responsibilities.

There was no mistaking the SBC stance in their final resolution on the subject: "*Resolved*, That this Convention does not deem it advisable to embarrass itself with any enterprise for the publication and sale of books."

Still various individuals and organizations explored the prospect of Southern Baptists publishing and distributing their own literature. The first plan to get off the ground was the Southern Baptist Publication Society, formed in Savannah, May 13, 1847, at a convention of delegates from Virginia, South Carolina, Georgia, and Alabama. Based in Charleston, the Publication Society had no official connection with the SBC, although its founders and supporters were members of the Convention. The society produced various Sunday school materials for several years though it never enjoyed wide exposure or influence. It operated until the outbreak of the Civil War, when wartime disruptions quickly put it out of business.

Overlapping the Publication Society was the Bible Board, begun in Nashville when the Convention met there in 1851. This gathering of messengers concluded that they should lift the burden of overseeing publications (supplied by others) from the home and foreign mission boards and give it to a group set up expressly for that purpose. Some of them thought that by being in Nashville, a central location and major printing center, the board would be more successful than the struggling Publication Society in far-off Savannah. Others feared that Nashville was a liability because of a Southern Baptist wild card named James Robinson Graves. There was truth on both sides.

Graves was a teacher when he moved to Nashville from Kentucky in 1845. One of his students was Morton Howell, son of Robert Boyte Crawford Howell, pastor of First Baptist Church in Nashville. Howell was so impressed with Graves that he helped him succeed to the pastorate at Second Baptist and made him associate publisher of Howell's periodical, *The Tennessee Baptist*. The two could scarcely have been more different. Howell was scholarly, sensitive, and eager to avoid conflict while Graves was a passionate debater who delighted in annihilating the opposition through *ad hominem* arguments, sarcasm, and stinging wit. Graves soon muscled control of *The Tennessee Baptist* from Howell and used it to advance his personal views, one of which was that non-Baptists should never preach from a Baptist pulpit. Reverend Howell and others routinely invited preachers from other traditions to deliver sermons to their congregations. Graves railed against it, establishing what soon became known as Landmarkism.

Based on Proverbs 22:28, "Remove not the ancient landmark, which thy fathers have set," Landmarkism held that the only church was the local church and that because only Baptists could trace their spiritual lineage back to the time of Christ, only Baptists could baptize or serve the Lord's Supper.

In 1849 Howell resigned from *The Tennessee Baptist* and a year later moved to a new pastorate in Richmond, leaving Graves to launch his Landmark movement on a wider scale. By 1852 Graves had installed one of his followers, Amos Cooper Dayton, on the Bible Board. Dayton was a New Jersey native, former dentist, and former Presbyterian who came to

Nashville from Mississippi and became Graves's mouthpiece on the board while Graves proclaimed his views and found contributors to his cause through *The Tennessee Baptist* and his own publishing company.

In 1855 the Convention expanded the Bible Board's mandate to include "religious and denominational book distribution" as well as Bibles. By that time Basil Manly Jr., pastor of First Baptist Church, Richmond, had organized a meeting of Sunday school leaders in a separate attempt to nurture discussion about a publication board. Manly put out the call during the 1853 Convention in Baltimore, and his meeting later that year in Richmond attracted more than one hundred delegates from several states. Though the group planned to reconvene in 1855, they never met again.

In 1857 Reverend R. B. C. Howell moved back to Nashville and to First Baptist, setting the stage for a titanic clash with Graves and his followers. Two pastors had served at First since Howell left, and both had departed at least in part on account of Graves's criticism. Serving his fourth term as president of the Southern Baptist Convention, Howell was an *ex officio* member of the Bible Board. In Richmond he hadn't spent much time thinking about the board or working with it; now reunited with it in the same city, he became more active. He could clearly see that Graves had taken over the Bible Board through A. C. Dayton and resolved this time, unlike in 1851, to challenge his younger former protégé.

Meeting in Nashville on October 3, 1857, representatives from the Convention, with Howell presiding, organized the Southern Baptist Sunday School Union. But Graves managed to get Dayton elected president of the Union and himself as secretary. Howell then turned on his own organization. With his popularity in Nashville and his position as president of the Convention, he evidently shook off his customary self-effacing reticence and got Dayton removed from office. Furious, Graves unleashed all his rhetorical fury on his old mentor, to the point where Howell's supporters filed charges against Graves at First Baptist. A church trial ruled in favor of Howell; then Graves and a handful of followers set up their own "true" First Baptist Church.

The row kept the full Convention from approving the new Union, which was postponed until another meeting in April 1858. That meeting too was postponed because of continuing argument until November. In "The Development of a Sunday School Strategy . . . ," historian Clemmons points out that for all the discord it caused, the Southern Baptist Sunday School Union (called in some sources the Southern Baptist Sabbath School Union) "aroused many Baptists to the potential of the Sunday school as the teaching agency which could shape the denomination" according to "a particular interpretation of Baptist theology." The controversy spurred both the Southern Baptist Publication Society and the Bible Board to publish and promote more. It also prompted proponents of every theological stripe to see that their views were represented or that they prevailed.

Dr. Howell weighed in with all the power he could muster to stop the Graves/Landmark juggernaut. During the liturgical trial at First Baptist, he testified: "The man who writes Sunday school books or upon whose judgement they are published, and put into the hands of our children, should be well instructed in the divine word, and scriptural in his doctrines. And as it is desirable that a Sunday School Union should be an enterprise upon which the whole denomination might unite, his theological knowledge and orthodoxy should be undoubted by all. Could the whole denomination unite upon the views and teachings of Graves and Dayton?"

The Sunday School Union was finally constituted in the fall of 1858 with Dayton confirmed as president. The next year Graves mounted a battle for Landmarkism against the Southern Baptist Convention and moved to abolish the Foreign Mission Board. With rumors of a denominational battle in the air, more than twice the number of messengers attended as the year before. Graves was solidly voted down but tried nevertheless to depose Howell as president. Howell won reelection on the second ballot, but even that opposition prompted him to decline the office. Richard Fuller was elected in his place.

The Sunday School Union, fragmented as it was, met annually until the Civil War put an end to the formal organization in 1863. The indefatigable Graves nurtured what embers remained of the idea, resuming limited operations in 1867, though with his publishing enterprise halted as a casualty of war, he never had the audience or the influence he had enjoyed in the past.

In 1862 Union troops occupied Nashville and President Lincoln installed a military governor. Within a year the Southern Baptist Sunday School Union and the Bible Board were history, their work partly folded back into the mission boards. But the same Convention that abolished the Bible Board resolved to keep looking for some way to produce and deliver publications and other study materials to Sunday schools.

A special committee appointed in 1861 to study the matter introduced a resolution at the 1863 meeting in Augusta that "the Bible Board of the Southern Baptist Convention be and the same is hereby abolished." The resolution carried. Then at the same session Basil Manly Jr. introduced a resolution that "a Committee of seven be appointed to inquire whether it is expedient for this Convention to attempt anything for the promotion of Sunday Schools, and if so what?" Here at last was a proposal encouraging in that it started with a statement of the need, not a proclamation of what the proposer wanted to do.

The committee, with Manly as chairman, met immediately and had its recommendations ready before the end of the Convention. Committee members believed that what one state convention prepared for Sunday school could be useful to another and that they could save money by joining forces and working for the good of all. As Dr. Manly would write in the *Religious Herald*, "There is now no general society among us actively engaged in the Sunday School work. From the institutions at the North, which we had chiefly depended on, we have withdrawn; and we can never again trust them to provide for the religious instruction of our little ones." To the Convention he declared, "Here is at once an open door, and an urgent claim, both opportunity and argument for activity."

Dr. Manly's committee recommended establishing "the Board of Sunday Schools of the Southern Baptist Convention" and charging it with "the duty of taking all measures adopted to promote the establishment, enlargement, and higher efficiency of Sunday Schools throughout our land; provided that the Board shall not establish a printing house."

In justifying his recommendation, Manly lifted up the importance of Sunday school to the future of the denomination:

> All of us have felt that the Sunday School is the
> nursery of the Church, the camp of instruction for
> her young soldiers, the great missionary to the future.
> While our other benevolent agencies relate primarily
> to the present, this goes to meet and bless the genera-
> tion that is coming, to win them from ignorance and
> sin, to train future laborers, when our places shall

know us no more. All of us have seen how Sunday
Schools tend to direct increasing attention to the
Bible, to elevate the ministry, to train young ministers
to build up Churches in destitute parts, to foster the
missionary spirit, to increase both our capacity and
willingness for every good work.

The Sunday School Board began operating in Greenville,
South Carolina, and soon raised $3,000 in seed money from
state Baptist organizations. Limited as their operations were
throughout the Civil War, by its end in the spring of 1865, the
Board had distributed ninety-two thousand books in Sunday
schools throughout the South at a cost of more than $46,000,
$11,000 of which came from receipts and the rest from dona-
tions. They got twenty-five thousand New Testaments free
from the American Bible Society, sent through the war-torn
countryside under a flag of truce.

A statement quoted by Barnes captures the Board's vision
in those earliest months to go far beyond teaching Bible
lessons to penetrate deep into the culture that was largely
rural, isolated, and decimated by years of civil war:

> A large proportion of the children of our coun-
> try have now no means of learning to read but in
> the Sunday School, and experience has shown that
> they can there readily learn both to read and write.
> Parents need the help of the Sunday Schools in the
> moral and religious training of their children in

these days of evil. And the numerous orphans, whose claims upon us are recognized by all, may find in the Sunday School a great orphan asylum, requiring no capital and little expenditure of any kind, interfering with no other scheme, but aiding them all.

When he launched the Sunday School Board, Manly depended on volunteers and established denominational organizations throughout the Confederacy to build its reach and capability. Soon he saw the Board had to have a full-time leader and hired his friend and Southwestern Seminary colleague, John A. Broadus, to do the job. Over the next two years the men published thirty-seven thousand copies of the *Confederate Sunday School Hymnbook* and other hymnbooks, thirty thousand copies of *Child's Question Book on the Four Gospels* written by Manly, and various other titles. With the end of the war, however, defeated and exhausted communities saw hymnbooks and children's lessons as luxuries they could no longer afford. Total receipts in 1865 came to $400 for the year, not enough even to pay Broadus's salary. He continued on as a volunteer.

In January 1866 the Baptist Sunday School Board introduced something refreshingly different in format and approach from anything they had published before. It was *Kind Words for the Sunday School Children*, a child-size newspaper written and designed to appeal directly to children rather than their teachers, parents, or whoever bought the Sunday school materials. It was also the cheapest Sunday school publication anybody could remember: ten cents a year in quantities of ten or more. John Broadus reported, "Children are rather pleased than otherwise that theirs should be a *little* paper, strikingly different from the papers for grown people."

Kind Words Volume I Number 1 opened with a poem by Basil Manly Jr., also titled "Kind Words":

> *Words are things of greatest worth,*
> *Thought often lightly spoken;*
> *Thoughtless, fleeting words of mirth,*
> *May wound the heart that's broken;*
> *Or words that pass forgotten by,*
> *May prompt to deeds that cannot die.*

This little paper was an instant success, one of the only bright spots in an otherwise dismal financial picture in the years after the war. The Sunday School Board owed the American Bible Society $2,000 for merchandise. Some of the Board's own stock of books and materials had been burned when Columbia fell, and some of the rest sold for now-worthless Confederate money. What remained had been poorly made with the inferior materials available during wartime. Transportation was scarce and expensive, and members of many Southern churches could barely feed themselves; church publications were far down their list. The one promising ray came from *Kind Words*, selling after its first year at a rate of twenty-five thousand copies per month.

Into this arena came the SBC's old nemesis J. R. Graves, who had moved from Nashville to Memphis and was trying to reenergize his Landmark movement, still alive under the old Southern Baptist Sunday School Union, which he had wrested from Dr. Howell years before. During the 1867 Convention in Memphis, Graves proposed uniting the Union and the Sunday School Board there in Memphis, the center of radical Landmarkism. After a long night of heated debate, the Convention voted to move the Board from Greenville to Memphis, arguing the Tennessee city had survived the war in better shape than other southern metropolitan areas. James P. Boyce believed the Board should be disbanded and that the Convention should get out of publishing and Sunday school promotion altogether because it would only lead to "endless trouble." Others thought Sunday school matters belonged with the individual state conventions.

As his opponents had feared, J. R. Graves soon muscled his way into effective control of the Sunday School Board in Memphis. Not only was Landmarkism a threat; Sunday school was far less well-known and less popular in the West than along the Eastern seaboard. The corresponding secretary of the Board, C. C. Bitting, was a South Carolinian without reputation or connections in the Mississippi Valley for soliciting donations. When he couldn't even raise his own salary in a year's time, he resigned.

Bitting was replaced by Thomas C. Teasdale, who happily reported to the Convention in 1870 that he had set up a contract with Southwestern Publishing Company to publish all the Board's materials and take all the risk, paying the Board 10 percent of all receipts. While this put the Board on firm financial footing for the first time, it also delivered it into the hands of one J. R. Graves, owner of Southwestern Publishing Company. This made Teasdale the enemy both of the antipublishing faction of the Convention and the anti-Landmarkism wing.

The American Baptist Publication Society, which had been supplying materials to Southern Baptists since the beginning, also weighed in, opposing the struggling Sunday School Board, and, some Southerners feared, would bypass the Board completely and sell their Northern wares directly to Southern congregations.

Whatever chance of survival the Board had at that point was wiped out by the financial panic of 1873. This nationwide depression dampened the demand for books as well as the generosity of donors. At the Convention of 1873, the Committee on the Present Condition and Future Prospects of the Sunday School Board reported that the conditions were miserable and the future prospects equally so. Sylvanus Landrum, then president of the Sunday School Board, moved that his Board be abolished and its work taken over by the Domestic and Indian Mission Board.

The motion carried, and the Sunday School Board disappeared altogether, to reappear eighteen years and a thousand miles distant in a Virginia preacher's dream.

CHAPTER 5

A Nip-and-Tuck Year

The first Sunday in Nashville was the most lonesome day of my life. Some who afterward became earnest personal friends looked on me then as an intruder and a disturber of the peace." So wrote James Marion Frost near the end of his life recalling his first week as corresponding secretary of the newly formed Sunday School Board of the Southern Baptist Convention in the summer of 1891. (Trying to step into his shoes a hundred summers later, I would have some of the same feelings.)

Though Frost had worked tirelessly for years to bring the Sunday School Board into existence, he never expected to lead it. He had spent his whole career as a pastor. He loved leading his congregation at Leigh Street Baptist Church in Richmond, and the members loved him in return. The day the Southern Baptist Convention voted the Board into existence, Frost had learned that J. B. Gambrell and Joshua Levering proposed to nominate him as corresponding secretary. He hurriedly convinced them to postpone filling the job and let the new Board elect its own secretary. Frost particularly asked that the Convention not consider him for the position, which would take him away from the pastorate he felt called to serve.

That request was a challenge to the Southern Baptist board of trustees meeting in Nashville on the evening of May 29, 1891, to elect their corresponding secretary. The 8:00 p.m. starting hour came and went with only ten present of the forty men expected to attend. How could only a fourth of the group confidently choose a leader, especially when the obvious choice, Frost, already said he didn't want the job?

These ten waited uneasily in the study of Dr. W. R. L. Smith, pastor of First Baptist Church. The room, with its polished woodwork, elegant Victorian drapes, and over-stuffed horsehair furniture, was nestled in an imposing church building on a commanding hilltop, looking down Broadway to the Cumberland River and across town to the state capitol on its own hill a few blocks away. The soaring bell tower, massive brick walls, and delicate stained-glass windows of First Baptist, Nashville, radiated a sense of confidence, permanence, and solidity from its high perch that the men inside could surely have used.

As president of the Board, Dr. Smith had dutifully contacted every man invited to this all-important meeting. After so many years of discussion, discord, and struggle, they were the ones charged with launching the Sunday School Board. The poor turnout was no doubt a disappointment. And of the thirty absentees only two had sent explanations: one was in Europe and another, Dr. A. D. Sears of Clarksville, Tennessee, was on his deathbed.

The corresponding secretary would be the Board's only paid employee, responsible for everything from editing copy to smoothing still-ruffled feathers among some state Baptist conventions over the very existence of a Board. It seemed a risk for so small a group to select him, but it would have been an even greater risk to put it off now that they had their long-awaited mandate. The ten prayed for divine guidance and forged ahead.

Charles S. Gardner, pastor of Edgefield Baptist Church in Nashville, nominated Lansing Burrows of Augusta, Georgia, who looked every inch the denominational sage with his wire-rimmed glasses and luxurious white mutton chops. E. E. Folk, editor of the *Baptist and Reflector*, nominated J. M. Frost. The first ballot produced a tie. The men prayed together and voted again. Another tie. After that, Folk, bending finally to his nominee's wishes, switched his vote to Burrows, who won the election on the third ballot. The men voted him a salary of $2,500 a year, though they didn't know at the time where the money would come from.

Two weeks later, nine of the same men plus one new addition from the original forty gathered in the same room to go through their paces again. Burrows had declined the offer. They prayed once more for guidance and filled out their ballots. This time they selected J. M. Frost unanimously on the first round. The news brought Frost an "ache of soul" at the thought of leaving his pulpit in Richmond and uprooting his wife and five children, knowing both that he was hesitant to leave his preaching and that he was God's man for the job. It's a feeling every pastor knows who has ever left a pulpit he loves because he feels God calling him to something else.

John A. Broadus, the Baptist senior statesman whose influence at the Birmingham convention had preempted debate over authorizing the Board, wrote to Frost encouraging him to accept the post. Ezekiel Robinson, preaching at Fifth Baptist, Philadelphia, where Frost was visiting, spoke from the pulpit about "how sometimes God crosses all our plans, turns our purpose aside, and constrains us into new lines of life." Historian Robert A. Baker wrote in his 1941 history of the Board that Frost admitted Robinson's message "went home to my heart as a message from God—a voice that would not be hushed." Baker also noted advice to Frost from Henry G. Weston, president of Crozer Seminary: "Don't you dare decline that call from your brethren."

In the end Frost accepted the call in spite of his reservations about leaving the pastorate and putting a strain on his family. Recalling the time years later, he wrote, "I came to my task July 1, 1891, sure of only one thing, namely, that I was doing what seemed my duty," moving to Nashville with "a deep sense of pain." He worried about his devoted wife, Nanney, sister of his college classmate M. M. Riley, who traded the role she knew and loved as a pastor's wife for a new home in a strange city and an uncertain future with the Sunday School Board.

The future was uncertain in every way imaginable. Frost's first day on the job he had nowhere to live (he and his family were staying temporarily with friends), no office, no staff, and not a cent of seed money to start operations or provide his salary. The Convention had authorized $2,500 annually for his work as corresponding secretary plus another $500 for editorial duties but left Frost to raise it himself. His friend E. E. Folk of the *Baptist and Reflector* loaned him an office where Frost set up shop with nothing but a small walnut desk from his study in Richmond—the same one he'd used to write the original proposal for the Board. Later he paid five dollars a month for the space.

Frost saw the immediate needs as twofold: first, to take over the *Kind Words* series of publications as authorized by the Convention; second, to build bridges with the substantial number of state denominational leaders who continued resenting the whole idea of a Southern Baptist publication enterprise. Some still personally felt the sting of defeat from the 1891 convention, others feared the Board would be a bottomless pit of financial losses, and yet others maintained strong ties to the American Baptist Publication Society, which had served Southern Baptists well for many years. In short, plenty of influential men believed the Baptist Sunday School Board was wasteful and unnecessary. Frost planned to go meet with them all over the South.

But to do anything took at least a little money. The Southern Baptist Convention launched the Board, in Frost's words, "absolutely without means." There wasn't even money for him to move his furniture or buy a train ticket. He could expect income in the future from *Kind Words* but not until January when editorial control would pass to him from the Home Mission Board in Atlanta.

In what seems a mysterious vein to modern readers, Frost explained, "Money which the Secretary chanced to have in hand, but which belonged to another, was used temporarily to meet immediate and pressing necessities." He wrote out of respect for the long-held practice of never putting ladies' names in print. Except for wedding notices and obituaries, the wives of honorable men seldom had their names in books or news stories or any other public record. There might also have been a tinge of embarrassment. For it was a $5,000 loan from his wife, part of an inheritance from her father, that allowed Frost to keep the Sunday School Board afloat that first year. The Board also took out two loans totaling $1,050 from First National Bank in Nashville. Eager to show a clean balance sheet at the end of the first fiscal year on April 30, 1892,

Frost repaid the bank before then. (In a 1966 interview with Board archivist Marian Keegan, Frost's children said he also repaid his wife, though no paper trail evidently ever existed. Reportedly when asked if her husband paid her back, Nanney Frost answered, "He said he did.")

During the fall of 1891, J. M. Frost maintained a grueling travel schedule to visit the various state conventions and drum up support for his Board. Historian Robert Baker reports that Frost traveled ten thousand miles in three months, sleeping in Pullman cars, eating in railroad cafés, and using the train stations as his office. His first stop was the Texas state convention in Waco, where he spoke to enthusiastic overflow crowds that heartily endorsed the new Board. Other conventions were more skeptical, and a few plainly hostile.

Reserved by nature, Frost warmed gradually to the challenge of defending his newborn enterprise. As he later recalled, "Timid and somewhat shy perhaps because of the delicate situation, I at first took my seat in the rear of the house and waited to be called; but soon it became manifest that the work which was my chief concern would never get to the front except as the Secretary put it forward. So I went to the front with the trust which had been committed to my care."

By January 1892 Frost had traded life on the rails for the hectic task of relocating *Kind Words* to Nashville. There were six publications in all, with the children's *Kind Words* magazine the oldest and best known, the "golden thread" that Frost believed tied this new chapter in Southern Baptist history to its publishing roots. The others were *The Child's Gem*, *Kind Words Teacher* (edited by Frost), and three quarterly magazines. Dr. Samuel Boykin, a University of Georgia graduate who had edited *Kind Words* since 1873, made the move to Nashville along with his magazine and became Dr. Frost's editor in chief.

Frost contracted with the Methodist Publishing House, a large printer operating in Nashville since 1854, to produce all the Board publications. He moved out of the *Baptist and Reflector* offices, first briefly to the Presbyterian Publishing House, then to the Methodist Publishing House, where he could be near the printing. As part of their bid to get the work, Methodists gave the young Board offices rent-free. Frost reported they also provided "every convenience and courtesy. Indeed the men in charge there almost carried the Sunday School Board in those early days."

Boykin and Frost both had a huge amount of work to do. Robert A. Baker lists Dr. Boykin's duties beginning January 1, 1892: "The preparation of the quarterlies for Primaries, Intermediates, and Advanced groups; *Kind Words* for Young People in three editions—weekly, semimonthly, and monthly, including a page for missions in two of these editions; Lesson Leaflets in single sheets; *The Child's Gem* for little folk; Lesson Cards and Bible Lesson Pictures for the infants; and other equipment for the Sunday School, such as reward cards, collection envelopes, question books, record books, and catechisms." Frost, for his part, published a catechism by John A. Broadus at the Convention's direction, and edited *Kind Words Teacher*, forty-eight pages of articles, lesson expositions, blackboard exercises, and other helps published once a month.

All these titles had been printed in Atlanta under a five-year contract that expired at the end of 1891. Early in the new year, the Methodist Publishing House in Nashville took over the work on the Board's behalf without missing a single issue. The first income across Frost's desk was $5,000 in December payments made for the January orders. Frost was elated and relieved. One of his opponents' most relentless arguments was that publishing Sunday school materials would be a constant drain on Convention resources. That had been true in the past, but Frost was determined to do everything he could to break even the first year. It was a nip-and-tuck year. "Sometimes," he wrote, "debt seemed certain, inevitable, as we worked, watched, and waited."

As much as a man so humble as Frost was able, he must have felt a real sense of victory on April 30, 1892. That day he reported to the annual Convention meeting in Atlanta that the Baptist Sunday School Board ended its first year not only solvent but with more than $1,000 in the bank. Far from being a drain on the denominational treasury, the Board almost immediately became a net contributor to Southern Baptist causes. Less than three months after its upbeat report in Atlanta, the Board voted to donate $3,000 over the next year to state organizations in support of Sunday school and missionary programs.

Seizing the opportunity, Frost followed his impressive financial report with a call for unqualified Board support from all Southern Baptists, painting a glowing picture of future prospects:

> Brethren, this great enterprise which you have entrusted to the Sunday-school Board is not a scramble and squabble for literature, but something in every way high and noble, and with your endorsement and support in Convention assembled and in your churches and Sunday-schools the Board may do a work of which the ages will be proud. Of course the literature is essential, but only as a means to an end—a powerful means to a noble end.
>
> And moreover, if the leadings of Providence can ever be read and interpreted, God's hand is surely in this movement, his favor has surely been upon the work. . . . We stand in the present, but we speak for the future; we work in the present, but shall gather and garner our harvest in the centuries and the ages and the eternities.

But ages and eternities notwithstanding, J. M. Frost soon surprised his brethren by stepping down from his leadership post at the end of the year. After only eighteen months, the new and promising Sunday School Board faced the challenge of finding another visionary so sound in his theology, so resilient in the face of criticism, and so tight with a dollar.

CHAPTER 6

The Forgotten Man

Dr. Frost had gone through a heartrending struggle in deciding to leave his pastorate in Richmond to lead the Sunday School Board. When First Baptist Church in Nashville extended a call for him to be their pastor, he had to relive that struggle all over again. He wrote later that he never intended to be away from the pastorate for long, but the opportunity from First Baptist Nashville came sooner than he expected. He "rushed for what seemed an open door," he admitted, though he felt a "deep sense of pain in taking up the new work" so soon after bringing the Board to life.

As Frost explained, "I entered the secretaryship at first with a mental reservation, supposing two years would suffice to show whether the Sunday School Board could succeed; if it did, then another could make it go; if not, there would be no need for a Secretary. In either case I would be free to return to the pastorate." He left for his new pulpit on a Broadway hilltop January 1, 1893, but also remained as interim secretary until May 1 when his replacement took over.

The new man was one the outgoing secretary knew well. Theodore Percy Bell had been a deacon at Frost's Leigh Street Church in Richmond and the first person Frost had ever shown his written proposal that eventually brought the Sunday School Board into existence. Bell was assistant corresponding secretary of the Southern Baptist Foreign Mission Board and editor of the *Foreign Mission Journal*. He had a lifelong interest in the mission field and, as a young pastor in his native South Carolina, had applied to be a foreign missionary himself. In 1881 he was assigned by the Foreign Mission Board to China, but when a trustee questioned his doctrinal standards, the appointment was withdrawn. Church historian Leon McBeth points out that the challenge to Bell's theological credentials was probably without merit since five years later he was appointed to his FMB leadership position. He had a heart for China for the rest of his life. For years he personally supported a Chinese missionary, and his daughter Ada was eventually appointed to serve there.

McBeth describes T. P. Bell as "often the forgotten man" in Baptist Sunday School Board history, his brief tenure overshadowed by the looming legend of J. M. Frost. But Bell was a skilled visionary leader God used to carry the Board through a critical stage of its development. He grew up in Columbia after leaving his home in Beaufort at age nine, just ahead of invading Yankee troops. He attended the University of South Carolina, Furman University, and The Southern Baptist Theological Seminary. As his pastor at Leigh Street Baptist, Frost took note of Bell's passion for the Lord's work as well as his writing ability.

When Frost left the Board for First Baptist Nashville, he made clear that he still wanted to assist the Board. One reason he accepted the call, he said, was that it allowed him to stay in Nashville (he lived in an elegant home near Vanderbilt University just to the west of downtown) where he could stay involved in Board affairs. The Board voted on March 13, 1893, to hire Bell beginning May 1. The Board also elected Frost their president and continued his appointment as editor of *Kind Words Teacher* at $500 per year. Bell was awarded Frost's former salary as Secretary of $2,500.

Southern Baptists were pleased to have another true Southerner replacing Frost. *The Baptist Courier* of South Carolina described Bell as "a man of sound judgment, wide information, fine executive ability, good scholarship, [and] deep spirituality," adding, "Traveling over the Southern States in the interest of Foreign Missions has given him a wide acceptance with his brethren everywhere, and he is universally and deservedly popular."

One challenge Dr. Bell faced was keeping his young organization solvent during years of nationwide financial upheaval in the 1890s that reached the crisis point just about the time Bell moved to Nashville. The red-letter date in the so-called "Panic of 1893" was April 21, 1893, right when the new secretary, one month a widower, was settling with his three children into a new house in a strange city.

The whole economic story is a confusing confluence of lean years for Western farmers, new higher agricultural tariffs, and artificial support for the price of silver. But the panic moment came when the amount of gold in the federal treasury dropped below $100 million dollars. In those years paper money was convertible into gold, and breaking this psychological barrier convinced some investors and bankers that there wouldn't be enough gold to convert the paper money of everyone who wanted to do so. Their fear became a self-fulfilling prophecy: so many people scrambled to convert their dollars to gold that many banks couldn't meet the sudden demand and went out of business. Since deposits weren't insured back then, the failed banks' customers were wiped out. They in turn laid off workers and closed their factories, producing a disastrous ripple effect.

It would be almost four years before revised economic policy, a presidential election, and the Klondike gold rush ushered in a new era of prosperity. So for the entire period of T. P. Bell's leadership, the Sunday School Board had to struggle with a weak economy. It may well be that Bell was better suited to navigate these unfriendly waters than Frost would have been. It's hard to imagine Dr. Frost, the patrician Southern gentleman and scholar, pressing debtors to bring their accounts current or sparring over prices. But Dr. Bell took up those duties without hesitation.

He wrote frank, unvarnished dunning letters to churches, individuals, and other Southern Baptist organizations calling on them to pay up. He was understanding with late payers if he thought they were doing their best but showed little patience to account holders who stiffed him or who promised to pay and didn't. Some of them he cut off completely. McBeth also notes that Bell "had to conduct a great deal of unseemly haggling with Baptist state papers who, Bell thought, were overcharging the Board for advertising space."

As Frost had done, Dr. Bell traveled widely, expanding his network of Baptist connections from his days on the Foreign Mission Board and promoting Board publications and study materials to the state organizations. Some Southern Baptists still resisted the whole idea of a publishing organization and kept buying their materials from the American Baptist Publication Society in Philadelphia. The ABPS stepped up efforts to minimize the Board's impact on their business. They had added a new office in Dallas the previous November to their St. Louis and Atlanta branches and still had influential friends throughout the Convention.

There were inevitable run-ins with unhappy customers. To a critic who claimed some of the youth material was too sophisticated for its audience, Bell admitted, "The fodder has been too high for the colts." One Baptist in Louisiana wrote to criticize lesson cards on Palm Sunday and Easter, complaining they promoted a "ritualism" too close to Catholicism. Bell answered that the Board bought the cards from a publisher in Boston and sent them out before anyone noticed the emphasis. "I will see to it that there is no repetition of the matter," he promised.

The same day he wrote the card supplier:

> I suppose it is a fact known to you, that Baptist folk do not believe in the observance of Easter, Palm Sundays & etc., but when these things slip into the cards which we send out to our schools, they give us trouble. I beg to call your attention to the enclosed card which introduces the idea of Palm Sunday and its observance. We are purchasing a large number of these cards from you now, and I hope to be able to continue . . . but if we do so it will be necessary that this kind of thing be avoided."

Under Bell's leadership, the Sunday School Board more than held its own through the years of depression. Total receipts for 1893 were just over $43,000, increasing to about $48,500 the next year and more than $58,000 in 1895. Bell kept up the pressure on past-due accounts and not only paid his own bills but over that time donated $15,000 to various state organizations, boards, and Southern Baptist causes. Some of the very people who predicted the Board would be a money loser now came to Bell hat in hand looking for support. Not only was the Board profitable, but it also represented a new type of financial resource for the denomination—business income rather than the donations the Convention historically depended on.

Bell's willingness to confront challenge head-on caused friction with his old colleagues at the Foreign Mission Board. As secretary of the Sunday School Board, Bell made generous appropriations to foreign mission work. The rival Publication Society also contributed to the Foreign Mission Board, and though the Society made one annual gift far smaller than what the SSB provided throughout the year, Bell thought the FMB gave the Society a disproportionate amount of publicity. In light of Bell's enthusiastic support, including the quarterly Missionary Day when a special Sunday school offering was collected for foreign missionaries, the secretary surely felt slighted. To his friend Annie Armstrong, one of the founders of the Woman's Missionary Union (WMU) in 1888, Bell confided, "I am tired of the Foreign Board assuming that it is everything and the rest of us nothing, except as we can be beneficial to them." The Sunday School Board, he added, would not "be tacked on as a tail to the Foreign Mission Board kite."

Bell believed the FMB promoted the Publication Society at annual conventions, giving them prime placement in the program and excessively highlighting their contributions. He chafed at the fact that several FMB staff members also worked

part-time for the Northern Society. He felt the Society was a
threat to the Sunday School Board on account of its influence over the Foreign Mission Board and its powerful friends
in the SBC. At the 1895 Convention in Washington, DC, the
FMB sang the praises of the Northern Society, then criticized
Bell when he refused to follow suit. Asked to introduce A. J.
Rowland, his Society counterpart, to the Convention, Bell
refused. R. J. Willingham, head of the FMB, teased him publicly, saying the hot weather had put him in a bad mood.

Bell couldn't see why his fellow Southern Baptists, only
four years after inaugurating their own publication arm,
would so willingly give their business to its Northern competitor. In a letter to Willingham, Bell asked what the FMB
would think if the Sunday School Board actively supported
the Gospel Mission, whose stated goals (and many of their
donors) were the same as the FMB. He saw the Northern
Society as a juggernaut preparing to snuff out a rival formed
by Southern Baptists for Southern Baptists—with the unwit-
ting help of Southern Baptists themselves.

In a letter cited in an unpublished paper by Norman W.
Cox, formerly head of the SBC Historical Commission, Bell
fumed, "I may be wrong, but I am very strongly of the opinion that the future of the Foreign Mission Board, and even of
the Convention itself, is by the logic of our situation, in large
measure wrapped up with that of the Sunday School Board."
For Southern Baptists to buy from the Northern Society
instead of the Board was "to cut their own throats." Maybe it

was those boyhood memories of flight in the face of Northern invaders, but he'd felt the same way when he was editor of the *Foreign Mission Journal.* Then, he said, "I refused to accept any advertising from that Society, and would not have done so at a thousand dollars a page."

At the same time he was fighting the American Baptist Publication Society for the hearts and pocketbooks of Southern Baptists, T. P. Bell was also fighting to define and promote a Southern Bible training curriculum for Southern young people. He was worried about a Baptist movement to form a national Baptist youth organization. In the spring of 1890, eighty Baptists met in Chicago for the purpose and the next year, in the summer of 1891, launched the Baptist Young People's Union of America (BYPUA). The Baptists were reacting to Christian Endeavor, an interdenominational youth program begun in 1881 by a Congregationalist minister. Christian Endeavor was popular with Baptist youth north and south, as well as members of other denominations in America and abroad.

The success of this ministry made Baptists realize that they didn't want their children drifting off to non-Baptist programs and that there was a high demand for a student-focused program with its own literature and weekly meetings. By 1893 state Baptist youth programs were under way in Texas, Arkansas, Maryland, and Virginia. That year the SBC adopted a resolution, based on Dr. Bell's suggestion, that in order to "secure the increased spirituality of our Baptist

Young People" including "their instruction in Baptist doctrine and history," their training should come from societies "strictly Baptistic" and "without interdenominational affiliation."

The Convention further resolved: "In order that such literature as may be needed in attaining the ends had in view in these movements may be easily available to the churches, the Sunday-school Board be requested to provide the literature suitable for the purposes above mentioned and place the same where it may be needed."

In response, Dr. Bell developed the *Young People's Leader* monthly and hired Dr. Isaac Jacobus Van Ness, pastor of Nashville's Immanuel Baptist Church and a Sunday School Board trustee, as its editor. Though a New Jersey native, Van Ness had graduated from Southern Seminary in 1890 and immediately taken up his duties in Nashville.

There was still the matter of whether the BYPUA, founded in Chicago and dominated by Northerners, was a threat to training *Southern* Baptist youth. J. M. Frost, T. P. Bell, and Isaac Van Ness wanted what Frost described as a "distinctively Southern movement in connection with our own Convention, with emphasis on the Southern, in a broad, lofty, aggressive sense." When the three met later with William Whitsitt and J. B. Gambrell, two men who would play important parts in the history of the Baptist youth movement, they agreed unanimously that they should work, in Frost's words, "together in the South for the establishment of a Southern Young People's Union, auxiliary to the Southern Baptist Convention."

The question was how to bring up a proposal when it was likely to create a firestorm of controversy on top of the existing conflict over where SBC churches should buy their Sunday school materials. Rather than bring it to the Convention floor, interested parties held a meeting before the 1895 annual conclave in Washington. Gathering at First Baptist Church, the group heard Dr. R. H. Pitt, editor of the *Religious Herald* of Virginia, propose a resolution calling for a distinct organization for Southern Baptist youth. The result was what Robert A. Baker called an "explosive discussion" that "sometimes exceeded proper decorum." After a season of heated debate, Pitt's resolution was defeated. One of the most vocal opponents was T. T. Eaton, a Landmarkist, editor of the Baptist *Western Recorder* in Kentucky, and longtime critic of T. P. Bell. Other opponents were men who preferred the existing Young People's Union of America to any sort of new, pointedly Southern effort.

Even Dr. Bell would have been lukewarm to the idea had not he feared the Southern identity of his Board and the Convention were about to be lost. As he explained in a letter to Annie Armstrong, "My own personal preference, if it was merely a question of a Southern organization, would be to have none at all, and my only reason for wanting one was a matter of self-preservation against the BYPUA."

Six months later the Georgia state BYPU sponsored a meeting in Atlanta to reconsider a Southern youth program. After another round of wide-ranging debate, the assembled group voted the Baptist Young People's Union, Auxiliary to the Southern Baptist Convention, into existence. It was an independent organization with no official connection to the SBC. This arrangement, they hoped, would allow them to achieve their goals of producing the programs and publications they thought Southern youth should have, without risking a bloody battle in the Convention.

By that time, the fall of 1895, Dr. Bell had a more immediate problem on his hands. The ABPS had slashed its prices, offering six months of Sunday school literature for the price of three. Bell refused to match the discount, exclaiming, "God forbid that I should try to buy any school or any church of the Lord's people to use our literature when they are using another." To a pastor writing to ask if he would lower his prices, he pointed out that the offer from the ABPS was good only for churches not currently using their publications. "Suppose next year I were to do the same thing, would you switch back and forth for the little saving it gives? . . . If you think it best to leave us and go over to 'our friend the enemy,' I shall have no unkind word or thought for you."

He vented his anger in a letter to his friend Dr. Lansing Burrows, secretary of the Convention and the man initially elected as the first leader of the Sunday School Board:

The American Baptist Publication Society is wealthy, and absolutely determined to have a monopoly of all Baptist publishing in this country. It is just as determined on the destruction of the Sunday School Board of the Southern Baptist Convention, as Grant was on that of General Lee's army. It adopts measures overhanded and underhanded, straight and crooked, and every way to accomplish its purpose. Some of its officials whom brethren would not suspect of so doing, have even told clear and positive lies about me and my family in their endeavor to injure the Board.

(Bell had recently remarried. His new wife was Martha McIntosh, a South Carolina native and the first president of WMU.)

Historian Leon McBeth sees a goal beyond profits in the Publication Society's aggressive attitude and suggests there might have been more to Bell's Civil War simile than even Bell realized: "The Northern Society . . . felt there was a chance to heal the schism of 1845 and restore unity in the Baptist family. This would include the dissolution of the Southern Baptist Convention and all of its Boards, but this seemed a small price to pay for healing the schism that divided the Baptist family. . . . [Bell] was just as intent on preserving the Southern Baptist Convention, and perpetuating the division, as the Northern Baptists were upon reunion."

Two months after Bell had resigned as assistant secretary of the Foreign Mission Board, the secretary also resigned and Bell was offered the job. He turned it down to stay in his new position at the Sunday School Board. Now he was thinking about making a change. In closing his letter to Dr. Burrows, four days before Christmas 1895, he wrote pensively, "I wonder sometimes if I belong to an old school that is too strongly Southern Baptist in its sentiment, and that the time has come when I had better get out of the way and let others of broader spirit take a lead in some things."

Despite all the turmoil, work at the Board was going well. Dr. Boykin edited the venerable *Kind Words* issues, Dr. Frost continued editing *The Teacher*, and Isaac Van Ness was in charge of the new and popular *Young People's Leader*. Finances were strong, and the subscriber list grew steadily even in the face of a poor economy and relentless competitive and political pressure from the American Baptist Publication Society.

It was, Theodore Percy Bell decided, a good time to move on.

CHAPTER 7

Fireworks

Scarcely a month after his reflective and revealing letter to Dr. Burrows, T. P. Bell bought the *Christian Index*, the Southern Baptist paper in Georgia. He resigned from the Sunday School Board a week later to move to Atlanta and edit his new publication. Isaac Van Ness resigned too and went with him. In announcing his departure, Bell explained:

> In 1893 I yielded to the solicitations of the members of this Board, who felt that my wide acquaintance with the brethren over the South, and the cordial relations sustained to them all, peculiarly fitted me for taking charge of the then "infant" Board. For three years I have done my best, while all through

the days I have looked forward to a time when the Lord would let me feel that I had done enough in this sphere of labor. I now feel that that time has come. The condition of the Board . . . is so good, and the work so prosperous, that I have felt I could drop out now without injury.

Quickly and unanimously, leaders of the Sunday School Board voted to offer Dr. Frost his old job back. Whereas the first time around he had stewed and worried over leaving the pastorate, this time he didn't hesitate. He "burned the bridge" behind him and, he wrote, "poured my life without reserve into this channel of denominational work" to benefit "our great Baptist brotherhood of the South. Herein is my joy and crown of rejoicing." The job now also included the position of treasurer, which had been combined with the corresponding secretary's position in 1894.

The Board Dr. Frost took charge of had weathered his absence well. Receipts were solid, morale was high, and demand for its publications grew steadily. Frost returned to his old office at the Methodist Publishing House and went to work. One issue looming large was the continuing political and marketplace pressure from the Publication Society. Perhaps to Dr. A. J. Rowland and the rest of the Society management, Frost's return was a sign of weakness. Scarcely five years old, the Board had already changed leaders twice; Frost spent only a year and a half on the job the first time around and his successor stayed less than three. The Board still didn't have a home of its own. Its assets were valued at something like $22,500, while the Society's equaled $700,000.

Yet the Board was growing, tenacious, and fiercely independent. One day it could be a real threat to the power of the Society. Now may have seemed a prudent time to extend an olive branch of sorts. Early in 1896 Rowland wrote to Dr. Bell asking whether he would "fight it" if the Society proposed some sort of cooperation with the Board. Bell informed him that Frost had resumed his old post as secretary and Rowland should write to him. Frost considered the proposal and wrote back that Rowland's suggestions would harm not only the Board but also the entire SBC.

Rowland wrote Frost again. In a letter dated March 18, 1896, he said his executive committee wouldn't take no for an answer, insisting that many Southerners supported the Society. He claimed, "There is an earnest desire on the part of many of our brethren in the South that our Society should make overtures to your Board looking to greater harmony in the publication of Sunday School literature." They were "renewing the propositions because we have been urged to do so and because we are desirous of entering into closer relations with our Southern brethren."

The Publication Society seemed to position their offer as a partnership or merger of equals, preserving the Board's editorial integrity. But there was a catch. As Rowland explained, "We propose the annual appointment by the Sunday School

Board, said appointment to be subject to the approval of our Society, of an editor who shall have sole charge of that portion of the Series which is continued without change, who shall cooperate with our editor of periodicals in the production of the other issues of the Series, said editor to reside at Nashville or Philadelphia as may be deemed best."

With an editor "subject to the approval" of the Publication Society and who would almost certainly work from Philadelphia, accepting Rowland's terms would clearly be the end of an independent Southern publishing organization, and both sides knew it. But if the Society thought the Board was on the ropes and ready to make a deal, they could scarcely have been more mistaken.

After consulting with other members of the Board, Frost wrote to Rowland that "we cannot accept your proposition, deeming such alliance neither desirable nor feasible. We have no thought whatever of surrendering the work entrusted to us by the Southern Baptist Convention. Under the blessing of God our work has had in these five years a success almost phenomenal and altogether without precedent in Baptist circles."

Failing to achieve his objective in private, Rowland decided to go public with his offer, replying, "I presume there is no objection now to the whole matter being laid before the public. Unless I hear from you contrary I will forward a copy of your reply to some of the brethren who wished us to make a proposition." Frost and others anticipated a showdown at the 1896 Convention in Chattanooga; in fact, the secretary asked J. B. Hawthorne to prepare a presentation on "The Educational Value to the Convention of Owning and Publishing Its Own Sunday School Periodicals." But nothing happened, though Frost commented that "the situation was painful in private circles." Rumor had it that even the great Southern Baptist figure John A. Broadus, who had died the year before, supported the Publication Society. The rumor proved to be false.

Though there was no standoff with the ABPS at the Convention, the Society intensified its efforts to oppose the Sunday School Board in the marketplace. Board representatives arriving to present their products sometimes found Publication Society materials stacked on church pews as they entered or colportage wagons at the front door. Frost "had to fight his way for every inch of ground," one early field secretary wrote. "It was a great fight and Dr. Frost was quiet and serene about it all, moving right on like an old ocean liner plowing the waves."

In the fall of 1896, Frost extended a helping hand to another Baptist body struggling for independence from the ABPS. As the Southern Baptist Convention had done, the National Baptist Convention (Negro) wanted to establish its own publication arm. After the Publication Society declined to help them, they turned to the Board, asking to buy rights to the printing plates of Bible expositions for use in their own new quarterlies and teacher materials. Frost readily granted permission to use the plates and would accept no payment for them. Afterward he fended off accusations that he and the National Baptists were in collusion to take business away from the Society.

The 1897 convention was in Wilmington, North Carolina, presided over for the ninth year in a row by Jonathan Haralson. That was where the fireworks everyone had expected the year before in Chattanooga finally went off. After a glowing report to the assembly from W. J. Northern on the Sunday School Board, including a healthy balance sheet and the purchase of a house in Nashville to use as a headquarters, a member of the Publication Society took the Convention floor and blasted both the Board and Frost personally. He particularly criticized the Board's Bible lessons. As he went on, his speech became steadily more strident and pointed and the murmuring audience got more agitated. Listening to the diatribe, Frost, Northern, and a few others huddled near the presiding chairman's seat to decide how they should respond.

Several of them told Dr. Frost someone had to answer the speaker. Frost insisted he could not do it. William Hatcher of Virginia leaned over to the secretary and asked, "Do you care if I make a speech about that long?" He indicated part of a finger length. Frost replied, "I cannot say. Do as you like."

Years later Dr. Frost described what happened next.

[When the ABPS speech was over,] many men made an effort to get to the floor. I never saw so many heavy guns unlimber so quickly and get ready for action. Dr. William E. Hatcher, of Virginia, got the floor, and in twenty-five minutes made a speech that was a marvel even for him. All of his powers with an audience came into play in that short time. He told how he had not favored making the Board at first; how it had won its place in the denomination; how the Baptists of the South had set it out as their policy; now with humor that convulsed the audience; now with pungent statement that shot like an arrow from a master's hand; now with pathos that swept like fire in a prairie; now again as he came to the close like thunder in the gathering storm. Can anyone who was present ever forget how he stirred and swept the people as he turned with a mighty sweep in the declaration: "I have been a life-long friend of the Publication Society, but it must not come here to interfere with our work. We have our way of doing things, and woe betide the man who crosses our path." He ended, and there was no need for anything further. The case was disposed of, and a calm followed the storm.

Another ploy the Publication Society tried in order to head off serious competition was to nominate and elect several of their sympathizers to places on the Board. Frost countered with a little parliamentary sneakiness of his own.

Rather than protest the new Board members, he persuaded the Board president to hold that year's annual meeting so late in the year that there wouldn't be any time to take action on much of anything. Dr. Frost also went out of his way to appeal one-on-one to Board members he knew still didn't endorse having a separate SBC publisher, inviting them to investigate what the Board was doing. Some of them he even asked to promote the Board to state agencies; many eventually became some of the Board's strongest supporters.

By now all the ABPS strategies had failed: under-cutting prices, a private takeover attempt, a war of words on the Convention floor, and infiltrating the Board with their own allies. It was clear that in spite of their history of supplying materials to Baptist churches in the South, there was a demand from the Southern Baptist Convention for products that reflected a specifically Southern point of view, written and edited by Southern Baptists. No doubt there was also a feeling that if there was money to be made supplying Sunday school materials, that money should go where it would benefit the work of the denomination rather than elsewhere. The Wilmington standoff marked the last serious challenge from anyone to the SSB as publisher of Southern Baptist Sunday school literature. The Publication Society was never again a threat. By 1910 they had closed all three of their Southern branch offices.

Besides holding off the Northern Society, another high point for the Board in 1897 was moving at last into a home of its own. When the SBC convened for its 1893 annual meeting, Frost was sorry he had no place he could point to as the Board's property, which, he noted, "gratified some" and "gave others grave concerns." By 1897 the Board had set aside enough money, in addition to all its charitable appropriations, to buy a building. They purchased a private home at 167 North Cherry Street (later renamed Fourth Avenue North) for $10,000. It was a solid but unpretentious house with a wrought iron balcony across the second floor and cheerful striped awnings above the front windows.

Up until that time the Board had never published a book. Back in 1846 the Convention had resolved not to "embarrass itself with any enterprise for the publication and sale of books" and had so far been true to its word. The Board's marching orders from the Convention were to write and produce Sunday school study materials and "not engage in any other publication work except as hereinafter instructed." Books had been an expensive failure for the SBC in times past, although P. E. Burroughs suggests that the book publishing ban was "a concession to the Publication Society and an agreement secured by its friends that the Convention Board should not invade the general publication field. That field was to be left clear for its competitor." Yet in 1897, poised to become a full-fledged replacement for the Publication Society in the South, the Board would have to venture into the unknown waters of the book trade.

The opportunity came ironically from a project the ABPS rejected. Matthew Tyson Yates was a Baptist missionary in China during the American Civil War, when the Foreign Mission Board was scarcely able to keep its doors open, much less support its men and women in the field. With almost no help from home, Yates preached the word faithfully in Shanghai and accomplished great works for the Lord over forty-two years in the field, some of them under very tough circumstances. Dr. Charles E. Taylor, president of Wake Forest College, was commissioned to write Yates's biography. Taylor offered his manuscript to the Publication Society, but they turned it down on the grounds that they didn't think it would turn a profit and already had several missionary biographies in print. The man who commissioned the manuscript, A. J. Barton (later first chairman of the SBC Social Services Commission), suggested sending it to Frost, though he was well aware that the Sunday School Board was not supposed to publish books.

Frost stayed up most of the night reading the "wonderful" and "charmingly written" manuscript, which stirred his soul "to the deepest depths." Excitedly he reported, "For three days I was as one who had been on the Mount of Transfiguration, and was left with the conviction that the book would move others as it had moved me; that it was a book which for every consideration should be published, especially by Southern Baptists, a book indeed which the Convention would want published whether it paid or not."

Friends and colleagues both inside and out of the Sunday School Board were divided in their opinion whether

to publish. They believed unanimously that the book was
as moving and important as Frost had thought. But some
believed it was wrong to publish a book when it was categori-
cally forbidden, while others thought the story's importance
outweighed any official prohibition. Frost tried and failed to
find an underwriter for the venture. "My heart would not be
still," he later recalled, "for I felt that we had come upon our
opportunity. My theory was that the Convention would want
the book published, [and] would commend the Board for its
publication."

Soon Frost concluded that if he couldn't get permission
he'd settle for forgiveness. On December 31, 1897, he approved
the project and a budget of $500. *The Story of Yates the
Missionary* rolled off the press in time for the 1898 Convention
in Norfolk, Virginia. Dr. Lansing Burrows received the cere-
monial first copy, which he had paid one dollar for in advance.
At the news of what the Board had done, Frost reported, "The
natural thing happened. Some thought it a serious money
risk and a breach of instructions; the Convention, however,
adopted unanimously and even with enthusiasm a report on
the Sunday School Board's work."

The report was written by Dr. George W. Truett, a young
Baylor graduate who had just begun what would be a legendary forty-six-year pastorate at First Baptist Church, Dallas:

> We express not only our hearty approval, but
> also our great pleasure in the publication of the life

of Dr. Matthew T. Yates. And in this connection recommend compliance with the request which comes
from the Board, namely, that it be allowed liberty in
the publishing of books as part of its work; using, as
indicated in the report, such money as it may deem
practicable to appropriate from its business, or such
money as may be contributed for this particular
object. We recognize the far-reaching significance
of this recommendation, but judging of the previous management of the affairs entrusted to its care,
we feel perfectly safe in consigning to the Board this
enlargement of its work."

The SSB was in the book business.

CHAPTER 8

Gaining Ground

Though Frost's calculated risk had paid off handsomely, he was still officially not allowed to publish books. So he looked for private benefactors. In January 1899 Benjamin E. Garvey, a boyhood friend whom Frost had approached about underwriting the Yates biography but who couldn't do it at the time, endowed the Eva Garvey Fund. This gift eventually supported publication of seven books, including the early classics *Baptist Why and Why Not*, *Doctrines of Our Faith*, and *The Moral Dignity of Our Faith*. These three titles alone sold more than thirty-five thousand copies, with all seven Garvey Fund books reaching almost forty-seven thousand in sales. Three years later Dr. P. D. Pollock, president of Mercer

University, set up the Constance Pollock Fund in similar fashion to publish a series of books on Sunday school organization and leadership training. Eventually both funds recovered all their investment, and the substantial profits after that went to strengthen the Board's bottom line.

The year the Garvey Fund began, Samuel Boykin, long-time editor of *Kind Words*, passed away. The Board persuaded Isaac J. Van Ness to return to Nashville from Georgia where he worked with Dr. Bell on the *Christian Index* and became Dr. Frost's principal assistant. Between the two of them, these visionary, dedicated, and faithful Southern Baptists led the Sunday School Board for the next thirty-five years.

As the turn of the century approached, Frost considered how he could reorganize and refine his work to bring better Sunday school programs to more Baptist congregations in the South. He declared:

> As the Convention has in mind a celebration for the year 1900 we would ask that earnest consideration be given for making that an occasion for decided advancement in the Sunday School cause throughout the States and Territories. . . . We need improvement in the Sunday Schools that we have, we need Sunday Schools in the churches that have not hitherto had them, and all along the line to improve our Sunday School condition, and to foster our Sunday School power.

Almost half of Southern Baptist churches, more than nine thousand congregations, had no Sunday school at all in 1900; but Frost believed Southern Baptists and their Sunday schools were on the brink of a great season of growth. Besides the Sunday School Board, the SBC that year included the Home and Foreign Mission Boards, Southern Seminary in Louisville, Kentucky, and the affiliated Woman's Missionary Union. Southern Baptist membership was growing by more than 5 percent a year, well ahead of the general US population increase averaging about 3¼ percent.

Frost believed the way to build the Sunday school program most effectively was to send somebody into the field to promote SSB materials and show churches how to use them. Obviously churches weren't going to spend money on Bible lessons or anything else if they didn't recognize the benefit. Of the congregations that had any sort of Sunday school, some still used ABPS products or other suppliers, some cobbled together lessons of their own, and some did without anything.

Frost suggested hiring a field secretary "who will give himself wholly and devotedly to the promotion of the Sunday school cause." He heard of a man who was doing in North Carolina what he wanted to see done across the country and spent a year watching him in action. By the time he got Frost's attention, Bernard Washington Spilman was already known in his native state as "the Sunday School man." In his biography of Spilman, C. Sylvester Green paints the picture of a jolly, gregarious dynamo of a man weighing upwards of three hundred pounds who loved people and was devoted to the Southern Baptist cause.

Spilman was a Wake Forest graduate who had also attended Southern Seminary. He had been a pastor but found his true calling as a "Sunday School missionary" crisscrossing the state to see how churches were doing with Sunday school and how he could help them improve. He found only six programs in the state that he thought were well run. He decided that the key to success was effective teaching. To that end he spent a lot of his time holding teacher training workshops to explain and promote better Sunday school teaching methods. He also promoted summer assemblies based on the popular Chautauqua retreats, which combined a vacation in the country with lectures, travelogues, and other cultural entertainment.

Spilman made impressive progress at a time when the North Carolina Baptists were struggling. Many pastors in the state withheld support from Sunday school either because they didn't see the point or felt a threat to their leadership. Some months the state convention couldn't scrape together the money for Spilman's salary. During one road trip John E. White, the state secretary, advised him to give up Sunday school work because "there is nothing but failure ahead." When he got back to his office in Raleigh, he opened his dictionary and scratched the word "failure" out of it. For him it simply didn't exist.

Spilman moved to Nashville and started working for the Board in 1901 under a five-point mandate: (1) improving Sunday school in the South; (2) coordinating his effort with individual state Sunday school leaders; (3) accepting no compensation other than room and board from state associations; (4) not entering a state except by invitation; and (5) not selling Sunday school literature. He was careful not to compete with state associations or try to make decisions for them; he was out to win them as allies. His job wasn't to pitch SSB material or organize new Sunday schools himself but to stimulate others to organize them and then demonstrate the worth of Board materials and supplies. As Dr. Frost explained, "Improvement in the Sunday school condition means advancement in everything else. A Sunday school campaign means a campaign for Bible study, for better knowledge of the Word of God among the people; in our thinking, it means enlargement of the Sunday school idea, while in practical work it means more schools, larger schools, and better schools. It is a marshalling of the army of the Lord for a forward movement."

After one look at what Frost described as a "dingy little office" in the only space available for him at Cherry Street, Spilman spent most of his time on the road and soon ended up moving his family back to Raleigh because his wife didn't like Nashville. As much as he traveled, it scarcely mattered where his base of operations was. This set the precedent for field secretaries to live anywhere they chose, though in theory they worked out of Nashville.

Somehow, amid all the traveling, Spilman found time in 1902 to write *Normal Studies for Sunday School Workers*, which the Board sold for 25 cents each or $1.80 a dozen. The same year Southern Seminary began teaching Sunday school pedagogy and eventually established an academic chair in the field. After more than half a century of haphazard development and expansion, Sunday school was finally getting some concrete standards and professional organization.

In 1903 the Board moved out of its home on Cherry Street to a far larger and more impressive house at 710 Church Street. Formerly the home of railroad executive and financier Colonel E. W. Cole, it featured a tile roof with a forest of chimneys and gables, and an elegant limestone staircase leading from the sidewalk to a spacious porch flanked by columns. Among other prominent figures of the day, President William McKinley had visited Colonel Cole there.

Dr. Frost had once turned down an offer of $12,000 for the Cherry Street house, which would have cleared the Board a $2,000 profit. Now the Cherry Street building was sold for what Frost called "about the same price" they had paid for it, $10,000; and the Board bought the Cole house for $60,000 in cash. Even with this expense on top of the cost of sending B. W. Spilman into the field, the Board in 1903 exceeded $100,000 in net assets for the first time.

With his jovial manner and single-minded resolve, Spilman was a great success at spreading the word about the value of Sunday school and how to teach it. His first seven months on the job he traveled twelve thousand miles. During his second year he met a state Sunday school committee chairman and one of his former employees, both of whom eventually became important players in the history of the Board. Spilman was attending the Mississippi State Convention in the summer of 1902 where they were trying to launch a statewide Sunday school program even though previous attempts had all fizzled.

A resolution to employ a state Sunday school secretary, introduced by Dr. T. J. Bailey of *The Baptist Record*, was referred to a committee chaired by a department store owner from Winona named Arthur Flake. Spilman, Bailey, and Flake endorsed the resolution; but there was stiff resistance from other committee members. When it looked like the issue might go in his favor after hours of argument, Flake opposed a vote because he didn't think they should go forward unless the committee agreed unanimously. The question was deferred from that Saturday to Monday morning.

Sunday afternoon Flake walked to the train station with a young convention delegate named Landrum Pinson Leavell, who was leaving town early. A faculty member of the Jefferson Military Institute near Natchez, Major Leavell planned to spend some time the next day recruiting new students. At twenty he had been a clerk in Mr. Flake's store and lived in his home. Now, after graduating from the University of Mississippi, he was carrying on the tradition of a military education for sons of the South. The two walked along the platform, Flake in his Sunday suit and Leavell in his dress uniform, talking about the prospect of having a state Sunday school secretary.

With a sudden start, Flake looked the young major in the eye and said, "Landrum, you ought to take that job."

"Why, I never thought of it before," Leavell answered. "I could not do it."

"Well," Flake shot back, "I never thought of it before; but we have both thought of it now, and you are the man. You must stay here until tomorrow. The Convention will elect you."

Leavell held out his train ticket and said he had to get on with his recruiting work, but Flake stood firm. Leavell agreed to stay the night. Between then and the next morning, Spilman and Flake worked their contacts, getting out the word that Leavell was willing to take the job. After the president of the state mission board spoke in favor of Leavell at the Monday session, Spilman took the podium for a solid hour. Barely visible above the lectern despite his enormous weight, he began his remarks with a radiant smile and an unexpected offer: "I am not sure whether I am taller standing up or lying down. If you cannot see me, I will try lying down."

He talked about the importance of teaching in Jesus' ministry, among His disciples, in the Old and New Testaments, down through the ages, and in Sunday school today. Preaching,

he insisted, had to be matched with teaching. Pastors and laymen alike not only withdrew their opposition from Friday
but pledged money toward a Sunday school secretary's salary.
When Leavell was called to speak, he told of dedicating his
life to Christian service during a YMCA conference, seeking
God's will in how best to serve. When he finished, many of
his audience were in tears. Leavell was heartily approved as
Mississippi's first statewide Sunday school leader.

That fall Leavell and Spilman preached "the gospel of
better Sunday School work" in twenty-two Mississippi towns
in twenty-six days. Spilman soon invited his young associate
to join him at the Sunday School Board, and the two combined their talents for the good of Southern Baptists everywhere. One of the highlights of their collaboration came in
1906 when the first Sunday school institute was held at First
Baptist Church in Nashville, bringing Sunday school teachers
from around the city to study teaching methods. In a novel
gesture of hospitality, the church agreed to feed all 250 participants; the whole week was an unqualified success.

To Spilman and others who had worked so long to
improve Sunday schools and who realized how far they'd
come in fifteen years, the closing night of the institute was
an emotional moment. As L. P. Leavell's son and biographer
Ronald Q. Leavell described it:

> Dr. Spilman was unable to speak. Tears streamed
> from his eyes. Finally he managed to say: "It has

come at last. It can be done. I thank God that I have
lived to see it. For 10 years I have been praying for
such a meeting as we have had. I knew it ought to
come. This week has come and I have seen it with my
own eyes. Today my heart is too full of gratitude to
God to talk about it." He stood there for a few minutes with tears rolling down his cheeks, then slowly
walked to his seat. At least some of them understood
with Dr. Spilman that they were on the threshold
of a new day in the Sunday school life of Southern
Baptists.

Along with fieldwork and teacher training, another way
to strengthen Sunday schools was to promote hymn singing.
Strictly speaking, since the Board couldn't publish books,
they couldn't produce a hymnal. However, predecessors of the
Board had tried their hands in the music field several times.
The old Southern Baptist Publication Society in Charleston
had issued *The Baptist Psalmist* in 1851. Though the SBC
recommended it, the songs were too hard to learn and gener-
ally too formal for Baptist worship. At the height of the Civil
War in 1863, an earlier Sunday School Board published *The
Little Sunday School Hymnbook* and the *Confederate Sunday
School Hymn Book* from their headquarters in Greenville.
Wartime disruptions doomed both those efforts. In 1871 a
hymnal titled *Kind Words in Melody*, modeled after the *Kind
Words* publications, sold for twenty-five cents a copy.

In 1904 Dr. Frost announced that the Board would publish a new hymnal. "The demand for its publication has been growing for years," he said, "and our people are in great expectation of it." Churches used a helter-skelter variety of songbooks; some had none at all. A good collection of hymns gathered with Southern Baptist preferences and worship traditions in mind would surely strengthen the worship experience. If the venture made the Board a profit, so much the better. But as historian Leon McBeth observed, "Board leaders saw their mandate as helping the churches fulfill their biblical mission and ministry. . . . If the proposed hymnal had not been profitable, and the churches still needed it, there is every reason to think the Board would have tried to meet that need within the limits of its resources."

Before the year was out, the Sunday School Board released *The Baptist Hymn and Praise Book*, a collection of 577 hymns, priced at 85 cents a copy or $55 per hundred. The annual report of the Convention described the new title as containing "many of the old hymns so rich in doctrine and spiritual power and sweep of music, and also some of the nobler songs which have gladdened the hearts and enriched the life of Christians in these modern times as Zion has awakened to sing afresh the story of redeeming grace." The collection was "suitable to all the services of the church, whether on Sunday or at a prayer meeting or in the Sunday school or in the special revival meetings." In seven years the Board sold

nearly ninety thousand copies, far and away its best seller up
to that time.

Recognizing the obvious—that book publishing was necessary, profitable, and ongoing—the SBC finally lifted its ban
against publishing at the 1910 convention in Baltimore. One
reason for the timing was that the American Bible Publication
Society had closed all three of its offices in SBC territory, leaving the field to the Board. Dr. Frost had often told churches
that the Board was grateful for 95 percent of their business
but wanted 100 percent. With the ABPS in full retreat, the
board had to broaden its produce line to include 100 percent
of what churches needed.

The resolution came from T. P. Bell, former secretary of
the Board and still one of its most enthusiastic supporters:

> Whereas, the removal of the branch houses of
> the American Baptist Publication Society from the
> South has left open a great field for the preparation
> and dissemination of Christian literature of many
> sorts, especially of the Baptist type; and,
>
> Whereas, somebody is going to occupy this field,
> more less, to the advantage of our Baptist interests;
> and,
>
> Whereas there is no agency, individual or other,
> so well qualified to occupy it to the satisfaction and
> profit of our people as is our own Sunday School
> Board, which has means, experience, business touch

with all our churches, Sunday schools, and pastors,
knows well the needs of our people and enjoys their
confidence and affection; therefore be it resolved:

The Board be authorized and urged to enter,
at as early a date as possible, on the work of supplying the brethren of our churches with books, tracts,
hymn and song books, and indeed all supplies for
churches, Sunday schools, missionary societies,
Young People's Unions, such as are suitable and
desirable.

In taking this step the Convention acknowledged the
current power and future potential of the Board to nurture
and shape Sunday schools across the SBC. The resolution,
approved unanimously, also unleashed a new wave of growth
and influence that would carry the Board to new levels of
success. The birth pangs were over; now the maturing process
began in earnest.

CHAPTER 9

The Track Is Clear

The Sunday School Board had outgrown its quarters again. Under B. W. Spilman, an energetic field staff—eventually eleven in all—rode the rails almost constantly, visiting churches, meeting with state leaders, and working to raise the quality and popularity of Sunday school. Among the new additions were Arthur Flake, the Mississippi store owner and state association stalwart, who joined the SSB staff in 1909, and Dr. Frost's daughter, Margaret, who came in 1910. Meanwhile, Frost and his editorial team headed by I. J. Van Ness oversaw an ever-increasing volume of books and publications. Adding in the required stenographers, shipping clerks, and other support staff jammed the old Cole mansion to capacity.

Frost set aside money every year to make gifts to foreign and home missions, add to a Bible fund, support state associations, and build up a reserve for a new office somewhere down the line. In 1912, crowded as they were, the Board diverted more than $20,500 to donate to the new Woman's Missionary Union training school at Southern Seminary. Its wealth gave the Board the potential to be a potent political force in the denomination, but Frost was always careful to look at the need and seek God's will on the matter; he never used the Board's prosperity for political advantage.

Also in 1912 the Board began a project that produced one of the most enduring symbols of Frost's leadership. They sold the Church Street headquarters for $200,000, more than triple what they'd paid for it in 1903, with permission to stay there until they had a new building. They already had a lot at 161 Eighth Avenue North, just off Broadway, and had held onto it even after offers to sell at a handsome profit.

An elegant four-story building was designed, framed in steel, and sheathed in Kentucky limestone. Two massive stone columns framing the front door were flanked by matching square pilasters at the corners, all four of them extending up from granite bases to Corinthian capitals supporting a heavy cornice above the fourth-floor windows. The design, Frost wrote, represented "the three-fold idea of business place, banking house and with temple effect—something of a Baptist Business Temple."

The Board moved into its new home in October 1913, less than fifteen months after selling the Church Street house.

The Eighth Avenue headquarters was solid and elegant without being overly showy. Frost located his office immediately inside the front entrance off the marble-floored lobby, accessible to anybody and perfectly positioned to keep a watchful eye on things. The building had hot and cold running water, an elevator, and coal-fired steam heat. There was a big, empty basement in case the Board ever wanted to install its own printing presses and a whole spare floor that they let the Tennessee State Mission Board use for the time being. "We wonder at the ways of God," Frost mused, "and count ourselves happy in the thought that His hand has guided in it all."

On May 16, 1914, the Sunday School Board building was presented to the SBC in a special service during the annual convention. For the occasion Dr. Frost wrote a booklet titled *The Sunday School Board, Southern Baptist Convention, Its History and Work*. It was the first comprehensive history of the early days of the Board and even today gives a valuable snapshot of its accomplishments over those first thirteen precedent-setting years.

The Board, Frost explained, "has its chief business in issuing Sunday school literature in such form and teaching as best suits the needs of the Baptist churches of the South. This was its purpose when first appointed, and is the line of its greatest business achievement. . . . All else in the way of publishing and merchandise is incidental."

The *Kind Words* series and all its various spin-offs were still going strong. To them the Board had added the

Graded Lessons, developed both to help standardize and organize Sunday school classes and to give Southern Baptists an alternative to interdenominational study materials. The series was produced for five age groups: primaries (under nine), juniors (nine to twelve), intermediates (thirteen to sixteen), seniors (seventeen to twenty), and adults.

The adult studies were targeted particularly at the popular Baraca classes for men and Philathea classes for women. Until 1908 Southern Baptists had collaborated with the International Lesson Committee in producing some materials. After the graded program was in place, following a theological split between the Committee and the SBC, Southern Baptists produced their own lesson series beginning in 1910. Dr. Frost wrote a spirited pamphlet challenging the Baraca and Philathea Union of Syracuse, New York, which opposed what it called "denominationalism" in favor of a nondenominational approach to Sunday school that it believed was "of tremendous value in attracting those who have grown tired of over-emphasis of dogma and creed."

The Union's pamphlet defending their position, "Let's Get It Straight," made J. M. Frost see red. Far from being nondenominational, Frost countered, Baraca and Philathea were "*anti*-denominational in their aim and effort." He continued: "It is not a fit message for Baptists, whether individually thinking for themselves, or for classes in Sunday schools of Baptist churches. Indeed, every denomination will come to feel sooner or later, and some are already realizing, that their interests are in jeopardy when entrusted to the care for forces operated from Syracuse and having the leadership of those who think it makes no difference what one believes or teaches." Stepping out of his cool editorial persona for the moment, Frost had no reservations about stridently defending his Baptist beliefs and redoubling his resolve to see that Sunday schools had the resources they needed to uphold those beliefs.

Other important publishing work continued. B. W. Spilman's popular *Normal Studies for Sunday School Workers* was combined with other small books by L. P. Leavell and Hight C Moore to produce the Convention *Normal Manual for Sunday School Workers*. This 1909 manual on Sunday school methods, pupil needs, and the Bible went through numerous editions over the next quarter century and was the foundation of teacher training for a generation. In 1913, keeping in mind Spilman's belief that good Sunday schools depended on good teaching, the Board hired Dr. Prince Emmanuel Burroughs, pastor of the Broadway Baptist Church in Fort Worth, as Education Secretary and spearheaded further new training materials for teachers. He also developed a popular system of diplomas and special seals to give children a sense of accomplishment as they worked through the lessons. (I've quoted widely from his fifty-year anniversary history of the Board, published in 1941.)

The Board had played a key part in the growth of the Baptist Young People's Union. L. P. Leavell began working with the organization in 1907; Arthur Flake turned his attention and enthusiasm to the BYPU starting in 1912. The Board developed a distinct curriculum for young people and began donating money to the BYPU. Between 1895 and 1916 the organization exploded from 500 unions totaling 20,000 members to more than 4,000 unions representing 153,000 young men and women.

Besides these key areas, the Board established a Home Department to make Sunday school teaching available to people who didn't or couldn't come to church. The Board also took a long look at the possibility of operating retail stores. However, the existing mail-order operation was very successful. Opening stores would be an expensive risk, and it could put them in competition with the many state associations that operated their own stores. Retailing was deferred for the time being.

Frost proudly included a table in his history booklet showing the Board's healthy financial condition. Between 1892 and 1914 the SSB had given more than $61,000 to the Bible Fund, money earmarked to supply Bibles free of charge to a variety of groups. They donated almost $600,000 in all to everything from WMU and the Baptist seminaries to the Chinese Publication Society. The generous contribution to the WMU reflected that group's early support for the Board, especially Frost's friend Annie Armstrong, WMU corresponding secretary during the Board's early years, who he said glowingly "in many ways helped to give the Sunday School Board its proper rank among the forces which make for denominational life." The largest gift, $212,000 was to local Sunday school operations through the field directors. This was all in addition to paying $160,000 for their new building, $60,000 for the Eighth Avenue lot, and having a $50,000 cash reserve in the bank.

According to P. E. Burroughs, Dr. Frost was a sick man by the time he showcased his fine new headquarters for the Convention. In his *Fifty Fruitful Years*, Burroughs wrote:

> The burden of the years had exacted their toll, and the strenuous pressure of the last two years in which the building had been under construction and the history [Frost's celebratory account of his years at the Board] had been written left its marks which could be seen even by the casual observer and which were all too clear to interested friends. The two years which followed were years of labor and sorrow. . . . After [his health failed] he struggled on in weakness and suffering for nearly a year. He kept at his post through sheer determination to live. If he could have given up his active and exacting service and sought rest in a more favorable climate, he might have pro- longed his days. He preferred to stay with his tasks, and chose to die in the harness.

Church men of the time often worked up until their last days. No doubt they did so because they felt called to the task and deeply loved their Southern Baptist cause. Also the cold truth was that unless they worked, these men had no income. This was before the days of Social Security or retirement pensions. They had to work as long as possible to keep bread on the table. Burroughs notes this sad fact in passing. Frost had built the Sunday School Board from nothing to an influential spiritual and financial powerhouse worth millions. But "he had unselfishly neglected his own fortunes. As he calmly faced the approaching end, he expressed regret that he had seemed unable to make suitable provision for those who had just claims upon him"—his wife and family.

Near the end his old friend T. P. Bell wrote: "Men talk as if your days were not to stretch very far into the future—our future. And if so what of it? When a man has finished a great work his Lord has given him to do, what if, some day, the same Lord should say: 'Enough! come up higher.' I know no man among us who has won and held the love, and admiration as well, of his brethren more completely than you have: and we have reason to believe, the Master's also." Neither man could have imagined then that Bell would finish his earthly work even sooner than his fading friend, succumbing to illness in North Carolina on October 2 at the age of fifty-four.

Prepared in heart and spirit to pass on, Frost lingered for a time in spite of the bronchitis that was slowly suffocating him. With wry humor he said, "I feel as if I were on a journey and the train is late. Why should I wish to stay? I have done all I can for my family and for my Lord." Though his doctor had warned him not to do any more public speaking, Frost preached the commencement sermon at Southern Baptist Theological Seminary in 1916. This, he insisted, was the highest honor of his life. He traveled briefly to French Lick Springs, Indiana, looking (evidently in vain) for some relief from his symptoms.

One of the last people to meet Dr. Frost for the first time was Gaines S. Dobbins, a young pastor from New Albany, Mississippi, whom I. J. Van Ness had invited to Nashville to interview for a position on the editorial staff. "He took me to see Dr. Frost, who was on his deathbed," Dobbins wrote years later. "The end was clearly approaching. . . . I shall never forget the pale, wan figure that lay on the bed nor the clasp of the thin hands as Dr. Frost joined in the invitation to me to become Dr. Van Ness' helper. His last words [to me] were, 'Young man, a great and effectual door is being opened to you.'"

It was typical of Dr. Frost that even in his last days he was identifying fresh talent for the Board and encouraging promising young Southern Baptists to put their shoulders to the wheel.

Just under eight weeks after his friend Bell's final letter, on October 30, 1916, James Marion Frost died in his Nashville home with his wife and children around him. The *Nashville Banner* declared, "In Dr. Frost's death, Nashville loses one of its most worthy citizens and the church one of its most sainted members. . . . At the time of his death, he was considered by many the greatest living man in the Baptist Church."

At the memorial service held in the First Baptist Church in Nashville, where the Sunday School Board had been voted into existence and where Frost had once been pastor, friends and colleagues came from all across the South. After a great service of thanksgiving, just before the casket was closed, Lansing Burrows, his great white mutton chops wet with tears, stood over the body and sobbed, "Good-bye, Frost. I will see you in the morning."

On one of his last trips out of town, Frost himself had chosen his burial site at Cave Hill Cemetery in Louisville near Southern Seminary, where J. P. Boyce, John A. Broadus, and other distinguished faculty members lay. His body was carried to Louisville by special train, where the funeral service was conducted by W. W. Landrum at Broadway Baptist Church.

Frost also wrote words that deftly define the Board's position as the Frost era came to an end. They were the words that concluded his celebratory booklet written for the dedication of the new building: "The track is clear. Everything is propitious. The possibilities are immense and capable of indefinite expansion. The past is full of promise for the future. The Baptists of the South should lead all other people for the coronation of the King and the bringing in of the kingdom."

CHAPTER 10

An Optimistic Age

A few days after Dr. Frost's funeral, I. J. Van Ness wrote to E. Y. Mullins, president of Southern Baptist Theological Seminary, to thank him for his warm personal comments about Frost during the ceremony. In his answer Mullins revealed, "We are of course greatly interested in his successor, and, confidentially, some of us think you are the man, all of us so far as I know."

Isaac Jacobus Van Ness had served briefly at the Board editing *Young People's Leader* before moving in 1896 to Atlanta, where he edited *The Christian Index* for T. P. Bell. Four years later he returned to Nashville as editorial secretary under Frost following Samuel Boykin's death. During his second tenure at the SSB, he wrote editorials for denominational publications, edited articles, tracts, and books, vetted book manuscripts submitted by others, and wrote books of his own. He eventually oversaw three weekly publications, one monthly, and sixteen quarterlies. And if all that didn't keep him busy enough, in 1906–1907 he was president of the Sunday School Editors' Association of the United States and Canada.

The last six months of Dr. Frost's life, Van Ness had been managing his official duties for him at the request of the Board. Van Ness brought issues and questions to Frost's bedside at his home on Terrace Place, then carried his recommendations back to the leadership. Church historian Leon McBeth observed, "The way Van Ness conducted himself during these troubled times gave the trustees more confidence in his leadership. He always scrupulously carried out Frost's wishes when they could be determined, though at times Frost was too ill even for that. Moreover, Van Ness was careful to act *for Frost*, never in his own capacity."

On November 28, 1916, the Board chose Van Ness as acting corresponding secretary. The next May the national Convention in New Orleans elected him permanently to the post as recommended by the trustees, despite a brief effort to open the floor to other nominations. Van Ness was a different sort of man and a different sort of leader from any of the major Southern Baptist figures who had gone before. He was from well north of the Mason-Dixon Line and on his way to a career in finance before answering the call to Christian service.

Isaac Van Ness was born in East Orange, New Jersey, in 1860, to parents of Dutch ancestry. He was baptized at seventeen by Edward Judson, whose father, Adoniram Judson, had been a legendary missionary in India and Burma and translated the Bible into Burmese. Isaac went to church with members of the Colgate family, whose patriarch, William, had founded a prosperous soap and candle company and endowed a university. (The invention of toothpaste in a tube, in 1908, would eventually make his company a household name.) Isaac's father was caretaker for Samuel Colgate, who served as Sunday school superintendent and encouraged Isaac to be his secretary.

After graduating from high school, Isaac got a job as a bookkeeper with J. P. Morgan & Co. in New York. Whatever interest he had in high finance was tempered after a while by his observations of his fellow workers. Sitting on his high bookkeeping stool, he could look down the long desk at his coworkers, many of them stooped and gray from their long years of service. "Surely there is something better in life for me than this," he said to himself. He pushed back his stool, hopped to the floor, walked to the manager's office, and resigned on the spot.

Feeling an interest in Christian outreach, Van Ness went to work for the YMCA in New York as, among other things, athletic director. His pastor asked him what good reason he had for *not* preaching. Intrigued by the way the question was worded, he thought about the prospect and decided that he was in fact called to Christian ministry. He asked the venerable Mr. Colgate for advice. The old gentleman told him he ought to go to a southern seminary because southern preachers were "warmer hearted and more effective" than northern ones. He picked Southern Seminary in Louisville, largely because it gave him a chance to study under the great Dr. John A. Broadus.

In later years Van Ness never tired of honoring Broadus or of repeating various stories about his gift for teaching. One of his favorites was about Broadus calling him to the blackboard to write a sermon outline. When Van Ness finished, he had covered the whole board with minute details. Broadus stood looking at it in silence for a moment, then declared jovially, "A very good skeleton, a very good skeleton—but not enough meat!" Another time Broadus summoned a brash student who kept interrupting him to the front of the room. He handed him a Bible and the class roll and said, "Here, you take over." The student tried to stammer out a response before standing flustered and silent. Broadus held his hands together in front of his face and mimed blowing up a balloon, then "popped" it with a forefinger and hissed as the imaginary air leaked out.

One morning after class, Dr. Broadus introduced Isaac to Dr. W. R. L. Smith, who had come from Nashville to find a pastor for the new Immanuel Baptist Church. The young

Van Ness had small experience in the pulpit: only a summer preaching at a mission church back home in New Jersey founded by his pastor. But on the strength of his interview with Smith and the strong recommendation from Broadus, Isaac was called to Nashville. A year later he married Francis Tabb, daughter of a socially prominent Louisville family who thought she could have done better. Francis insisted her life was far richer and fuller than it could ever have been with any other match.

Between the time Isaac Van Ness first moved to Nashville in 1890 and the day in May 1917 when the convention elected him executive secretary, the Sunday School Board and the culture around it had undergone a historic transformation. Only a controversial idea in 1890, the Board had grown into a strong and purposeful organization that had not merely paid its own way but subsidized other Southern Baptist ministries and operations as well. It had a magnificent limestone headquarters in downtown Nashville. Its books, tracts, magazines, and other publications articulated and reinforced Baptist doctrine and at the same time helped unify Southern Baptist congregations across the country.

Like the rest of the nation, Nashville was a far different place than it had been a generation earlier. In 1890 much of the commercial traffic in town came by riverboat. Automobiles were unknown, and electric light was a novelty. By 1917 the city blazed with electric signs, electric streetcars crisscrossed the business district and near suburbs, and cars outnumbered horses in the street. A large and magnificent Romanesque train station of gray stone proclaimed the importance of railroads as river commerce faded. Even the street names were different: Vine Street, Market Street, Cherry Street, and all the rest had given way to numbered avenues in 1904 as city leaders strove to be more cosmopolitan.

It was a time when America flexed its international muscle with newfound confidence. A month before Van Ness was elected, the United States entered World War I. It was the beginning of a historic shift in world power and wealth away from Europe and toward the New World. In such an optimistic age anything seemed possible. The Sunday School Board was established on firm footing and branching out.

The same war that gave America new clout in world affairs presented the Board and every other enterprise in the country with new challenges. With military enlistments rising and the available workforce shrinking, the Board had a harder time finding workers and had to pay more to get them. On top of that, the influenza epidemic of 1918 closed churches in many communities, reducing the demand for Sunday school materials. Yet even as demand fell and the cost of materials and postage shot up on account of wartime shortages and government policy, the Board prospered. Between 1917 and 1919, while Southern Baptist Sunday school enrollment dropped by about twenty-five thousand as church members left for military service, Board receipts increased by more than $100,000. Part of the increase came in producing popular and inexpensive Bibles for soldiers.

The Board's prosperity and the wartime conditions it operated under brought I. J. Van Ness two of his first major challenges as corresponding secretary. At the 1917 convention, surplus funds were lively topic of discussion. The Board submitted a policy statement proposing that instead of giving money to various denominational programs and projects as in the past, they would among other things develop their own field operations in Sunday school and BYPU, support state boards, distribute more free tracts, and contribute to the Foreign and Home Mission Boards to the extent that their work involved publications and church building.

Some members of the Convention were wary of the Sunday School Board moving into the other boards' ministry areas. Yet there was also a resolution that the SSB should pay administrative expenses of the Foreign and Home Mission Boards. To that suggestion the Sunday School Board replied: "This proposal is contrary to sound administrative principles." The Board went on to assert that each board of the Convention should be responsible for its own expenses, that Southern Baptist entities not receiving support would feel slighted, that the Sunday School Board had no assurance of future surpluses and if they had them, they should be available for emergencies. They also pointed out the need to spend money helping "our backward country churches."

The Convention approved the Sunday School Board's statement, and that was the end of the financial controversy.

The second challenge to Van Ness in those earliest years was US government policy on spiritual ministry to men and women in the armed forces. To simplify matters the government wanted to combine several Protestant denominations under the umbrella of the YMCA. Van Ness and the president of the Convention, J. B. Gambrell, led denominational opposition to the idea. Formed on regional and cultural grounds, the Southern Baptists had a historic policy, reinforced during the 1914 Convention, against "entangling alliances with other bodies holding to different standards of doctrine and different views of church life and church order," insisting on "a complete autonomy at home and abroad."

Later Van Ness further expanded on the official Southern Baptist position, affirming that the Convention would maintain complete control of its work, opposing "organic or official connection" with other denominations, and denying "any interdenominational agencies the expressed or implied sanction to approach our schools."

When he was elected secretary, I. J. Van Ness prayed, "Lord, make me big enough to work with other people and let them get the credit." Van Ness was not the grandstander type. He was quiet, cautious, deliberative almost to a fault (according to people impatient for him to decide an issue), and led others by suggestion and consensus. Accustomed as he was to editorial work, he spent most of his time at Board headquarters and seldom traveled. He kept his office where J. M. Frost had had his, on the ground floor immediately off the entry foyer, available anytime to anyone.

The beautiful new building had room to spare. In 1917 there were only fifty-eight Board employees scattered throughout the space, plus the vast empty basement. One whole floor was occupied by the Tennessee State Mission Board. But all that was about to change.

Dr. Frost had operated with what Leon McBeth called a "skeleton crew" in Nashville editing and shipping materials, while field staff covered the South encouraging Baptist churches to start Sunday schools and then to buy their literature from the Board. Six field secretaries established headquarters wherever they wished and worked their own hours. As the idea of Sunday schools took hold and the Board grew larger, Van Ness reorganized the operation to centralize and coordinate it more efficiently. Another contributing factor to the change was that Frost had the strong and forceful personality required to manage people well at a distance. Van Ness's more passive and reflective style worked better when more of the senior staff was close at hand.

Van Ness and the trustees departmentalized the Board in two stages. The first was in 1917, when they divided the business activities among the Bookkeeping and Cashier's Department, Order and Mailing Department, and Sales Department. Within two years the Board had established five more departments, some of them led by men who would become key figures in Southern Baptist history.

The new Editorial Department took over the core duties of editing and publishing. Hight C Moore, a North Carolina pastor and editor of the state *Biblical Recorder*, came as coeditor when Van Ness left the Board editor's chair to become corresponding secretary. Moore was familiar throughout the denomination as recording secretary of the Convention and later served in various other capacities as well as a director of the American Baptist Theological Seminary. His distinctive name came from the Southern tradition of adapting family names to first names. His uncle and namesake, who died a Confederate soldier, was named Hight in honor of a Grandmother Hight and C for Seay, another ancestor. (This explains the riddle of why his middle initial is never followed by the customary period: it isn't an abbreviation, it's a cypher.)

His collaborator was Edwin Charles Dargan, former pastor of First Baptist Church, Macon, Georgia, past Convention president, and Dr. Broadus's successor to the chair of homiletics at Southern Seminary. These two would serve shoulder to shoulder, writing, editing, and supervising a growing stable of publications until Dargan's retirement ten years later at the age of seventy-five. After that Moore carried on alone as editorial secretary.

Another member of the editorial council was L. P. Leavell, who had finally given in to Arthur Flake's urgent request to be the first state Sunday school secretary in Mississippi, then came to work for the Board the next year in 1903. Though he taught at Southern Seminary and wrote or contributed to several books, his greatest achievement was in writing and editing materials for the Baptist Young People's Union, including its student manual, annual yearbook, and *B.Y.P.U. Quarterly.* Handsome and energetic, Leavel looked healthy even though he knew for years that his blood pressure was dangerously high. In 1925 he suffered a massive stroke while playing golf with Dr. Van Ness in Nashville. Bravely but with limited success, he spent the next four years trying to recover sufficiently to resume his duties before his death at fifty-five.

A separate Department of Missionary Publications came into being in 1919, headed by Gaines S. Dobbins. Whatever residual sensitivities there were regarding surplus funds and the Sunday School Board muscling in on Foreign Mission Board territory, they seem not to have affected establishing a separate group specifically to encourage and support mission workers in distant lands. *Home and Foreign Fields* was Dobbins's main regular publication, though he also prepared material for special missionary days in Sunday school and supplied stories about missionaries to other publications.

One of Van Ness's more ambitious new ventures was a Church Architecture Department. In 1919 he explained, "The development of modern Sunday-school ideas, and especially the growth of the graded and departmental idea, has made it imperative that the Board as an element of its campaign of

Sunday-school education should make some effort to secure buildings adapted to modern Sunday-school work."

Baptist churches had improved their worship spaces over the years, but progress was slow. At the end of the Civil War, only about half the Baptist congregations in the South had any building at all. By World War I many more church families had a place to worship; but the large majority were, in historian Leon McBeth's words, "one-room affairs designed for preaching with no thought or provision for Sunday School classes. From the first, Board leaders recognized that if Southern Baptists were to develop effective Sunday Schools, they must adapt their buildings for that purpose." The way a building was designed had a big influence on the kind of worship experiences that took place there. Or as one unidentified Board employee put it, "The pickle takes on the shape of the jar."

To lead the Architecture Department, Frost tapped Prince Emmanuel Burroughs, a native Texan and Baylor graduate who took a succession of pastoral calls before settling at Broadway Baptist Church in Fort Worth. He had been at the Board since 1910 in charge of teacher training. Burroughs's initial interest in building came at a point of crisis. His church and his home nearby were both destroyed by fire. Out of the ashes he built the first modern Baptist church educational building in Texas. In 1917 he wrote *Church and Sunday School Buildings*, which was revised and reissued in

1920 and followed by two more books by Burroughs on the subject.

Acting on a 1917 Convention recommendation, the Board set up the Organized Class Department specifically for reaching adults. Many Baptists still associated Sunday school with simple Bible stories and songs and games for children. The Convention wanted to make sure adults knew they had opportunities as well. For this department Van Ness selected another energetic former state secretary, Harry L. Strickland of Alabama. A Tennessee native, Strickland was educated largely by his school principal father. After he moved to Nashville, Strickland joined Immanuel Baptist Church, where Van Ness had pastored, and served that congregation as a deacon and Sunday school superintendent.

Strickland's emphasis was on finding and equipping great leaders for adult Sunday schools. He also championed graded Sunday schools when that was still a novel idea. Rather than teach everybody in church the same lesson the same way, Strickland's approach was to write a range of lessons for each level of age and spiritual maturity. "The determining factor," he explained, "is the pupil."

Like his friend Landrum Leavell, who first encouraged him to make a career of denominational service, Harry Strickland died tragically. A "seemingly trivial accident" at an evangelistic meeting brought on a fatal case of blood poisoning in 1924 when Strickland was only forty-eight.

Leavell, by the way, was appointed secretary of another new department, this one to run the BYPU. Ever since the Young People's Union was formed in 1895, it had existed independently of the Southern Baptist Convention even though the Convention soon began appointing the BYPU executive committee every year. In 1918 the convention appointed the Sunday School Board to lead and manage BYPU activities.

Ernest Eugene Lee, stationed in Dallas and promoting BYPU west of the Mississippi, was Leavell's associate in the field. Lee had come from Virginia and was a direct descendent of "Light Horse Harry" Lee, George Washington's favorite general and father of Robert E. Lee. Ernest was a successful hardware salesman who switched careers to become an insurance agent. Talking with prospective clients about insurance, he also shared the gospel with them. In 1901 he volunteered as the first BYPU president in Indian Territory (Oklahoma). Five years later he took a dramatic pay cut to enter Christian service full-time as secretary of the Texas BYPU. His remarkable success produced an offer to join the Sunday School Board in 1908.

By the time he became associate secretary of the BYPU Department ten years later, he was renowned for his "boundless energy, vibrant personality, unexcelled intellect, masterful teaching, and deep consecration wrought for God." Over his long career at the Board he would cover more than

2.5 million miles by train and car, and make twenty-one thousand speeches. He also loved working at Baptist summer camps throughout the South, where in time three generations of admiring campers came to know him as "Hot Dog."

CHAPTER 11

Solid Progress

More growth lay ahead in the Van Ness years. But just over the horizon was a crisis that only decades of prudent management in the past and firm-handed leadership in the present could overcome. The Roaring Twenties were a time of optimism and promise for the SSB; yet by the end of the decade, the Board would be hanging on to fiscal solvency by its fingernails with the rest of the Convention holding fast to the Board's dangling coattails and shoelaces.

The twenties also saw the rise of the Department of Survey, Statistics, and Information; a Convention-wide Baptist Student Union headquartered in Memphis (it was folded into the SSB in 1928); Vacation Bible School under Homer Lamar Grice; an advertising department under Kentuckian George W. Card; a Sunday school administration department under Arthur Flake; and a modest experiment in book retailing by buying half-interests in several state convention bookstores.

The classically columned stone headquarters on Eighth Avenue hummed with activity, all the empty offices filled within two years after the end of the First World War. A building that seemed adequate for the foreseeable future in 1918 was suddenly too small by 1920. Because of its sloping lot, the building stepped down halfway back, so that from street level the back portion looked about two stories lower than the front. The Board added two stories to fill in the space and soon built another six-story building across from the back door entrance on Ninth Avenue. This brick-faced building was more modest and functional than the original headquarters, built for storing, packing, and shipping merchandise. By 1924 the Board built yet another building, a two-story one that they leased to their printing contractor.

Noble Van Ness, Isaac's son, worked forty-three years at the Sunday School Board beginning in 1922. His early memories paint a colorful picture of a work environment that combined crusty old long-timers with field directors who flitted in and out at all hours.

He wrote about Mitchell E. Dunaway, the Board's first purchasing agent, whose photograph shows a taciturn face

behind wire-rimmed glasses, close-cropped fringe around his
bald head, and a high, stiff, detachable collar that had been
out of style for years:

> In 1891 M. E. Dunaway wrapped the first pack-
> age of Board literature. His temperament was such
> that he would have wrapped the last one if possible.
> He was of the old school that kept their counsel, their
> reasons, and their business knowledge strictly to
> themselves. To this day I do not know how he decided
> on the quantities of each periodical to offer, except
> NEVER too many. . . . I can see him now in shirt
> sleeves and long dark green canvas apron addressing
> labels by hand, putting them on packages and sorting
> them to mail sacks, and saying nothing.

The younger Van Ness also described the high-level hum
of activity surrounding the Board in general:

> We were around six days a week from eight to
> five, except that we wasted Saturday afternoon by
> going home. This was slightly suspect as being against
> God's will. And who ever heard of air-conditioning,
> pension plans, job descriptions, evaluations, or salary
> scales?
> Dunaway ruled the order and mailing depart-
> ment in his separate world. We had no worries
> there nor any chance to have them. B. W. Spilman,

the first field secretary, would occasionally bounce
into Nashville like a fat little Brer Rabbit. Prince
Emmanuel Burroughs whistled through his dentures
as he talked on church architecture [Board workers called him "Whistling Pete"]. John L. Hill edited
books, without ever editing manuscripts, between
audience-moving speaking engagements. L. P. Leavell
lived B.Y.P.U. George Card took care of advertising
and had a hard time getting periodical cover pages
away from editor Hight C Moore.

The Lord must have been with us, for we grew
like Topsy.

The end of the World War in the fall of 1918 marked a
surge in prosperity and optimism throughout America and
among Southern Baptists. The 1919 Convention endorsed
the $75 Million Campaign, a push to raise $75 million in
five years to support programs of the Convention and of
state boards that were not funded by churches. Besides the
huge cash goal, the campaign promoted unification among
Southern Baptists, teaching and defending the "fundamen-
tals of Bible faith," increasing Sunday school enrollment,
and bringing more people into full-time Christian service.
L. R. Scarborough was campaign chairman.

Pledges came pouring in to the $75 Million Campaign
until they reached $92 million. Knowing the Convention
had that level of financial support, and watching the Baptist

churches and Sunday schools growing "like Topsy" across the South, the Sunday School Board added still more departments and more gifted leaders in order to keep pace.

One legendary figure of the time was Arthur Flake, the Texas native who had a successful career as a traveling salesman before settling down in Winona, Mississippi, to run his department store. He had already had a varied and distinguished career. In 1895 he founded the first BYPU in the state and gained a reputation as an inspired speaker and church builder. In 1909 he accepted J. M. Frost's offer to work for the Sunday School Board in the field. After years spent promoting Sunday school throughout the South, Flake found himself in charge of BYPU. His job description changed, but his heart remained with his old work.

In 1919 after ten years at the Board, Flake resigned to take the new position of "church manager" at First Baptist Church, Fort Worth, Texas, under outspoken fundamentalist pastor J. Frank Norris. Announcing Flake's arrival in Fort Worth, Norris explained that the new hire would be in charge of all church organizations and activities and receive the same salary as the pastor. The current church membership was more than three thousand and Sunday school membership more than four thousand; Norris expected Flake's arrival to double both numbers. As Leon McBeth noted, "Though this title was not used, Flake was one of the earliest ministers of education in a Southern Baptist church."

While he hadn't reached his radical peak at that point, Norris was already a burr in the denominational saddle and Van Ness wondered how Flake could go to work for such a person. In letters to his former boss, Flake made clear that Sunday school work was what he wanted to do and not BYPU; furthermore he and his family disliked the constant travel his Board job had required, which aggravated some health problems. Flake also thought he needed more hands-on experience in Sunday school work to make his fieldwork more productive.

But within months Flake decided Pastor Norris was too tough to work with, left First Church Fort Worth, and moved back to Nashville and the Board. He was appointed secretary of the new Sunday School Administration Department where, at the age of fifty-eight, he began his most enduring work. In the field, and especially during his brief tour in Fort Worth, Flake tested and refined his technique for building a Sunday school. Now he summarized them in five simple points that became famous as "Flake's Formula."

According to Landrum Leavell, the formula increased attendance in Flake's Winona Sunday school by 500 percent. In his 1920 Convention report, Van Ness called it "one of the most far-reaching of our recent plans, and we confidently believe that it will work a revolution in our methods."

As P. E. Burroughs wrote years later, "A simple formula it was: (1) take a census and find out where the people are, (2) make a new organization classifying along with present pupils those who are possibilities, (3) train the workers, (4) prepare space for all classes, (5) send the workers out to win and bring in those who are without. A simple ordinary formula, indeed. But it had in it enough dynamite to blow up the Sunday school world and rebuild it on new lines."

By 1924 Sunday school enrollment was up by 600,000 members to almost 2.4 million. In five years BYPU nearly doubled to 495,000 participants. Board receipts grew from $634,000 to $1.42 million between 1919 and 1924. The combination of the $75 Million Campaign and Flake's Formula was dynamite indeed.

Vacation Bible School was another big success of the 1920s, with the Daily Vacation Bible School Department organized in 1924. The idea behind this program was to extend Sunday school-type instruction to children through the week during summer vacation. The movement actually began a generation earlier in 1898, when a transplanted Virginian in New York City, Mrs. Walker A. Hawes, conducted an "Everyday Bible School" at Epiphany Baptist Church for poor children on the East Side. The school grew more popular every year; and in 1901 Robert G. Boville, secretary of the New York City Baptist Missionary Society, promoted it in East Side missionary churches.

By 1907 Boville had resigned his position as secretary to form a national interdenominational society to promote VBS for, as he said, "using idle college students and idle church buildings in which to teach idle children the Word of God."

In 1922 the International Association of Daily Vacation Bible Schools joined the International Council of Religious Education. That year five thousand schools were conducted worldwide but only fifty in the American South. Through its Sunday School Department (formerly the Organized Class Department), the Sunday School Board began promoting Vacation Bible School and began designing literature for Southern Baptist VBS programs.

One man who caught the spirit of VBS was pastor Homer Lamar Grice of First Baptist Church in Washington, Georgia. He read about it in the local paper not long after his church had built a large and expensive educational building, which now sat dark and empty six summer days a week while the children of the community sat around with time on their hands. Leon McBeth picked up Grice's line of reasoning:

> He decided to start such a school in Washington. Despite his inexperience, Grice felt that his background as a former public school teacher would help. He wrote to the Sunday School Board in Nashville to ask them to send VBS literature and guidebooks. M. E. Dunaway responded that the Board had heard of the VBS but had no literature in that field [though it was likely under development]. He referred Grice to the ABPS in Philadelphia [the Board's old Northern rival], which in turn referred him to a Presbyterian

publishing house [Presbyterians in 1910 were the first denomination to endorse and promote VBS]. The upshot was that Grice gathered all the materials he could find, none of it from Baptist sources, and playing by ear devised his own VBS about 1922.

The pastor and his wife publicized the event and opened the doors. More than five hundred children from all denominations attended. Except for its length (four weeks) much of what Pastor and Mrs. Grice cobbled together from their makeshift curriculum would be familiar to VBS students today: Bible stories, memory verses, music and singing, crafts, and refreshments. On the last day there was a packed house for the commencement exercises, where parents and children alike marked the achievement. They also took a missionary offering.

When the Sunday School Board got wind of Grice's success, they established a VBS department and invited Grice to lead it. Grice agreed under the condition that he would always report directly to Van Ness and no one else. Grice joined the Board in September 1924, and he and his wife set to work writing and producing separate VBS guidebooks for beginners, primaries, and juniors in time for summer 1925. They wrote, edited, and typeset them without another pair of eyes seeing the pages. For the next year they wrote four books, adding an intermediate level, and four more the year after that. In later years the somewhat slapdash designs were redone from scratch a little more carefully. But Homer Grice became the founder of Southern Baptist VBS and a fixture at the Nashville headquarters for years to come.

During the 1920s Van Ness steered the Board seriously toward book retailing for the first time, though Southern Baptists had tried bookselling on a smaller scale at various points, as Leon McBeth's research reveals. The Bible Board ran a store in Nashville that went out of business during the Civil War. In the years that followed, several state conventions operated supply stores for their churches. The one in North Carolina was supposed to subsidize B. W. Spilman's salary as state Sunday school secretary (which it didn't). It may have been the first ever named Baptist Book Store. Occasionally denominational papers also ran a small bookshop, or a church would have its own store.

When J. M. Frost first considered the prospect of operating bookstores back in 1910, he believed they weren't necessary and that they would compete with independent stores already up and running. He wrote, "It seems a wiser policy and more just to encourage these several houses in every possible way and to foster their interests in putting out good literature and in making our people a reading people."

Traditionally Southern Baptists had not been a reading people; at the turn of the twentieth century more than half of all Southern Baptist congregations were still rural churches that met only once a month. But as the century progressed, the demand grew for items other than books that a denomi-national store could sell: maps, chalkboards, class record supplies, choir robes, offering plates, and more.

The Board's first stab at retailing was in selling books and supplies at state and associational meetings. Based on overwhelmingly positive response, Van Ness believed Sunday School Board bookstores could provide an important service to Southern Baptist churches and furthermore could do it at a profit. The Board bought a half interest in several state convention bookstores and by 1928 owned thirteen stores outright. Van Ness was especially proud of this prosperous and promising commercial enterprise, claiming, "Among the various ventures of the Sunday School Board none is more interesting and more far-reaching in its possibilities than this chain system for supplying our people with good books." By this time the Board had enlarged its role as a publisher too, setting up the Book Publishing Department in 1922 under Dr. John L. Hill, formerly president of Georgetown College near Lexington, Kentucky.

As the twenties roared along, the denomination grew, and the Board grew with it. But there were some warning clouds on the horizon. The optimistic $75 Million Campaign, which took in $92 million in pledges so quickly, had collected only $59 million by the end of the official five-year campaign period in 1924. As a result, as Robert A. Baker reported in *The Story of the Sunday School Board*, "Money which had been expended in anticipation of receiving the total amount from the campaign had been borrowed and necessarily must be repaid." For all their indebtedness resulting from the $75 Million Campaign shortfall, the Convention moved ahead on momentum, at least for the short term. In 1929 the Board published thirty-nine books and distributed more than twelve million periodicals.

Van Ness led by consensus and suggestion. No one characterized him as a "strong" leader, but everyone admired his solid progress forward and willingness to let department secretaries take care of their responsibilities with a minimum of oversight from him. He found enthusiastic, dedicated, experienced men, gave them a job, and stayed out of the way.

Van Ness put denominational harmony and cooperation ahead of taking a potentially divisive stand, as a set of principles he presented to the Board in 1929 makes clear: "The work of the Sunday School Board should be constructive and for the promotion of the generally established views of our denomination. . . . Our periodicals are not for the exploitation of personal or peculiar views on the part of the individuals who may be selected as writers. . . . They shall avoid the discussion of questions, at any time, which are unsettled, and the occasion of sharp issues among our people."

This policy kept the Board from taking a vanguard position on denominational issues. But the sense of unity it produced helped them survive the tough economic years that followed when the denomination, like the nation as a whole, teetered on the edge of financial disaster.

CHAPTER 12

Lean Times

In 1930 Isaac Jacobus Van Ness was seventy years old. Up to then he had been a steady, respected, and successful leader even if his style had been quiet and reflective rather than flamboyant and heroic. But about that time his colleagues couldn't help noticing Dr. Van Ness beginning to decline. He became physically weaker and seemed to fade in and out a bit. As the months passed, Van Ness's advanced age and his limitations became more obvious.

In a 1988 interview, Keith Von Hagen, a long-time Board sales and merchandising director who worked closely with Van Ness, said frankly, "He got senile. He was still on the job, still trying to carry on, but actually he was quite senile and problems developed." The Board did what it could to ease Van Ness's responsibilities. In 1932 they hired their first business manager, largely to take some of the pressure off the secretary.

Board trustees also stepped into the emerging power vacuum from time to time, especially W. F. Powell, pastor of First Baptist Church in Nashville and chairman of the elected board for thirty-three years. Evidence supports McBeth's conclusion that during these last five years of Van Ness's leadership, "Powell's hand appears in every major decision, and he apparently at times overstepped the proper boundaries from trusteeship to administration. Having moved into leadership partly from necessity, Powell apparently sought to continue his daily involvement in administrative affairs at the Board."

Like Frost before him, Van Ness hung on because he had no real economic alternative. It would be twenty years before the Board instituted a plan that gave retiring workers a pension substantial enough to depend on. However, sick or incapacitated employees received generous paid leaves up to six months or more, and perhaps it was in this spirit that everyone agreed Dr. Van Ness, in light of his long and selfless career at the Board, could stay on the job as long as he wanted.

The Board was wiser than they knew to surround their aged leader with the best help they could find. It was a time to think fast, save your pennies, and hunker down. The economic slump that began in the summer of 1929 didn't seem unusually foreboding at first, but within a few years the Board found itself trying to survive in the middle of the worst economic depression in the history of the industrialized world.

Historically the American government didn't interfere when the nation's economy hit a rough patch, depending instead on natural market forces to bring on a recovery. It had always worked before, but this time the situation was more than market forces could deal with. Speculators had bid up the price of stocks far higher than they were worth. When investor confidence wavered, stock prices tumbled. To keep prices up, banks and other institutions bought up huge numbers of shares. That worked for only a few days: on "Black Tuesday," October 29, 1929, the US stock market collapsed completely.

Between 1928 and 1929, receipts fell for the first time since the Sunday School Board had been in business. Book sales of all kinds declined nationwide, and denominational giving also dropped, giving churches less money for tracts and periodicals. Over the next three years the financial crisis worsened as overextended businesses failed and defaulted on their loans, causing banks to fail, which meant all the depositors lost their deposits. Unemployment rose as agricultural and industrial output dwindled lower and lower.

Finally admitting the market was never going to correct itself this time, President Herbert Hoover began setting up special government programs to pump money into the economy and make credit easier to get. But it was too little too late. He still hesitated to take crucial steps, vetoing direct federal relief programs even after it was clear that churches and local governments were swamped with hungry, homeless people.

The Sunday School Board had to tighten its belt: between 1929 and 1933 receipts fell almost $400,000, a drop of about 20 percent. But this was a far milder decline than in areas of Baptist life dependent entirely on contributions. Donations to local church work dropped by 40 percent during the same period while gifts to missions fell more than 42 percent from $40 million in 1929 to $23 million four years later. The Convention, having spent money for several years in anticipation of collecting $92 million in pledges, was dangerously overextended. They issued bonds to cover part of the shortfall and stretched their resources to the limit. The SBC never defaulted, but it would be 1943 before it finally climbed out of debt.

Several factors helped the Board weather these tough financial years. First, the Board had dutifully added money to a reserve fund every year, which provided a cash cushion as sales tapered off. Second, they redoubled their efforts to run their business as frugally as possible, wasting nothing, carefully bidding out work, controlling costs as well as possible. Another advantage was the new business manager, Dr. James T. McGlothlin, an Alabamian and Board trustee, who had taken on responsibility "directly for employment, purchasing, and printing" according to the 1932 annual report. "In the development of this new position," the report continued, "the business manager assumed, with the executive secretary and treasurer, the responsibility for joint signature on checks and documents, following in this the best precedents of modern business."

McGlothlin's presence, along with the Board's unusually healthy cash position and its sterling track record over the years, gave the Board what was possibly its best advantage during the Depression, which was an excellent relationship with local banks. As the national economy hit bottom in 1932 and 1933, unemployment across the country surged to 25 to 30 percent or twelve to fifteen million people. Those who had jobs earned on average about half of what they had in 1929. As a result, many churches couldn't pay their invoices to the Board, which meant the Board had to draw down its savings to make its payroll and pay its own suppliers. One employee from that era even recalled being paid in company scrip for a short while. But because of the Board's solid financial history and fiscal diligence during the national crisis, its bankers offered a line of credit up to a million dollars.

This allowed the Board to move ahead on an even keel even as other denominational work suffered and literally hundreds of American publishers went bankrupt. The Board kept supplying churches whether they kept their accounts current or not. Some eventually paid in full, others paid fifty cents or less on the dollar, and some never paid at all. At some point later in the decade, the Board wiped the slate clean, forgiving all outstanding debt for church literature.

The handful of Baptist Book Stores remained solvent. Many secular bookstores that survived the business downturn had to contend with new schemes from desperate publishers experimenting with book clubs, gift coupons, and other sales techniques that circumvented the retailer. The times produced at least one lasting innovation. After several false starts in the past with poorly designed and cheaply made products, the idea of paperback books caught on, first in England with the Penguin Library and then in the United States with the New American Library.

It seemed an inauspicious time to introduce a new publishing imprint, but that was what happened. Since opening the publication department in 1922, the Board had always had plenty of manuscript submissions. Through the Depression years the situation remained at least somewhat like the book editor, Dr. John L. Hill, described it earlier: "More people are writing, more manuscripts are coming to this office, and more prospective authors are in touch with us by correspondence than in any previous year. Our open invitation to all, our uniform contract to all, and our democratic policy of dealing with all authors, appeal very strongly to Southern Baptists."

Sharp marketing managers know that if they can gain market share during a downturn by spending and producing products when others have pulled back, they're likely to keep a significant part of that share once the market grows back. Dr. Hill and others in the Book Department were looking for new outlets for SSB books. For years they had used Judson Press as their imprint but thought a new name might help them break into wider markets. But they could never come up with a name everybody could get enthusiastic about.

The name appeared at last, and the way it arrived became a favorite story around the Board: it came by Pullman car, which most people under fifty have never heard of. Pullmans were special coaches leased from the Pullman Company by the railroads. During the day they looked like a typical passenger car, with row after row of padded benches, an aisle down the middle, and big windows along the walls. But at night, while passengers were away in the dining car, porters folded the benches flat to form lower bunks, pulled hidden beds down from the ceiling to form upper bunks, made up the bunks with sheets, blankets, and pillows, then divided them with canvas panels into private areas, each with one upper and one lower bed.

This was the way most businessmen traveled long distances, including Dr. Hill, who was shaving in the bathroom at the end of a Pullman one morning as his train pulled into Greenville, South Carolina. Handling his blade with extra caution as the car rocked with the motion of the tracks, we can imagine this distinguished former college dean standing in his undershirt, his suspenders wagging around his legs, intent on not nicking himself, concentrating supremely on the task at hand.

Suddenly "like a flash" he had an inspiration. Why not name the new publishing imprint in honor of the great Southern Baptist figures John A. Broadus and Basil Manly? These were names Southern Baptists revered but which also would have a substantial, solid feel. As P. E. Burroughs later wrote, "Why not honor these men and in doing so honor ourselves by blending into one the first syllable of their names?"

As Hill himself wrote from Greenville to Noble Van Ness, at that time managing editor of the Board, "Why not *The Broadman Press*?" A committee studying the idea soon approved: "Realizing the possibility of making a much larger sale of our publications of a general nature, if these publications should bear a press name rather than the name of our Board, we therefore recommend that such a name be established . . . the *Broadman Press*." The Sunday School Board had a new imprint to go along with Judson Press and with titles released under the SSB marque.

The relative financial health of the Board helped the Southern Baptist Convention during the lean times; in spite of all that went on, the SSB managed to turn an operating profit every year. Not only did the Board pay its own way, but it also continued contributing money to the Home and Foreign Mission Boards, kept the conference center at Ridgecrest afloat, gradually replenished its cash reserves, and prayed for better times. Many years later James L. Sullivan, who headed the SSB beginning in 1953, told me that "every existing agency" of the Convention was saved from bankruptcy during the Depression by the Sunday School Board. A lot of this help evidently never appeared on the books.

Two forward-thinking operations also played a part in these historic years. First was the Relief and Annuity Board, formed in 1917 at Van Ness's suggestion and seeded with $100,000 in Board contributions. Though it was nothing like retirement benefits of the present day, this was the first attempt at a comprehensive program to care for elderly pastors, their dependents, and survivors. Through careful management the Annuity Board remained solvent and operational without interruption. Second was the Cooperative Program, set up in 1925 at the end of the $75 Million Campaign to give local churches a hand in supporting general denominational boards and programs.

The only time anyone remembered seeing Isaac J. Van Ness in an uproar was in March 1933 when the newly inaugurated president, Franklin D. Roosevelt, declared a "bank holiday." By this time eleven thousand of the nation's twenty-five thousand banks had failed. As more of them went under, pressure increased on the ones still open. Cash continued pouring out as customers closed their accounts for fear their bank would go under like so many others, not realizing (or not caring) that taking out their cash only made the bank weaker.

To stop these panicked withdrawals, Roosevelt closed the banks on March 5 and kept them closed until March 13. This "bank holiday" probably wasn't legal, and it certainly wasn't a "holiday." Rather it was a desperate last-ditch attempt to avoid complete banking system meltdown. But it worked. The day the banks reopened, the system took in more money than it paid out. Soon the Federal Deposit Insurance Corporation was founded to protect depositors from ever losing their money again in a bank failure. Roosevelt instituted direct federal relief to families and set up huge programs to put the unemployed to work.

As the American economy began to rise from the depths, Dr. Van Ness graciously requested the Board appoint his successor and allow him to retire. On June 6, 1935, his friends and colleagues hosted a farewell banquet that, P. E. Burroughs recalled, "was one of the most brilliant and one of the most largely attended affairs of its kind ever given in Nashville." Burroughs continued:

> No man could retire more gracefully than did
> Dr. Van Ness, and surely no man could deport him-
> self more nobly in retirement. Right well he knew that
> he carried with him the love and the grateful esteem
> of the people whom he had served through nearly
> fifty years. Right well he knew, in particular, that he
> carried with him the sincere and devoted affection of
> his colleagues and of the great Sunday School Board

family. He must have known too, deep down in his heart of hearts that he had given his best, in honesty, courage, and efficiency to the Sunday School Board and to Southern Baptists.

Dr. Van Ness's retirement marked the end of an era in the history of the SSB. He was the last "founding father" to lead the organization, the last head who had lived through those exciting, uncertain, early years when Frost, then Bell, then Frost again set the course. Van Ness had been of the younger generation, at his first pastorate in Nashville, a skilled writer and editor full of ideas and willing to take charge. He had absorbed much from his predecessors and, as Dr. Frost's longtime associate, was the ideal man to take the reins from his hands.

Van Ness guided the Board through a phenomenal period of growth and modernization. He managed to rework the operational side of the Board to its great advantage while still keeping his eyes fixed on the mission and message of Southern Baptist Sunday schools. Even in his final years as secretary, Van Ness was a figure his fellow Baptists loved and respected. He represented denominational tradition, fidelity to a goal, and steady, selfless leadership during a time when much of the printing and publishing world seemed turned upside down.

After his retirement he lived in a modest hillside home overlooking downtown Nashville and the Sunday School

Board he had done so much to build and preserve. For a number of years he returned to the Board for special events and ceremonies and always had a steady stream of callers ready to honor him for his years of service. After his death in 1947 at the age of eighty-six, his colleague William Phillips wrote: "In any company in which Dr. Van Ness moved his presence provoked confidence. He was never insistent, but so often right that his colleagues feared to go counter to his ideas. He was never precipitate in action but always cautious, preferring to wait and give any matter time for fullest thought and consideration. Dr. Van Ness was a master executive, but never demanding. Only a suggestion was necessary to one of his department executives, so great was their confidence in their gentle and gracious leader."

This gentle leader's successor was a far different sort of man, though, like Van Ness, the right man for his time. He was also the first secretary of the Board to win a contested election and, at least so far, the only one to receive the news of his victory in the hospital.

CHAPTER 13

Speeding Up the Machinery

In June 1934, as soon as the ailing I. J. Van Ness indicated he wanted to retire the following year, the board of trust began looking in earnest for his successor. The chairman of the trustees, W. F. Powell, appointed a five-member nominating committee that solicited recommendations from other Board members, employees, college and seminary professors, and pastors. Board minutes of March 13, 1935, contain the nominating committee's report of its final meeting on January 18 at the Hotel Peabody in Memphis. They also reveal something of the committee's deliberations and the standards they set in their search:

After [a] season of importunate prayer, the committee then entered into a discussion of the necessary qualifications of the man to fill this important place. It was agreed upon that the nominee should be a pastor of recognized standing among Southern Baptists, that he should have intellectual, executive and business ability, that he should be humble, spiritually minded, and that he should have a fair understanding of world conditions, and that he should be sound in his doctrinal views and not an extremist on any one point.

The committee chairman read a list of nineteen names that had been suggested, then asked for any further names from the committee. There were none. Then they took up the candidates one by one, discussing some, and dropping several by common consent. As the minutes stated:

Then the committee unanimously agreed to vote by secret ballot on the names retained, each individual listing them in the order of his choice. So by the process of elimination on this secret ballot, Dr. T. L. Holcomb of the First Baptist Church, Oklahoma City, Oklahoma, was the only man receiving a majority (five to one [including the committee chairman's vote]). A motion was made to make the nomination unanimous. On this motion and second, Dr. Holcomb was accorded a hearty and unanimous vote. We, therefore, come today recommending to this

Board, Dr. T. L. Holcomb to be elected as Executive
Secretary and Treasurer of the Sunday School Board
of the Southern Baptist Convention. [The position
had recently been retitled "Executive" rather than
"Corresponding" secretary.]

It was a historic event in that it was the first time the
Sunday School Board had proposed a new leader without any
participation from its founder, Dr. Frost. It also turned out to
be the first time the recommended successor had a challenger
for the position.

After the search committee presented its unanimous
recommendation, some trustees at the meeting wanted to
propose other candidates. The discussion produced a show
of support for Jerome Oscar Williams, a trustee and former
pastor of First Baptist Church, Bowling Green, Kentucky.
Williams had helped set up the office of business manager
for J. T. McGlothlin, who had come to the Board as its first
business manager in order to relieve some of the day-to-day
pressure on Dr. Van Ness. When McGlothlin died suddenly in
1934, Williams left his pastorate to take the job.

According to Leon McBeth (whose unpublished manuscript *Celebrating Heritage and Hope* forms the basis for this
account of Holcomb), Williams came to the Board believing
he would be Van Ness's successor. In a phone conversation
with McBeth in 1989, James L. Sullivan said Williams told
him he had "a verbal commitment from a group of trustees to

that effect, and without that assurance would not have taken the job as business manager of the Board."

R. Kelly White nominated Williams for executive secretary, and Wallace M. Rucker seconded the motion. Both men spoke on Williams's behalf. But when the vote was taken, there were only three votes against Holcomb.

As a trustee himself, Holcomb should have been in Nashville to get the news of his election first-hand. But he was temporarily stranded about two hundred miles to the west. At the age of fifty-three he had never learned to drive (he never would), and his wife, Willie, was driving him from Oklahoma City to the meeting. They had a wreck in Memphis, and she was in the hospital there. Dr. Holcomb got a phone call in his wife's room with the news that he had been tapped as the new executive secretary.

"Roll in another bed!" he shouted to a nurse. "I'm in worse shape than my wife!"

Thomas Luther Holcomb was born in Purvis, Mississippi, in 1882, and grew up in the small churches of the rural countryside where his father was pastor. In 1908 he graduated from Southeastern Seminary where, according to Robert A. Baker, he "witnessed the Sunday School giants in action," hearing both Frost and Van Ness preaching or lecturing. His first pastorates were small communities in his home state—Durant, Yazoo City, Pontotoc, and Columbia. During World War I, Holcomb worked as religious director for the YMCA in France, then took the pulpit at First Baptist Church of Sherman, Texas. After seven fruitful years there, he spent a year as executive secretary of the Baptist General Convention of Texas. In 1929 he answered the call to pastor First Baptist in Oklahoma City.

Holcomb's tenure as executive secretary in Texas made him familiar with the workings of state organizations and how they collaborated with the Convention and the Sunday School Board. His six years in Oklahoma City showcased his ability to build programs successfully and to put theory into practice. He wasn't a professional writer like all his predecessors at the Board had been, and he wasn't often drawn into deep theological discussions. He was a preacher, an evangelist, a doer, an implementer. And he got to work without delay.

During Dr. Van Ness's last several years at the helm, field directors were left pretty much alone (even more so than usual) to do what they wanted whenever they wanted to do it. In Nashville the lines of executive responsibility were muddled by the business manager position and by activist Board executives trying to assist the secretary with his work. Department heads competed for the secretary's attention to promote their pet projects. But the whole atmosphere was about to change, as a Baptist Book Store manager in Oklahoma City who knew Dr. Holcomb well predicted: "Well, I'll tell you one thing, when he gets there you're going to find out who is in charge."

As P. E. Burroughs described the transition:

The early days of the new order under
Dr. Holcomb witnessed, both at headquarters and
on the field, a quickening of spiritual purpose and a
strengthening of spiritual fellowship. Along with this
development came a speeding up of the machinery,
a girding for larger achievement. No special authority was exercised, no commands were issued, seldom
was there direct appeal. Rather there grew a new
atmosphere, there came a sense of comradeship, there
developed a will to win.

Another Board employee said simply, "He was a 'take
charge' man and he took charge."

Everyone who knew or wrote about Dr. Holcomb always
mentioned certain prominent characteristics. First was that
he was usually the shortest person in the room, standing
only a little over five feet tall. When he preached or spoke, he
often stood to one side of the lectern or pulpit so his listeners could see him. He used the pulpit or speaker's stand as a
prop, leaning his hand against it or draping one arm over it.
Another characteristic was a deep, rich, room-filling voice
that seemed like it could not possibly come from so small
a frame. Listeners sometimes compared him to the biblical
character Zacchaeus, the short man in Luke 19 who climbed
a tree to see Jesus over the heads of the crowd—a man who
got things done in spite of his stature.

Holcomb was also noted as a snappy dresser who was always immaculately groomed. His wife helped him buy his clothes, making sure everything fit well and went together stylishly. In pictures he is invariably tastefully dressed in the latest fashions, complete with a crisp and spotless pocket handkerchief. He also indulged in a weekly haircut and manicure, which was done at the same time as the haircut from a small table the manicurist rolled up to the barber chair. McBeth reports that Holcomb "was said to have the best manicured fingernails of any man in Nashville."

He may have been small and a bit of a dandy, but there was no doubt from the first that he would be "speeding up the machinery." He hung a picture of a small rural church in his office as a reminder that *every* Southern Baptist church needed the denominational, spiritual, and organizational support of the Board.

The first order of business was to tighten up the management and operation of the Board in big ways and small. With agreement from the trustees, Holcomb brought N. R. Drummond, his educational director at First Baptist, Oklahoma City, to be his "right hand man," what we would probably today call an executive vice president. Drummond had been a professor at Southwestern Seminary, where he had graduated, and was a proven success at keeping the operational machinery running smoothly at First Church Oklahoma City. He was also one of Holcomb's closest friends. In a time when all the leaders and many trustees of the Sunday School Board went by the courtesy title, "Doctor," Drummond was the first worker at the Board with an earned doctorate. Spiritually well-grounded, he could also handle the nuts and bolts of managing the Board, leaving Holcomb to concentrate on his strengths: pressing the flesh, personal encouragement and exhortation, inspiration, and motivation in the field.

Holcomb and Drummond lost no time making some important management changes in Nashville. J. O. Williams, the business manager for Dr. Van Ness who had expected to take his place as executive secretary, had gotten used to handling a lot of his boss's duties and evidently assumed he would continue in that role under Holcomb. The new secretary acted fast to show him otherwise. Though no one ever described Holcomb as power hungry, he made clear from the first who was in command.

Holcomb transferred Williams from business manager to head of the Education Department, replacing him as business manager with Harold E. Ingraham, Arthur Flake's associate in the Sunday School Department. Ingraham didn't want the job because he had expected eventually to succeed Flake as head of the Sunday school programs. But instead Holcomb appointed his friend Jasper Newton Barnette as Flake's assistant and successor. Neither Williams nor Ingraham was happy with the arrangement, but both of them learned their new jobs and performed them responsibly. Ingraham eventually served forty-three years at the Board in several capacities.

One example of the many small changes he made was to invade the turf of Mitchell E. "Mitch" Dunaway, the famously reclusive and curmudgeonly head of the shipping department since the Board opened for business in 1891. The Wednesday before the last Sunday in every quarter had become notorious as Big Wednesday, the day when regular shipping department employees plus a host of temporary workers labored from 7:30 in the morning until late at night to get out all the Sunday school materials in time for churches to start the new quarterly lessons. The problem was that Dunaway waited until the last minute to send out renewal notices. Because he never spoke to anyone and the whole staff avoided him, it wasn't until Holcomb started poking around that the problem was uncovered. The new secretary instituted changes that made Big Wednesday a thing of the past.

For all of his focus and intensity—and a temper he struggled at times to control, leaving tense meetings to walk up and down the hall until he regained his composure—Holcomb enjoyed a joke at his own expense. He told the story of conducting a wedding ceremony where, as always, he had written down the names of the bride and groom to make sure he didn't forget them. Concentrating hard on the name of the bride, Miss Legg, he said to the groom, "And do you take this woman whose leg you hold?" Another tale that made the rounds was a time Holcomb was speaking at the Baptist assembly in Virginia and assigned to share a room with Dr. C. Oscar Johnson, a pastor from St. Louis who was six and a half feet tall. Holcomb arrived first, hung up his clothes, and went about his business. When Dr. Johnson spoke that night, he began by saying, "I don't know who my roommate is, but judging from his suits, he must be a Boy Scout."

Holcomb traveled more than any Board secretary since Frost had during his first years on the job. Many afternoons and most Fridays, his wife would arrive at the Board with a freshly packed suitcase to drive him to the train station for a round of field visits. He reestablished close contact with the field directors, visited state and regional associations, talked with pastors and other leaders, and gathered a sense of what Sunday school could do for the churches and how the Board could assist them. The vast majority of Southern Baptist congregations were in small rural churches like the places where he himself had worshipped growing up in Mississippi. The Depression had bottomed out, but money was still tight, and churches needed to stretch their meager resources as much as possible. (In 1935, the year Holcomb took charge of the Board, only 10 percent of farm households in the United States had electricity.)

As Leon McBeth observed:

> Perhaps no head of the Sunday School Board
> knew less than T. L. Holcomb did in 1935 about the
> production of Sunday school literature. What he did
> know was Southern Baptists; he knew the churches,
> the pastors, and the people. And he knew how to talk

to people, how to get them to see what he saw, how
to motivate them to action. He was, in short, a *promoter.* For some that word may have a negative image,
but not for Holcomb. He believed the Sunday School
Board had worthwhile products and services to offer.
However, due to the Depression and other factors, the
churches were not using Board literature and materials as they could have.

Throughout the South, the churches became
more aware of the Board and what it had to offer
them. And with Holcomb's well-known loyalty to
the Bible and to Baptist doctrines, his powerful
preaching, and his persuasive spirit, he led many
churches to begin or resume using Board literature
and materials.

Early on Thanksgiving morning 1935, five months after he
moved to Nashville, Dr. Holcomb chaired a meeting of Sunday
School Board department heads (Burroughs adds "at their own
request") to talk and pray about the direction the Board should
take going forward. Burroughs described the scene:

> The burden of their prayer was that they might
> be led into a fuller fellowship and that God would
> send them out on some concerted mission worthy of
> the Sunday School Board and the ministries in which
> they served. The hours passed, and as they waited
> in quietness, the idea emerged that they might join

their comrades in the various states in a co-opera-
tive Southwide effort to "carry from the steps of the
Sunday School Board Building to the last church all
that we have come to know about Sunday School
and Training Union methods." This phrase, carved
out by Dr. Holcomb, became the accepted slogan. A
period of five years was staked off and agreement was
reached to designate the new effort, "The Five-Year
Sunday School Board Promotional Program."

At Holcomb's request the Board trustees voted on
November 26 to recognize "the district association as the
major unit promoting every phase of Sunday school and
Baptist Training Union work." On December 31, at a meeting of state leaders and Sunday School Board representatives
at First Baptist Church, Birmingham, the assembly agreed
to promote Sunday school and Training Union for five years
through the nine-hundred-plus existing district associations.

There would be two statewide conferences in each state
during each of the five years, one for Sunday school and one
for Training Union. District associations would send representatives; drivers of carloads of representatives would get two
cents a mile from the Board to defray expenses (it likely paid
for the gas). These conferences would train thirty thousand
volunteers in Sunday school and Training Union work and
get them excited about expanding established programs and
starting new ones across the denomination.

According to the 1936 *Annual*, when the Five-Year Promotional Program was launched, there were "24,537 churches in the Southern Baptist Convention, of which 15,000 are one-fourth time, and 5,000 one-half time." Using the district associations to run the program would make it possible to reach even small churches who couldn't send anyone to a state meeting and had no means to start a Sunday school program on their own. The associational leaders went to the state meetings, then shared their knowledge in local clinics for church volunteers on organizing Sunday school and Training Union, Vacation Bible School, keeping records, visitation, recruitment, and more.

McBeth observed:

This approach, simple as it sounds, was far more innovative than it looks at first. With only a little exaggeration, one close observer called it "the most daring effort ever undertaken by any denomination in America." . . . The genius of the plan was to approach the churches through the local associations and partly by means of volunteer workers. For all his travels, Holcomb could not go to every church, nor could his associates. But by enlisting and training capable lay people, helping them to know what the Board had to offer by way of literature and services, and convincing the lay volunteers of the *value* of what the Board offered, the Board thus had a direct entry to all of the churches.

"The churches responded," McBeth continues. "These were not remote and distant officials seeking to sell something; these were their own people who had made an exciting discovery about all the good things the Sunday School Board had to offer." At the end of the program in 1941, the fiftieth anniversary of the Board, there were more than 1,800 new Sunday schools with over half a million new members, and more than 2,000 new Training Unions adding 250,000 to the rolls. Vacation Bible School and teacher training also saw big gains.

Certainly the improving national economy played some part in this growth. The Social Security Act of 1935 set up retirement funds for the elderly and boosted public confidence in the future. The start of another war in Europe in 1939 created a huge demand for American war supplies and thus a huge number of new jobs, vastly accelerating recovery from the Depression. But Holcomb's bold initiative and unwavering focus were still responsible for the greater part of the Board's success.

He had other big ideas too, one of which was that good music was essential to good worship. This led to more new projects for the Board, including a book that would become, next to the Bible, the most indispensable item in the Southern Baptist pew rack.

CHAPTER 14

Onward Christian Soldiers

By the time T. L. Holcomb took charge, the Sunday School Board had published at least half a dozen hymnbooks or songbooks, beginning in 1904 with *The Baptist Hymn and Praise Book* edited by Lansing Burrows. But the choices were few, literally a drop in the bucket compared to the enormous amount of literature the Board published every year. And despite an on-again, off-again interest in music going back to the days of Manly and Broadus, the Board had never had a department to promote or publish music.

As a pastor, Dr. Holcomb had seen the power of music to inspire and comfort, and he believed it was an important worship tool that was underrepresented at the Board. His son Luther told the story of going to visit the city manager of Oklahoma City when Dr. Holcomb served at First Baptist there. It was the worst time of the Depression, and the suicide rate in town had spiked to a frightening level.

Luther picks up the story:

> As soon as [the city manager] saw my father in the reception room he said, "Come on in, Preacher. You've come down here to talk about the suicides, and there is nothing I can do about them." My father told him that he wanted permission to go on the streets of Oklahoma City after the Sunday evening services. "I don't want to preach. I want a truck, and I want a choir, and I want that choir to sing hymns like 'How Firm a Foundation,' 'Blessed Assurance,' and 'Amazing Grace.' All I want to do is stand up on the back of that truck and read verses such as 'God is our refuge and strength, a very present help in trouble.'"

In the same way the Board pointed the way to specific Bible stories and their application to daily life, it could lift up the great hymns of faith for the same ends.

One of Holcomb's first new hires was B. B. McKinney, the Board's first ever music editor, starting December 1, 1935. Baylus Benjamin McKinney had spent the last four years as assistant pastor in charge of music at Travis Avenue Baptist Church in Fort Worth and knew Holcomb from times when they had worked on several revivals together over the years. McKinney's job was to help "produce and promote through our periodicals the right kind of music for our churches" and to lead the music at training schools, assemblies, and conventions.

McBeth notes that the idea of a music department had floated around the Board for years without any concrete action. Up to the time Holcomb became executive secretary, professional music directors in Southern Baptist churches were "almost unknown," though a few had paid choir directors or, even more rarely, a paid quartet. Churches got their music from some of the hymnals the Board had published in years past, or books from other suppliers. In 1909 Robert H. Coleman, an assistant pastor at First Baptist Church in Dallas, formed a company to publish religious songbooks and released thirty-three of them over the next thirty years. His biggest customer was the Sunday School Board, which sold Coleman hymnals and songbooks in Baptist Book Stores.

In 1925 the Convention appointed a Committee on Better Church Music to "make such recommendations as it may deem wise and proper for the advancement of music in Southern Baptist churches." The committee affirmed that music was "the handmaid of religious worship" but discovered through their research that music overall in the denomination was in sad shape. They reported that 90 percent of the music leaders in Southern Baptist churches were volunteers and that of the 10 percent who were professionals, fewer than half were doing an acceptable job.

The report concluded that "50 per cent of the 28,000 churches use music of an inferior grade both in text and in musical arrangement, and 40 per cent of them use music of a medium grade, and that only 10 per cent of them use the very best grade of church music." The committee also pointed out that, except for courses at the three Southern Baptist seminaries, nothing much was being done to improve the situation. McBeth added, "They insisted that hymns should reflect accurate biblical truth in their text and that the music should be suitable to worship, 'not mere jig tunes,' they said, 'or what might be called musical doggerel.'" (Sounds like some of the discussions I hear today!)

The committee recommended to the Convention that they have the Sunday School Board "give careful consideration at its earliest convenience, to the advisability of establishing and fostering a Church Music Department for the purpose of improving the musical conditions" in church, Sunday school, and BYPU services. Board trustees had recently decided not to form any new departments for the present, and so they put the matter aside. The request came around again in 1933, when the Convention requested that the Board "consider the need and advisability of promoting a church music program that will aid the churches of the SBC." The economics of the Depression probably made it impossible to consider at the time.

But according to William J. Reynolds, who was head of the Board's Church Music Department from 1971 to 1980,

Dr. Van Ness's wife, Frances, was also partly responsible for the delay. Born into a distinguished Kentucky family who had its doubts about her marriage match, she liked high-church music and not what she considered lowbrow gospel or folk hymns, certainly not anything likely to be recommended by I. E. Reynolds of the School of Gospel Music in Texas (chairman of the 1925 "better music" committee). Homer L. Grice, head of Vacation Bible School work at the Board, thought the holdup might have been a combination of Depression-era caution and the preoccupation with Van Ness and the office of the secretary as his abilities faded.

McBeth wrote, "The fact that Robert H. Coleman . . . had a flourishing business in publishing songbooks for Baptist churches may have entered into the picture also. The Board has always been reluctant to enter into fields in direct competition with well-known Baptist individuals." The Board already had Coleman's books to sell, along with music from Hope Publishing Company in Chicago, which also gave the Board a small royalty. While Van Ness evidently was satisfied with the Hope Publishing deal, Holcomb was not and thought the Board should publish its own music.

B. B. McKinney was Holcomb's man for the task. McKinney had taught at the School of Sacred Music at Southwestern Seminary for twelve years before taking his position at Travis Avenue. He was also Coleman's music editor, and Coleman was his publisher—McKinney had been a prolific hymn writer for years. In 1937 the Board published

Songs of Victory edited by McKinney, and *The Song Evangel* three years later, also under McKinney's direction. His job allowed him to leave Nashville for extended periods to conduct revivals and lead music at various music conferences and events. One year in the late 1930s he traveled more than twenty-five thousand miles through seventeen states.

Some of the places he visited had a good selection of hymns. Championing variety, McKinney said, "Southern Baptists should by all means sing the great songs of the virgin birth of Christ, his miracles, his atoning death, his victorious resurrection, and his glorious second coming; saved by Christ through faith and saved forever—not saved by his beautiful life, but saved by his sacrificial death." Other stops were not so promising, as one Baptist college proved to be whose hymnbooks had no reference to the redemptive blood of Jesus because its editor didn't believe in it.

T. L. Holcomb initiated other musical programs at the Board. From First Baptist Church in Bessemer, Alabama, he got the idea of setting up a graded choir program for children. Walking into the church and seeing all the young singers in their uniforms, he later remembered, "Well, I knew right then that there was too much good looks about that group of young people that that thing was going to spread. . . . I knew just as well as I knew the ABCs that [graded choirs] was going to take."

McBeth saw this as a good example of Holcomb's intuitive leadership style. "He *knew* and he knew *immediately* that this innovation was important and that the Sunday School Board should promote it." A long article on graded choirs was prepared for the December 1937 issue of *The Sunday School Builder*, including photos of children dressed in choir robes. Any sort of robes in church were suspect in the minds of some Baptists, and the author of the article asked Holcomb if he felt "safe to publish choirs with robes on in this paper." His intuitive answer: "I know I feel safer than I do to let it go by without doing anything about it." Graded choirs soon became a hugely popular program.

In 1940 the Board began sponsoring Church Music Week, headed by I. E. Reynolds. The next year the Board turned the week over to McKinney. For years Church Music Week also devoted time to various other topics, though McKinney lobbied every year for a full week exclusively on music. Finally in 1948 he planted a young church musician (William J. Reynolds, quoted above) at the closing ceremony to request from the floor a full week of music. The next year he got it.

B. B. McKinney became a familiar figure at Southern Baptist revivals, conferences, Convention meetings, and Music Weeks—a tall, big-boned man with glasses and a shock of silvery hair who gravitated toward double-breasted suits. He conducted with enthusiasm, hands high over his head and singing along with the choir or congregation. Through the 1940s music became a major component of Board literature and outreach, and McKinney was the engine that drove it all. When the Department of Church Music was formed in 1941,

McKinney moved from music editor to department head. He developed the Church Music Training Course in 1946 and launched *Church Musician* magazine in 1950. He prodded the Board to help state conventions set up music departments by supplementing the salaries of state music directors as they had directors of Sunday school and Training Union.

Without a doubt, McKinney's biggest impact on the Board and on Southern Baptist churches everywhere was his work as editor of *The Broadman Hymnal*, published in 1940. His goal was to present a wide range of music but one with high artistic and theological standards. In his introduction McKinney wrote, "If music is the universal language, and it is, hymns of confession, of petition, of hope, of comfort, of adoration, of consecration easily become the mediums through which all devout souls may join in giving expression to their deepest emotions. . . . Here we have the stately, soul-stirring hymns dear to the hearts of all Christians, the best of more recent hymns, some of which make their initial appearance, and a number of very popular choruses."

McKinney himself wrote 149 hymns and composed the music to 114 more with words by others. Some of his new pieces were in *The Broadman Hymnal*, and some from his years at Coleman he received permission to publish in the new book as well. McBeth observed, "This hymnal probably has influenced Southern Baptist worship more than any other book than the Bible itself. . . . This became almost the official hymnal for Southern Baptist churches for a generation." It also cast Southern Baptist church music in the mold of the gospel hymn, which Frances Van Ness no doubt would have found shocking and thoroughly unacceptable. But it was what McKinney called "Heart Music for the masses."

B. B. McKinney was a man full of love for his denomination and for music as a means of praise and worship. He left a great legacy behind in 1952 when he died, at age sixty-six, following a car wreck on the way home from Church Music Week at Ridgecrest.

While setting up a music department under McKinney may have been T. W. Holcomb's most innovative step in reorganizing and reenergizing the Sunday School Board, it was only one of a long list of changes he made. In December 1939, as the Board looked ahead to its fiftieth anniversary, a study committee recommended dividing the Board into three divisions, each headed by a "special director" reporting to the executive secretary, in order to streamline operations and strengthen overall management. The divisions were:

1. Editorial Division, headed by Hight C Moore, who had been publications editor for years. The division was divided into the Periodical section, responsible for all the graded materials for Sunday school and promotional periodicals for Training Union and Vacation Bible School; and the Book section, in charge of study courses, music, and books.

2. Education and Promotion Division, directed by P. E. Burroughs, former head of the education department. This division wrote, edited, and published all the Board's

educational materials and took charge of church architecture and statistics.

3. Business Division, led by J. O. Williams, business manager for the Board during the later Van Ness years. All orders, purchasing, sales, advertising, accounting, and similar responsibilities were grouped here.

About the same time, based on the success of the Five-Year Plan, the Board decided to follow it with a new Four-Year Plan beginning in 1941 and ending in 1945, the centennial year of the Southern Baptist Convention. Meeting in Nashville on January 2, 1940 (even though the old program wouldn't conclude until December 31), state representatives decided to work again through associational channels, holding a one-day conference promoting Sunday school and Training Union in each of the more than nine hundred association areas once a year. Dr. Holcomb's friend J. N. Barnette, who had taken over management of Sunday school operations when Arthur Flake retired in 1936, was to head up the operation for Sunday schools, and Chester L. Quarles directed the Training Union efforts.

As the annual revenue of the Board grew to $2.3 million in 1940, the staff grew and was again cramped for space. At one point, part of the art department worked inside a plywood "penthouse" on the roof of the Frost Building until the fire marshal ordered it dismantled. In 1938 the Board bought a tract of land on Ninth Avenue next door to the Shipping Building and the next year broke ground on a new two-story office building. Planning ahead, the Board had the building designed so that an office tower could be added later. The Board also owned a building nearby on Commerce Street that was leased to its printer.

As promising as the Board's future seemed, prosperity and planning were no match for the upheaval that shook the whole nation in December 1941 when the United States entered World War II. Assumptions and projections and Four-Year Plans went out the window as the Board readjusted to a new set of circumstances.

Sunday school lost some of its momentum as churches focused more on the war effort. Congregations were depleted as young men and women left for the armed services. Eventually about 480,000 Southern Baptists would serve in World War II. Many older members, especially women, reentered the workforce, leaving less time for church activities. Though Vacation Bible School enrollment increased almost 20 percent between 1940 and 1944, Sunday school attendance dropped by more than 200,000 to just under 3.4 million.

More than thirty employees of the Board left for the service; a number of young women resigned their jobs to follow their husbands to military assignments. It was also a period when some of the legendary leadership figures chose to close out their careers. B. W. Spilman retired on the first day of 1941. In December of that year, M. E. Dunaway wrapped his last package in the shipping department after fifty years. P. E. Burroughs and Hight C Moore both retired in June 1943.

Fortunately for the Board, the new Administration Building at Ninth Avenue and Commerce Street opened on March 13, 1941. On account of the war economy, within a few months after that they couldn't have bought building materials at any price or found men to do the work. Tires, gasoline, and other products were strictly rationed. The War Production Board set regulations for how much material could go into a new suit and a long list of other consumer products.

The Board's biggest practical worry was getting enough paper for all of its books and periodicals. Some quarterlies came out with reduced page counts or were printed on lower quality paper if nothing else was available. Occasionally they were issued without covers. Where there had been two or three staples holding a copy together, the printers made do with one to save metal wire. As well as cutting back, the Board contributed lead, copper, and zinc from printing operations to the war effort. They even answered a request from Washington for typewriters, donating a number of them though the Board scarcely had enough to go around. Shortages notwithstanding, the Board added a new publication for military audiences, *On Duty for God and Country*, and a booklet titled *On to Victory*, that combined Scripture verses, inspirational quotes, hymns (including one of B. B. McKinney's favorites, "Onward Christian Soldiers"), and brief sermons.

Throughout the war Dr. Holcomb kept refining and expanding the Board, producing several important new services and ministries. One example was the 1941 inauguration of the Church Music Department. Two years later the Board began the Church Library Service to help churches set up, maintain, and use a library. In January 1944 the Visual Education Service was founded to add a new dimension to the Board's long history of print communication. Its first project was *The Romance of a Century*, a 16mm film on the history of Baptists in America.

Though the idea first surfaced in 1940, it was 1946 before the Board introduced the Department of Home Curriculum to help Baptists strengthen their marriages, nurture their children, and promote Christian character at home. The home curriculum concept started as a Christian Home Week event built around Mother's Day. It was such a success that the Board expanded it into a full-blown ministry. In January 1947 the department began *Home Life* monthly magazine. Its message struck a chord: soon it was the most popular periodical at the Board with more than a million copies a month in circulation.

In 1947 the Historical Commission was formed to safeguard two historic treasures. One was the Dargan Library, the core of which was the magnificent private library donated by Edwin Charles Dargan, editorial secretary of the Board from 1917 to 1927. The other was a collection of historical documents and data assembled by William O. Carver, chairman of the Southern Baptist Historical Society, which he founded in 1938. The Historical Commission agreed to merge and manage the two, naming the new archive the Dargan-Carver Collection. Upon Holcomb's recommendation the Board developed plans for a spacious modern library to house it, which was finished in 1953; Holcomb spoke at the dedication on June 16, two weeks after his retirement.

By then every vestige of war rationing and personnel shortages would seem a distant memory, and the Board would follow the Convention in a season of unprecedented growth and prosperity. In almost every way the time between the end of the war and the end of the Holcomb era were very good years indeed.

CHAPTER 15

New Programs, New Places

O ver its first twenty-five years the Sunday School Board took in a combined total of just over $4 million. In 1945 alone, Board receipts totaled more than $4.15 million. With the end of the war, veterans came pouring back home, war workers left the factories to return to their families and children, and churches across the country welcomed a flood of new members. Seminaries filled up with eager students going to college on the GI Bill, a government-funded program for veterans. Churches went on a building spree, many of them adding purpose-built Sunday school rooms for the first time.

What should have been a time of unbridled growth of the Board was hampered by a combination of postwar inflation and government price controls. The government still had to approve all paper orders, and just because the order was approved didn't mean it would be filled any time soon. The Board needed plenty of paper: in 1945 they printed an aggregate total of twenty-four million periodicals.

Though a period of strong expansion lay just ahead, the years immediately after the war gave T. L. Holcomb some knotty administrative challenges. He had never gotten used to delegating authority. In the late 1940s he still signed all the Board checks and set the salaries of many employees. The *Annual* for 1948 warned, "With production and distribution costs continuing to rise, it is essential that every possible economy, consistent with the effectiveness of our ministry, be sought and achieved."

One economy Holcomb had mastered, according to longtime workers, was keeping salaries low. McBeth wrote, "Many senior staff members recalled that they barely made a living during the Holcomb era. Capable workers, especially secretaries, were often lured from one department to another by the offer of a pay raise." Department heads poached top employees from each other. A few brave souls marched into Holcomb's office and asked point-blank for a raise. More often than not they got instead a "stern lecture" about living within their means.

Finally in 1950 the Board raised its minimum wage to seventy-five cents an hour but only under government pressure and the threat of unionization. As postwar prices rose and wages stayed the same, employee morale took a nosedive. Workers felt that management ignored them and had no sympathy for the financial squeeze so many of them were in. In the late 1940s the Teamsters Union tried to organize the shipping department. It was a powerful step for the union and a frightening one for the Board: if the shipping department went on strike, it would shut down the whole operation. Outside organizers came to Nashville, carrying placards and buttonholing employees on the sidewalk trying to encourage them to demand a vote to unionize, a vote that the administration by law had to allow if employees insisted.

Holcomb fought back by railing against unions during Friday morning chapel services at the Board and having anti-union leaflets circulated around the building. In the end a few members of the board of trustees, particularly a successful, high-profile Nashville businessman named Maxey Jarman, convinced Holcomb and the other leaders that they had to be more sensitive to employees' needs; they had to hire, manage, and compensate them in a more fair and structured way according to modern business practices. Jarman eventually convinced Holcomb to set up a personnel department in 1949.

The following year, as soon as building materials were available, the Board began a nine-story tower atop the center section of the Administration Building to ease the postwar office space shortage. As church membership mushroomed and demand for the Board's materials increased, Holcomb continued adding services to keep up.

Over the years the Sunday School Department had split into six semiautonomous departments, one for each age group, that made it hard to coordinate curriculums or even to know what was going on. One worker called them "six little islands floating in the same sea." Holcomb combined all of them, plus Vacation Bible School, back into one department headed by his good friend Jasper Newton Barnette, who had worked with Arthur Flake since 1927 and took over the Sunday school program after Flake retired. Homer L. Grice, who along with his wife had developed the idea of Vacation Bible School from the beginning, worked easily under Barnette. Though the duration of the sessions shrank from four weeks to two, participation continued to climb.

Training Union also dramatically expanded in the years following the war (in 1934 the name had been changed from Baptist Young People's Union to Baptist Training Union). Most of the country still had no television or professional sports, and few people worked on Sundays. The postwar economic boom allowed many young people to live at home years longer than their parents had been able to do. For millions of Southern Baptists, Sunday night was church night, and Training Union was an ideal combination of fellowship and Christian teaching. In charge was Jerry Elmer Lambdin, who led the department for thirty years beginning in 1929. All together, he spent forty-two years in Training Union work interrupted only by military service in World War I.

A new program in 1948 was the January Bible Study, in which participating churches set aside two Sundays and the week in between for an intensive study of the same Bible book or book segment. The first study, on Ephesians, was a huge success with more than six thousand congregations participating. Over the years the January Bible Study has remained one of the most popular and widely used of all the Board's programs.

Also in 1948, at the national convention in Memphis, a prominent minister to Baptist youth named Chester Swor delivered, in McBeth's words, "a stirring message on the need for a Christ-centered, church-integrated program of recreation that would challenge Baptist youth and adults to consecrate their entire lives, including their leisure, to Christ." Eyewitnesses called it a "thrilling address" that moved and excited its listeners. Swor specifically recommended a department of recreation, run by the Sunday School Board, to "provide leadership, research, plans, and materials to help local churches provide for recreation as a part of Christian education."

Caught up in the excitement of the moment, Dr. Holcomb rose from his seat on the platform, walked to Swor at the lectern, and shook his hand. "If the Convention authorizes it," Holcomb declared, "the Sunday School Board will accept the responsibility for the establishment and direction of the program you have suggested." The Convention duly gave its authorization. But like the music program that had been announced with enthusiasm in 1935 and then stalled for years because no one was sure what to do or who should do it, the recreation program was a long time being born.

Professor Agnes Durant Pylant of Wayland Baptist College in Plainview, Texas, was in the audience and thought Swor had a great idea. She immediately envisioned establishing courses in Christian recreation at Wayland and offering a major in the field. The components, she believed, were already in place:

> From the physical education department we could supply all the sports needed. Crafts would come from the art department. We knew Shelby Collier [director of the college choir] could provide a course in the leadership of community singing. Play production could be lifted from the speech and drama department. I would teach story telling and all phases of social recreation. Oh it was a beautiful plan. And it worked.

But it wouldn't be working for a while. Some churches strongly objected to any sort of church-sanctioned socialization program. To them church was a place for study, contemplation, prayer, and evangelism, not for eating hot dogs and ice cream and playing softball. Then there were hotly contested questions about what specifically was appropriate for Southern Baptist "recreation." One argument swirled around swimming. In Florida and California, church-sponsored beach parties for teenagers were common-place. In Arkansas, Oklahoma, and elsewhere, the tradition was far different: mixed bathing was not allowed. Boys and girls swam separately and wrapped up thoroughly while walking to and from the pool.

Dr. Holcomb didn't want to feed the controversy and didn't want to take sides, so he did nothing to help the new program get started. Finally after years of discussion and delays, Professor Pylant herself won the honor of being the first head of the recreation department. Holcomb's successor, Dr. James L. Sullivan, shrewdly decided that having a woman in charge would reduce the chance of divisive controversy. By that time Pylant had not only developed her Christian recreation courses at Wayland College, she had also led recreation programs at state assemblies and at Ridgecrest and written a book on the subject, *Play Time*. After her husband's death in a plane crash in 1953, she welcomed such a career change. She was hired at the end of Holcomb's tenure and began work early in 1954.

One of the most important developments during Dr. Holcomb's watch was the flowering of Southern Baptist retreat centers. Though the process was under way before Holcomb took office and continued long after he retired, key events took place in the 1940s and early 1950s that make this a good time to take a closer look at these popular, valuable, and versatile assembly grounds.

The idea of church-based "camp meetings" goes back to frontier days. In 1874, John H. Vincent, chairman of the

International Sunday School Lesson Committee, refined and expanded this early American tradition by adding teacher training courses in a vacation setting to church assemblies at Lake Chautauqua, New York. These so-called "Chautauqua meetings," sponsored by a variety of groups, quickly became popular across the country and added Bible studies as well as secular entertainment—travelogues, science lectures, literature discussions, and other cultural programs. Some even qualified for college credit.

Around the turn of the twentieth century, B. W. Spilman and other Baptists found out from experience that holding summer teaching clinics in the Chautauqua mold was a popular way to train Sunday school leaders. By the time Spilman left his position as state secretary for North Carolina to join the SSB as its first field secretary in 1901, he was convinced that Baptists ought to have a place to conduct these summer sessions. Earlier he had teamed up with Robert H. Coleman in Texas and tried to establish an assembly at La Porte, Texas, on the Gulf of Mexico. It never caught on, probably at least in part because the weather was hot and sticky, the sand flies were merciless, and it was too far off the beaten path for most Southern Baptists. Spilman tried again with a summer program in Knoxville, Tennessee, in 1902, but again it never attracted any significant number of participants.

In August 1902, Spilman took an option on a tract of land for sale in the Swannona Valley of the Appalachian

Mountains, eighteen miles east of Asheville, North Carolina, near a tiny town on the ridge called Terrell. The property, with breathtaking views and a cool mountain climate, was in Swannona Gap at the eastern entrance to the valley at the crest of the Eastern Continental Divide. Early settlers had called the area Eden Land. In 1905 the state convention authorized purchasing the 940-acre site as an assembly center as long as the convention didn't have to pay for it. Spilman, Hight C Moore, and a few others formed a nonprofit organization and bought the property for $8,500, paying $500 cash down and borrowing the rest.

On March 8, 1907, they incorporated as the Southern Baptist Assembly. Their charter stated that their plans were to "establish and maintain in the mountains of Western North Carolina a municipality of Baptist Assemblies, convention conferences, public worship, missionary and school work, orphan homes, manual and teacher training and other operations auxiliary and incidental thereto; also a religious resort with permanent and temporary dwellings, for health, rest, recreation, cluster work and fellowship."

In the beginning the place was a well-kept secret; six people attended the first worship service there. Spilman complained that Southern Baptist involvement was "pitifully inadequate" and that they acted like they were running a peanut stand. The Southern Baptist Assembly first christened the new place Blue Mont, then changed it to Ridgecrest. They began constructing buildings in 1908 and by 1910 had forty-two buildings on the property and a full seven weeks of programs. Participant fees allowed them to break even on operating costs. For a while beginning in 1916, Ridgecrest offered summer seminary courses for credit, but they were discontinued after a few years. Other programs such as Sunday school and BYPU training, missions, music, and Bible study drew ever-increasing crowds.

In those early days Ridgecrest almost went under more than once. Leon McBeth tells of the time a banker rode the train out from Asheville to say he would have to start foreclosure proceedings the next day if the Assembly couldn't bring its loan current. After the banker left, Spilman and some others raced back to Asheville in a Model T and conveyed most of the property to Spilman personally before the banker could get back to town. Eventually the notes were paid off, and Spilman deeded the property back to the corporation.

Spilman was delighted when, in 1920, the Education Board of the SBC took title to Ridgecrest, expecting to operate it out of funds designated from the $75 Million Campaign. But by the time the Education Board was disbanded in 1928, Ridgecrest was in bad repair, poorly managed, half empty, and the Board couldn't even keep up with the interest on the debt. In the optimism of the early 1920s, the Education Board had borrowed money for a variety of purposes using Ridgecrest as collateral, expecting to pay it back when the $75 Million money came in. But much of the money never came. In 1920 Ridgecrest carried a debt of about $9,000 and a value of more than $300,000. Seven years later the property was worth more than half a million dollars, but the debt had grown beyond $300,000.

Some Southern Baptists thought Ridgecrest should be sold, and during the Depression it was put on the market at a fire sale price just to relieve the debt load. But nobody stepped forward to buy it. Spilman said later, "Only the hand of God saved the assembly for Baptists." When the Education Board went under, the Convention turned Ridgecrest over to the Executive Committee, which ran it as best they could for three years and then proposed to sell it to the Sunday School Board—the most financially stable part of the Convention— for the rock-bottom bargain price of $200,000. Wary of taking on such a debt in hard times, the SSB declined but agreed to operate it for the Executive Committee.

In the early 1940s the Convention again asked the SSB to take Ridgecrest, and again the Board declined. Dr. Holcomb knew what a drain the assembly had been on every group that had owned it, and he didn't want to add the Board to that list. But in 1944 the Convention did a procedural end run around the Board and *assigned* Ridgecrest to the Sunday School Board. Holcomb admitted that the next trustee meeting after that was one of the gloomiest in memory. Maxey Jarman broke the spell by explaining, "What they have given us is a liability. Let us turn it into a denominational asset."

J. N. Barnette went to Ridgecrest every summer to over-
see operations and look for ways to improve them. Wartime
shortages added an extra burden; sometimes he had to buy
food for the cafeteria on the black market. In 1945 there was
no Convention meeting on account of the war, and Ridgecrest
programs were cancelled as well. But beginning the next year,
the Sunday School Board invested time and money improving the facilities and programs, streamlining management,
and promoting Ridgecrest throughout the denomination.

In handing Ridgecrest over to the SSB, the convention
had given them lemons; Holcomb and his able leadership
turned them into lemonade. By the mid-1950s Ridgecrest
was teeming with activity and was a jewel in the crown of
the Convention. In later years, programs expanded to run
year-round, and in 1972 the name was changed to Ridgecrest
Baptist Conference Center.

During the postwar boom of the late 1940s, Southern
Baptists began looking for a place to build a second assembly
center. On the best roads of the day, it took a family from the
West a week to drive to Ridgecrest and another week to drive
home. T. L. Holcomb had actually been thinking of a western
assembly center since the 1937 Convention in New Orleans,
when he met with a young pastor from New Mexico named
Harry Perkins Stagg, who proposed a "western Ridgecrest."
Many new Southern Baptist congregations were forming
outside the southeastern states where the denomination had
historically been concentrated, and they felt cut off from the

mainstream. Holcomb resolved on the spot that as soon as the Depression was over, he'd pursue it.

The Executive Committee studied the matter for several years. But in light of the continuing economic slump, the denomination's heavy debt, and the financial failure of Ridgecrest up to that time, the Convention of 1940, meeting in Baltimore, voted to drop the idea.

In 1945, the year there was no national convention, the state convention in Texas invited representatives from western states to talk about the prospects for a new assembly ground. All the representatives agreed that it was a good idea, and each one wanted the new facility located in his state. In 1947 this western alliance convinced the Convention to set up a committee to reconsider the idea. At one point the Convention wanted the Sunday School Board to choose the location, but Holcomb, typically, would not step into the middle of a controversy. There was a call for another committee, but due to some confusion the Executive Committee and the SSB both appointed committees; they solved the matter by combining both committees into one.

It was 1949 before the committee, in a contentious split vote, recommended building a new assembly at Harrison, Arkansas, in the Ozark Mountains. After the messengers voted against the recommendation, the committee "dropped the molasses jug," in Davis Woolley's words, when it let slip that the committee had already taken an option on land in Harrison and told the people there an assembly would be

built. Then an Albuquerque pastor named Philip C. McGahey
rose to offer a minority report recommending that the new
assembly be built in Glorieta, New Mexico. His motion
passed by a wide margin.

Behind the New Mexico resolution was Harry Stagg,
who had first proposed a western assembly to Dr. Holcomb in
1937 and who was now executive secretary of the New Mexico
Convention. Stagg and a few fellow New Mexicans argued
that a Southern Baptist outpost there would be good for
reaching Indians and Hispanics and improve Baptist witness
between the Mississippi River and California (where Golden
Gate Seminary had opened in 1944).

One of those New Mexicans was Aunt Ruth Baker, my
mother's sister, who was on the committee that looked at various pieces of property and finally selected Glorieta. I was thirteen years old in the summer of 1949, living in Jacksonville,
Texas, where my father pastored a church, and probably had
never heard of any place called Glorieta. But Aunt Ruth was
assistant editor of the state Baptist paper, the *Baptist New
Mexican*, and right in the middle of denominational affairs.
She also worked as a secretary to the governor in Santa Fe.

The committee's first serious prospect was the Pecos
Valley Ranch near Pecos, New Mexico, outside Holy Ghost
Canyon, which was on the market for $90,000. But before
they could make an offer, the Roman Catholic Archdiocese of
Santa Fe heard about their interest and snapped up the prop-
erty at a higher price. What seemed a disappointment turned

Published by the Sunday School Board of the Southern Baptist Convention.

VOLUME 1]   GREENVILLE, S. C., JANUARY, 1866.   [NUMBER 1

Kind Words.

Words are things of greatest worth,
  Though often lightly spoken;
Thoughtless, fleeting words of mirth,
  May wound the heart that's broken;
Or words that pass forgotten by,
May prompt to deeds that cannot die.

Kind words quell the angry soul,
  But bitter railings never;
Love can soothe with sweet control,
  And kindle love for ever.
Watch well your words, both old and
  young,
For life and death hang on the tongue.
             B. M., Jr.

Don't Waste too much Steam on the Whistle.

What a wonderful thing is a loco-motive! How Doctor Franklin or Sir Isaac Newton, or any other of the old gentlemen who knew so much, but who lived before Rail-road times, would have opened their eyes if they could have seen a loco-motive. I never get tired of look-ing at one. Here it is now at the station, all ready to start. How it hisses and blows and looks like it wants to be gone; and now it is agoing. Hear the whistle shouting out to everybody: "GET IN, GET IN, I'M AGOING, GET IN OR I'LL LEAVE YOU." And now off it rolls. Puff—puff—puff—puff—puff—puff, along the straight track as fast as a bird can fly; and now so gracefully and carefully it goes around the curve; and now, there's an old brindle cow on the track. Listen to the whistle: "LOOK OUT, LOOK OUT, OLD COW, GET OUT OF THE WAY OR I'LL HAVE TO RUN OVER YOU, I'M GOING SO FAST I CAN'T STOP." And now it comes near another station, and out shouts the whistle again: "HERE'S A STA-TION. EVERYBODY GET READY, MAKE HASTE, I CAN'T STOP LONG." Is it not first rate fun to ride on the rail-road?

Do you know what it is that makes the whistle blow? Why, just the same thing that makes the locomotive go along. It is the steam blowing through the big whistle, just like you blow with your breath through a little whis-tle, that makes all the noise. Now, suppose the locomotive kept on blowing and shouting all the time; don't you see it would not have steam enough left to make it go along. I have seen some men, and some boys, too, that let most of their steam go through the whistle. Is there any work to be done? Oh, they are the very fellows to do it, if you only listen to them. "Whoop, hurrah, get out of the way, every-body; we are going to do all the work." But they have wasted so much steam on the whistle that there is none left for work.

Now, boys, don't talk too big, or promise too much. If you do, some-body may say: "He's wasting too much steam on the whistle."

            GRANDFATHER GREY.

Baptist Church at Greenville.

Here is a picture of the Baptist Church at Green-ville, S. C., the town where this paper is printed. It is a prettier church than the picture represents it. But the outside of the church is not nearly so pretty as the inside, at least on Sunday mornings, when the Sunday school is assembled. Alto-gether, the school numbers three hundred and twenty-six. The average attendance this winter is two hundred and fifty-two. And the pret-tiest part of this Sunday school is the Infant Chil-dren. It's one hundred and nine scholars itself, and the average attendance, even in this cold weather, is eighty. Our Infant Class don't care for Jack Frost.

Rain or wind, or frost or snow,
To the Sunday school they go.

What Can I Do?

The family were moving. Every-body was busy packing—except Jack. Jack was sitting on the door-step, whittling a stick; and when his mother called him, and said, "Jack, my son, can't you help us?" he only grumbled out: "What can I do?" and never stirred. He looked very sulky, and, I thought, very silly.

Not long after, little Mary ran up and said, "Mother, I've finished what you told me. What else can I do?" She looked so bright and rosy with her exercise, and so hap-py, with the consciousness that she was doing something to help, and the desire to do more, that even looking at her smiling face cheered and helped me in my work. It was like a sunbeam shining out sudden-ly on a rainy day.

So you see there are two ways of asking "What can I do?" Which is your way?   HENRY HINTER.

Basil Manly (top left) hired John A. Broadus as the first employee of the Sunday School Board in 1863. Three years later they introduced *Kind Words* for children. Though this early Board folded in 1873, *Kind Words* continued for decades.

J. B. Gambrell (top), an early opponent of the Board, and James Marion Frost (bottom), the Board's founder and first corresponding secretary, hammered out the final differences among members of the Convention in a special private session. After a brief return to the ministry, Frost led the Board until his death in 1916.

When Frost accepted the call to preach at First Baptist Church in Nashville in 1893, Theodore Percy Bell (left) succeeded him as Board secretary. Three years later Bell resigned and Frost returned.

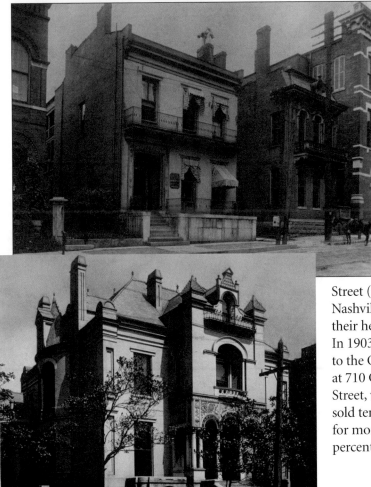

The Board bought a house at 167 North Cherry Street (above) in Nashville in 1897 as their headquarters. In 1903 they moved to the Cole House at 710 Church Street, which they sold ten years later for more than 300 percent profit.

Weighing in at 300 pounds, Bernard Washington Spilman famously told his audiences, "If you cannot see me standing up, I'll try lying down." Hired as the Board's first field secretary in 1901, Spilman tirelessly crisscrossed the South to promote Sunday school, whether by teaching (middle), speaking, or spitting watermelon seeds at Ridgecrest in 1908 (Dr. Spilman at center).

—LAUGH—
—AND—
GROW FAT.

A LECTURE BY

B. W. SPILMAN.

Spilman envisioned a retreat center for Southern Baptists and optioned 940 acres in the Swanonnona River Valley near Asheville in 1902. The North Carolina Southern Baptist Convention established Ridgecrest Assembly there in 1907. The Southern Baptist Convention took title in 1920 and assigned it to the Sunday School Board in 1944.

Arthur Flake (right), a former department store owner, revolutionized Sunday school with "Flake's Formula" for building attendance.

Landrum Pinson Leavell (left) was a college professor when Flake convinced him to enter Christian service. Leavell was key to the early success of the Baptist Young People's Union.

Homer Lamar Grice (right) originated Vacation Bible School and built it into one of the Board's most popular activities.

In October 1913 the Sunday School Board moved to an elegant new headquarters at 161 Eighth Avenue North, replacing the overcrowded Church Street house. Frost found its classical design well suited for a "Baptist Business Temple." Faced in Kentucky limestone, the building cost $160,000, paid in cash.

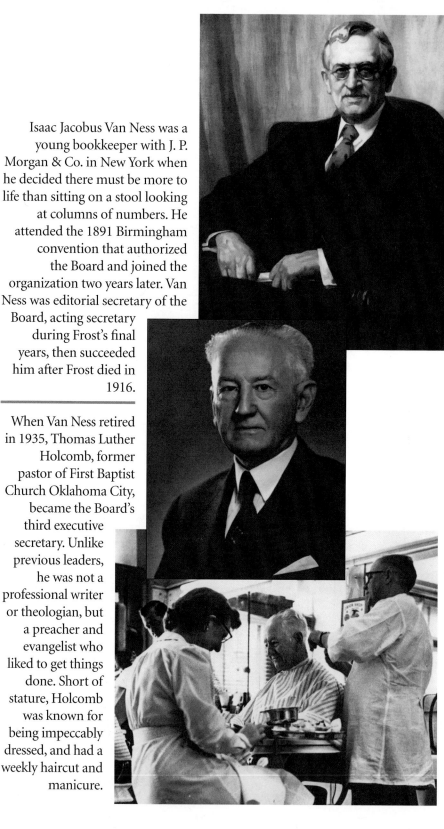

Isaac Jacobus Van Ness was a young bookkeeper with J. P. Morgan & Co. in New York when he decided there must be more to life than sitting on a stool looking at columns of numbers. He attended the 1891 Birmingham convention that authorized the Board and joined the organization two years later. Van Ness was editorial secretary of the Board, acting secretary during Frost's final years, then succeeded him after Frost died in 1916.

When Van Ness retired in 1935, Thomas Luther Holcomb, former pastor of First Baptist Church Oklahoma City, became the Board's third executive secretary. Unlike previous leaders, he was not a professional writer or theologian, but a preacher and evangelist who liked to get things done. Short of stature, Holcomb was known for being impeccably dressed, and had a weekly haircut and manicure.

The New Mexico Baptist Convention bought the Breese Ranch near Glorieta in 1949 to build a second denominational retreat center. The first major event there was Pioneer Week during August 1952, when 1,400 enthusiastic Southern Baptists slept in tents and unfinished dormitories to help kick off a major building campaign.

James Lennox Sullivan (right) and Grady Coulter Cothen led the Sunday School Board's transition to a modern corporation. During Sullivan's tenure (1953–75) the Board embarked on an unprecedented expansion program and weathered a tumultuous era of racial tension and theological debate. Though Cothen's presidency (1975–84) was cut short by ill health, he led the Board during the historic conservative resurgence that re-shaped the SBC beginning in 1979.

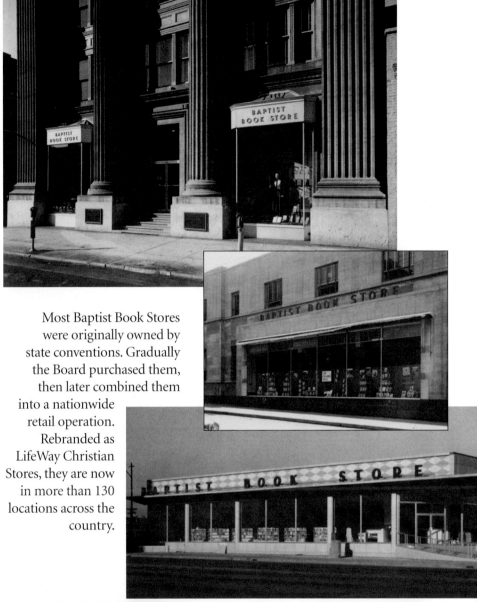

Most Baptist Book Stores were originally owned by state conventions. Gradually the Board purchased them, then later combined them into a nationwide retail operation. Rebranded as LifeWay Christian Stores, they are now in more than 130 locations across the country.

Prentice Lloyd Elder ended his term as Board president (1984–91) in a swirl of controversy. Of the range of projects he inherited from his predecessors, history proved him right for nurturing the Genevox music publishing business and for closing down the Baptist Telecommunication Network, an expensive failure hampered by low interest, lackluster programming, and a $60,000 a month satellite contract.

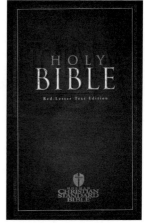

Writing "James Thomas Draper Jr." here is
consistent with the rest of the presidential
photos, but most people call me Jimmy. In the 1990s we dove into the
computer age with a series of upgrades and new systems including
on-line Bible study (below). Perhaps the most important project of
my presidency (1991–2006) was the release in 2004 of the complete
Holman Christian Standard Bible, an all-new translation combining the
readability of the most popular versions with unsurpassed scriptural
accuracy.

Originally the Board was not allowed to publish books for fear they would lose money and bankrupt us. Recently our Broadman & Holman imprint has made a major impact on contemporary culture with books by speaker and conference leader Beth Moore (above). The biography of pro golfer Payne Stewart by his wife Tracey and writer Ken Abraham was our first *New York Times* best-seller. A novel by retired marine colonel and popular broadcaster Oliver North (bottom) was our second.

LifeWay employees today serve on short-term mission trips around the world, including Africa (top; that's me standing on the left), Bangladesh (center), and Bosnia (bottom).

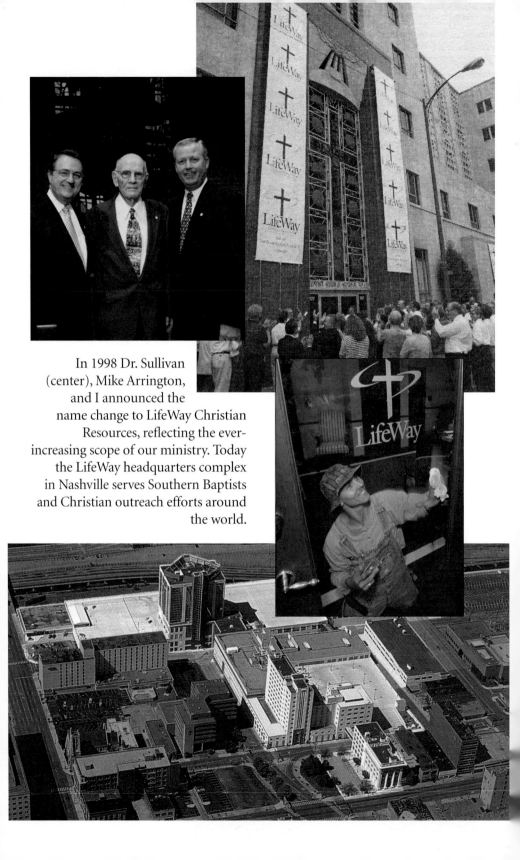

In 1998 Dr. Sullivan (center), Mike Arrington, and I announced the name change to LifeWay Christian Resources, reflecting the ever-increasing scope of our ministry. Today the LifeWay headquarters complex in Nashville serves Southern Baptists and Christian outreach efforts around the world.

into a blessing later when Clint Irwin, a Santa Fe pastor, called Stagg with some important news. James and Irine Breese, who lived outside Glorieta, were getting a divorce. Irine won the 880-acre ranch in the legal settlement and wanted to sell it quickly for $50,000 cash—an astonishingly good value compared with the Pecos Valley property.

The Breese Ranch, which had included a dairy farm, cattle operation, and apple orchard, was on the historic Santa Fe Trail and adjoined thousands of acres of national forest. Recently the property had been neglected and reportedly teemed with rats and rattlesnakes. Even so, Lewis A. Myers, editor of the *Baptist New Mexican* and Aunt Ruth's boss, declared, "The Glorieta area is the Mecca for the fisherman. It is the painter's paradise, the hunter's second Heaven. It is the tired man's haven and the live man's lift and joy."

Stagg sold a lot the state convention owned in Albuquerque for $30,000, borrowed $10,000 more from local banks, and raised the rest. So the state convention owned the property, thanks to Stagg's absolute refusal to give up, but when he invited members of the national Convention committee to come look at the site, no one wanted to. Only two or three ever visited the place That may have been one reason the committee recommended the Arkansas site in 1949 on a five-to-four vote.

But when the messengers voted down the recommendation, Vaughn Rock, a Phoenix pastor, and Philip McGahey submitted their minority report, talking up the cool mountain breezes to the stifling crowd that sat melting in the Oklahoma summer heat. As far as I know, this is the only time a minority report has ever been presented at the convention. But it worked. A motion by Duke McCall was passed for the Sunday School Board to study "what is involved in the development of the site at Glorieta, New Mexico, and no other site."

This was both good news and bad news for Stagg and the rest of the Glorieta contingent. The Board would accept the property, but they wouldn't pay anything for it and wouldn't even take it as a gift until they had checked out road access, the water supply, and other matters. The Board also required the New Mexico Baptists, who had swallowed a huge financial obligation considering how small the group was, to donate a new administration building. More than once the state Baptists decided to forget the whole thing, but Stagg somehow talked them out of it. The Board also insisted on owning about five hundred acres surrounding the Breese Ranch. The Board did agree to pay for this land, though Stagg had to negotiate the sales. By now word was out that the Baptists were trying to assemble a big parcel, and some landowners held out for big windfalls—which they got, to T. L. Holcomb's dismay no doubt.

At last in September 1949, Holcomb, SSB business manager Harold Ingraham, and church architecture head W. A. Harrell met with Stagg and a few others at the famous La Fonda Hotel in Santa Fe. After a season of discussion and prayer that lasted until nearly midnight, the Board agreed to develop Glorieta. As Ingraham remembered, "Half of the men in that room were crying. Back of that was the yearning of the West for recognition and the realization of the leaders that if they didn't get it, the Convention was likely to split. I don't think posterity or any of us will ever realize what Glorieta actually meant to the unity of the Southern Baptist Convention and to the saving of the West with all of its potential for Southern Baptists." Glorieta was dedicated on October 29, 1949, and plans for building got under way.

The first Convention-wide event there was Pioneer Week during August 1952. By then not a single permanent building was finished, but the fourteen hundred Southern Baptists who came out for a look from seventeen different states didn't seem to mind. A few of them slept in unfinished dormitories, but most lived in tents. Food was trucked out to the temporary dining hall every day from a restaurant in Santa Fe. There was a spirit of adventure, of being the first at something, that made the week a wonderful experience. And in contrast to the rustic facilities, the preaching was of the highest caliber, with speakers including W. A. Criswell, Herschel Hobbs, and Texas pastor James L. Sullivan, a former SSB trustee soon to succeed Holcomb as executive secretary, who enthusiastically supported the Glorieta project.

As Glorieta developed over the years, it became the third largest tourist destination in the state, with a picturesque lake, beautiful buildings, and gardens laid out over eight years by Cecil Pragnell, a world renowned horticulturist whose father had worked for Queen Victoria. The centerpiece of the complex was the worship center, appropriately named Holcomb Auditorium.

In 1953 T. L. Holcomb was seventy years old. He planned to continue on several more years with his work, since his predecessor had served until age seventy-five even though his health was poor, and Holcomb's health was excellent. But the trustees had other ideas. Then, as in the past, the executive secretary was officially elected year after year to one-year terms. In 1953, the trustees decided not to reelect Holcomb.

They never gave an official reason for their move, though McBeth gathered from interviews years later that they didn't want to risk repeating the last years of Van Ness's term when he was too sick to lead and the trustees too compassionate to turn him out. Another reason was that in spite of the Board's phenomenal growth during his eighteen years of leadership, Holcomb didn't have the management skills demanded of a business as big as the Board had become. He had always managed by means of intuition and personal relationships; but as the Board became more complex, it wasn't enough.

A story about Holcomb's retirement dinner comes from several eyewitnesses. As a retirement gift the Board gave him a new car. It was a Studebaker, then a popular model, made by a distinguished American company in business more than ninety years, having originally built the iconic covered wagons pioneers used to cross the continent in the 1800s. Something about it didn't please Dr. Holcomb's wife, Winnie, who would be doing the driving. In front of the assembled guests, she slammed the keys down in a huff. It was, McBeth reports, "an embarrassing and much discussed scene." He adds, "What became of the Studebaker is not recorded."

Still full of energy after his retirement, Holcomb spent three years as executive secretary of the Southern Baptist Foundation, then accepted the call to be assistant pastor at his son's church in Dallas, Lakewood Baptist. He retired in 1961 at the age of seventy-nine and died in Dallas eleven years later.

Meanwhile the Sunday School Board, though still a ministry above all else, had also become a big business. The next man to lead it would have to be not only a pastor and a visionary but a businessman as well.

CHAPTER 16

Into the Middle

As the next executive secretary of the Sunday School Board, James Lenox Sullivan presided over both a watershed era in the denomination and a historic upheaval in American culture. In many ways, everything that came before appears mild by comparison, and much of what followed seems absolutely radical. For the first time since the Southern Baptists established themselves in 1845, theological differences produced sharply divided public debate during the Sullivan years that affected careers and friendships from then until today.

The debate became even more strident later on, but it was at this point in the history of the SSB that the first big, meaningful, public cracks appeared defining and separating different theological factions. What was so disorienting and stark about this time is that it marked a transition from a long history of concord to a state of discord that went on for decades. The norm had always been accommodation and mutual respect for others within the Board and the Convention; henceforth the norm would include some degree of tension and suspicion.

As well as tracing this historic change among Southern Baptists, the Sullivan years spanned a transformation in American culture unlike anything that has happened before or since. America's social and cultural perspective in the 1950s was remarkably like it had been in the 1750s. Traditional America revered faith in general and Christianity in particular, self-sufficiency, patriotism, the simple joys of home and hearth, respect for authority, modesty and discretion in personal relations, humility, thrift, and accountability. By 1970 that traditional culture had all but disappeared from the public square, replaced by free love, free sex, draft dodging, college professors encouraging students to "tune in, turn on, drop out," Academy Award-winning films about subjects like homosexual prostitutes (*Midnight Cowboy*), and songs asking quite literally, "Why don't we do it in the road?"

This roiling cultural mainstream began flowing dramatically away from mainline Christianity. Beginning with the 1962 Supreme Court decision declaring prayer in public schools unconstitutional, America's courts and legislatures turned the nation's traditional notion of freedom of religion on its head. The same government that had chosen "In God We Trust" for the national motto in 1956 decided six years later that while we might officially trust Him we couldn't officially pray to Him. The First Amendment, which had always been used to preserve citizens' freedom to worship God, was recast as a means for taking that freedom away.

It was a puzzling and challenging time. And by God's grace, James L. Sullivan was the man chosen to lead the SSB through it all. Sullivan considered himself a man open to change but solid in his moral and spiritual foundation. The Bible, he wrote later in life, "played a vital role in the shaping of early attitudes," giving him "bearings and a sense of values" which he held fast. He continued, "While I could not argue that none of my attitudes have changed in the course of these years, I have to insist that those basic biblical beliefs are still the dearest I possess. With maturity and experience all of us take the teachings of others and make them our own through personal experience and application."

James Sullivan was the first Board secretary born in the twentieth century, in 1910 at Silver Creek near Sullivan's Hollow, Mississippi, where his father's family had lived since colonial times. His mother's kin had settled nearby not long after the Sullivans arrived, on a land grant signed by John Quincy Adams. Over eight generations the Sullivans became one of the biggest and best-known families in the state, renowned for excellence in their chosen field whether it was farming, gunsmithing, or moonshining.

Jimmy was the second of four children. His father was a successful building contractor, inventor, and business-man who raised his two sons and two daughters to love learning and to think for themselves. He also raised them to revere the Bible and apply its teachings to their daily lives. Jimmy grew up riding horseback in the country, spending summer days at his favorite swimming holes and fishing spots and winter months at the local school where he was an outstanding student. He joined the high school football team as a strapping 150-pound eighth grader. By the time he graduated, he was captain of the team as well as class valedictorian.

When he started high school, his father told him that if he got through all four years without failing a class, he would buy him any watch he wanted. When the day came for him to make his choice, he surprised his father by say-ing he'd already picked his favorite: the watch his father had carried since before he was married. Without a word his father took it out of his pocket and handed it over. Here was a boy who already showed a strong appreciation for his heritage and a keen ability to identify a goal, then work toward it.

Perhaps the only treasure young Jimmy appreciated more was the conversion experience he later described in his memoir, *God Is My Record*. A sermon one Sunday morning seemed directed specifically at him. After church he told his mother he wasn't hungry for dinner and rode his horse up to Lover's Mountain, a lookout where he and his friends went to fish, hunt, and swim.

> I tied my horse to a nearby tree, and spent literal hours in meditation and prayer trying to come to that point of a personal decision on my own. The day was drawing to a close. Still I felt that I had not received the answer for which I was questing. . . . I mounted my horse and was riding home alone. I had gotten in sight of the church when I actually experienced a change of mind, heart, attitude, and feeling. Burden was turned to joy. Doubts were removed by a vibrant faith which has continued with me throughout my years. . . . I'm convinced that God was impressing me also at that moment that He wanted me in the gospel ministry. I began to feel immediately that my life should be cast in that direction although it was years later before I ever told anyone even in confidence or made a formal announcement to that effect.

Jimmy went to Mississippi College, where he continued to excel as a scholar and athlete. He played on the football team, taking long and exciting train trips to play in Mexico City and at Colgate University in New York. His senior year he was captain of the team and president of the student body. One memorable college photo shows a handsome, solidly built young man in a football stance with a no-nonsense look on his face and a bandage over his right eye.

To help with his expenses as the national economy began its downward spiral, he got a job doing office work and running errands for the college president. Years later he credited his supervisor, Miss Addie Mae Stevens, secretary to the president, with teaching him "sound management practices" that he would put to work later as SSB executive secretary. From 1932 to 1935, Sullivan attended Southern Baptist Theological Seminary in Louisville, gaining more theological training than any previous Board secretary had received.

While still a student at Southern, Sullivan was invited to preach at the Baptist church in Beaver Dam, Kentucky, as a last-minute replacement for a sick pastor, who himself was serving temporarily since the former pastor had died. Within weeks the chairman of the deacons called offering this twenty-three-year-old seminarian the pastorate. Sullivan asked if the call had been unanimous. The deacon explained that it had not. Six members who were retired pastors and had all lost their jobs to seminary-trained men voted no. They wanted a "God-made" preacher, not a "man-made, Sears and Roebuck" variety who was considered a minister just because he had a seminary diploma. "Under those circumstances," Sullivan said, "I accepted and went to Beaver Dam with the avowed purpose of making these six ex-pastors my best friends. I think I succeeded."

With his wife, Velma, whose family were longtime Sullivan neighbors, Sullivan began his pastoral career in Beaver Dam, where he spent five of his "happiest years." During the early 1940s he pastored churches in Mississippi and Tennessee (married, a father, and thirty-one when World War II began, he saw no military service). In 1947 he came to Belmont Heights Baptist Church in Nashville, where several Sunday School Board employees attended. During those years he was also a trustee of the SSB and counted his fellow board members as his friends; they noted his steadiness, open-mindedness, and organizational skills.

In 1950 Dr. Sullivan accepted a call from First Baptist Church of Abilene, Texas. Founded in 1881, the same year the town was incorporated as the new western railhead for shipping Texas cattle, First Church Abilene was a historic institution in the region. George W. Truett had preached the dedicatory sermon, and Lee R. Scarborough went from the pastorate there to head the Evangelism Department at Southwestern Seminary. Of his coming Sullivan observed, "Indeed the pastor of that church was accepted, sight unseen, as the No. 1 citizen of the city the day he arrived."

The church was already filled to overflowing on Sunday morning when Sullivan began his ministry. Before long he found himself leading a million-dollar project to build a new sanctuary, declaring that the result was "one of the finest church structures in the Southern Baptist Convention."

The new church was still unfinished when Dr. Sullivan got his first call from Maxey Jarman, a prominent Nashville layman and shoe company executive who headed the search committee at the Sunday School Board for a new executive secretary. T. L. Holcomb, fit though he was and willing to continue, was being retired. Jarman and other trustees had come to know Sullivan when he pastored at Belmont Heights, and they wanted to assess his willingness to take Holcomb's place.

Like all who preceded him in the post, Sullivan initially resisted the offer because it would take him away from what he believed to be his calling. He wrote, "Leaving the pastorate was a painful experience for me because I loved everything about my years of close relationship to local congregations." W. A. Criswell, another member of the nominating committee and high-profile pastor of First Baptist Dallas, 190 miles east of Abilene, telephoned to encourage Sullivan to take the job.

Sullivan traveled to Nashville to meet with the nominating committee. It must have been an interesting exchange. Sullivan states that throughout his career he never negotiated his salary. The figure the Board offered was less than he earned in Abilene, but he agreed to it anyway. He did however insist on other conditions, all of which the committee accepted. Chief among them was that he could bring along his associate pastor from Abilene, John Marvin Crowe, as an administrative assistant (he eventually became executive vice president). Sullivan and Crowe had known each other since Sullivan was in seminary. Throughout his tenure at the Board, Sullivan depended on Crowe to take care of details, organize the leadership ranks, and implement his policies and decisions.

Dr. Sullivan was elected in March and took office June 1, 1953. Dr. Holcomb's last day was May 31, so there was no overlap, no break-in period. According to historian Leon McBeth, Sullivan was all but ignored when he arrived for work: "On the first day he was refused a parking place for lack of a SSB permit. He walked in the front door, unrecognized by workers milling about. Inside, he asked directions to his own office. There was no welcome, official or unofficial, and no installation service. He just walked in and started to work."

As he had done when moving to a new pastorate, Dr. Sullivan expected to spend as much as a year getting a feel for how the Board operated, talking with seasoned Board workers, watching the systems and employees in action, and developing ways to make them better. That wasn't possible. Dr. Holcomb was a gifted visionary and promoter who over time had allowed the operational machinery of the Board to work its way into a state of confusion. "The elected board was administering," Sullivan recalled, "and the hired managers were making policy. It should have been the other way around."

Holcomb frankly admitted that things were out of kilter. "I reorganized the Board once, and it nearly killed me," he said. "If I tried it again, I believe it would take my life. So I decided to leave it to my successor." And so without any time to plan or any predecessor to mentor him, James Sullivan jumped into the middle of things and started transforming the Baptist Sunday School Board into a modern operation.

He appointed a Plans and Policies Committee to help reorganize the way work was done. Probably for the first time ever, the new secretary brought in an outside management consultant—Booz, Allen, Hamilton—to analyze the way the Board operated from top to bottom and make recommendations. On what some employees later called Bloody Saturday, departments were realigned and responsibilities shifted on a massive scale. Sullivan believed he couldn't change things piecemeal because an organization partly old and partly new would never be able to function. But he believed change had to come for the Board to keep serving the denomination. He agreed with a consultant who warned him that such a broad-based restructuring was like changing a tire on a car speeding down the freeway.

When the dust settled, the Sunday School Board was reorganized into four divisions: Education, headed by William Lewis Howse, former professor of religious education at Southwestern Seminary; Service, under longtime

Board executive Harold Ingraham; Business, managed by Robert L. Middleton; and Merchandise and Sales, under Keith Von Hagen. Sullivan was the strategic planner for this enormous restructuring, and J. M. Crowe was the hands-on facilitator.

Four officers reported directly to Sullivan: Crowe; Norris Gillam, in charge of contracts and investment; personnel manager Leonard Wedel; and editorial secretary Clifton J. Allen, who transferred from head of the old editorial division and was now general editor over all publications.

For the first time Board job descriptions were standardized, as were pay scales. An employee credit union was formed. Sullivan and others scrutinized how jobs were done and looked for ways to do them more efficiently. They streamlined the organizational chart from top to bottom, separating each division into departments, then the larger departments into sections, with a formal description of who reported to whom. The Board revisited its contracts with suppliers, looking for competitive pricing, volume discounts, more efficient mailing and shipping methods, and other cost savings.

The Board found itself expanding as Southern Baptist churches prospered during the surging postwar economy. By the end of World War II, the Convention had paid off all its crushing Depression-era debt. The 1950s ushered in a season both of material prosperity and religious conviction. At the 1953 Convention in Houston, messengers launched a Sunday school expansion called "A Million More in '54" with a goal of adding a million members to the Sunday school rolls in a year.

The next year, at St. Louis, was Dr. Sullivan's first time to address the convention as secretary of the Sunday School Board. Only weeks before, the US Supreme Court had ruled in *Brown vs. Board of Education* that maintaining segregated schools for black and white children was unconstitutional, reversing the "separate but equal" policy the Court had affirmed in 1896 and upheld ever since. The timing gave Southern Baptists the opportunity to be one of the first large organizations of any kind to comment on the historic decision.

While carefully skirting an explicit endorsement of integration, the SBC affirmed that all people deserved to be treated as children of God. Sullivan sought a middle ground—in race relations in particular and on culturally divisive ideas in general: "As the Sunday School Board continues to grow, it is my prayer and determined hope . . . that it will never veer from the truth either to the right or to the left."

Sullivan saw this defense of the center not only as the Board's responsibility but as essential to its survival. He later explained: "Under our polity any church can veto any decision made by the Board or denomination. If we ever move too fast or too far, or veer to the right or the left unduly, churches that wish to do so can reject our materials, refuse our programs, and move in any direction they choose. We have no recourse. When such happens, school is out for us."

As a leader determined to discuss and consider all sides of a volatile issue, James L. Sullivan was doubtless the right man to lead the Sunday School Board through the rocky years that followed. He was also a dedicated chief executive whose commitment to balance was sorely tested during the cultural and denominational battles that shaped those times.

CHAPTER 17

Desegregation Tightrope

D r. Sullivan had scarcely gotten his massive reorganization plan under way—working on it into the wee hours
night after night in order to tend to his regular responsibilities during the day—when he had to face the crisis of desegregation. Because Southern Baptist churches were concentrated
in the part of the country most affected by the 1954 Supreme
Court ruling, they were especially apprehensive about what
the new laws would mean.

Sullivan's own feelings seem to have been that desegregation was a Christian step to take, but that stark, frequently
confusing, and too often conflicting federal laws and man-
dates made the process harder and more contentious than

it needed to be. It was an issue Southerners had been struggling with for generations. His stance was remarkably reminiscent of a letter General Robert E. Lee wrote to his wife, Mary, the last Christmas before the Civil War began: "In this enlightened age, there are few I believe, but what will acknowledge that slavery as an institution is a moral & political evil. . . . [However,] their emancipation will sooner result from the mild & melting influence of Christianity, than the storms and tempests of fiery controversy."

The year Sullivan took charge, which was the year before the *Brown* decision, he mandated that blacks and whites be paid the same wage for the same work. (While there was no resistance to that change, he opened a hornet's nest of controversy by paying men and women equally.) Sullivan also opened the employee cafeteria to blacks, making it the first integrated company cafeteria in Nashville. Only two white employees complained about eating with blacks, both of them retired preachers working temporarily at the Board until they could qualify for Social Security.

These policies produced goodwill among black employees and their families that helped the Board tremendously as arguments over desegregation became more strident. Radical pro-integration activists, many of them black, accused the Board of dragging their feet. In light of the Southern Baptist belief that every church acts independently, the Board steadfastly declined to set up or endorse any wide-scale program for integration. When radicals ratcheted up the political and public relations pressure, staging demonstrations outside the Nashville offices, the Board's own black employees stepped in, Sullivan said, and "silenced the criticism by denying that there was any justification for such aggressive attacks. They contended with their own people that the Sunday School Board was doing vastly more than most institutions of the nation and was doing so without creating issues or ill feelings on the part of anyone."

Because desegregation was so prominent in shaping the culture of the Sullivan years and because he thought and wrote about it in such depth, it's worth the time to look at a more comprehensive view of the controversy in Sullivan's own words. A reader can almost feel his hand on the SSB wheel, straining every muscle to steer a middle course. In *God Is My Record*, he declared:

> We knew the Supreme Court decision of 1954 was going to bring tremendous social upheaval the entire nation over and create immediate tensions in churches throughout the nation. Drastic changes of a revolutionary nature like that cannot be made instantaneously without corresponding emotional upheavals. Such would be disconcerting in the Convention. It could be catastrophic in some of the churches.
>
> The Sunday School Board has always stressed the importance of human personality, the worth of

persons, the equality of mankind before God. We
had championed the idea of the Bible that nationality
and racial extraction make no difference to the eyes
of God. The song, "Red, and yellow, black and white,
they are precious in his sight" was taught to nearly
every child in most every church. But in 1954 some
of the churches began to feel that they were being
coerced by government and law in matters related
to their internal church operations. Because of the
tradition of separation of church and state for which
Baptists had contended since the Constitution's first
amendment, written largely on Baptist insistence, the
feelings were intensified. Already they were feeling
there must be an easier and better way to correct a
national wrong than by violent or military means to
which government seemed to be resorting.

While Christians would have to agree with the
ultimate objective, there were conscientious disagreements as to method used to bring such to pass.

The Sunday School Board was thrown into
the dilemma of charting its course so as to help the
churches maintain balance and make judgments that
were right and lasting, that they would not regret later.
So we followed a pattern by which we hoped transition could come without violent revolutions in the
churches. Such could create irreparable breaches of
fellowship.

Very few of the thirty-four thousand churches
among Southern Baptists had any constitutional limitations on membership. This meant that officially
they were not segregated. In fact, many of them practiced some degree of integration already. But in many
areas only white prospects were visited during enlist-
ment times and invitations were extended only to the
white people of the area to come to Sunday School
and to unite with the church. Such a practice was
followed by many churches out of courtesy to strong
black conventions which insisted that our churches
not practice "sheep stealing" among their members.

This same noninterventionist policy that had attracted
criticism and protests by radical blacks also angered radical
whites on the other end of the integration seesaw.

Because the Sunday School Board did not
announce avowed opposition to the government's
position and did not openly attack integration on
moral and scriptural grounds, there were extremists
who organized against us to try to force us into the
position of arguing in our printed materials that God
made us different and therefore wanted to keep us
separate.

There are evidences that at least three extremist organizations, the Ku Klux Klan, John Birch

Society, and White Citizens Council, were looking for grounds of a major attack against the Sunday School Board.

These radical white supremacist organizations attracted large followings at times in the 1950s and 1960s, a time when a popular lapel pin in the South read simply, "Never." The Ku Klux Klan, founded in Pulaski, Tennessee, in 1866 as a white vigilante organization, was outlawed after Reconstruction, then re-formed in 1915 for the purpose of intimidating blacks and their supporters. In 1920 the KKK had four million members, but by the 1950s its membership and influence had diminished dramatically. The civil rights movement reignited the group, which then set up new chapters throughout the South.

The John Birch Society, founded by a retired Boston candy company executive in 1958, was originally a virulently anti-Communist organization that soon embraced other radical causes including opposing desegregation. Ironically, it was named in honor of John Birch, a Baptist missionary and US Army intelligence officer. The founders considered Birch's death, on August 25, 1945, to be the first casualty of the Cold War.

The White Citizens Council, organized at Indianola, Mississippi, in 1954, was often called the White Collar Klan or Uptown Klan. Publicly renouncing violence, it organized economic reprisals against people and businesses that supported desegregation.

Over the next decade the Board picked its way through the minefield of race relations with reasonable success, even as its downtown Nashville neighbors took a turn in the national spotlight. Nearby dime-store lunch counters were the sites of some of the nation's first sit-in protests. Black students came in and sat at the counter to be served. Told the store didn't serve food to blacks, the students stayed put and were arrested. Activists kept up the pressure from both extremist positions, assailing the Board on one hand for moving too slowly to endorse desegregation and on the other for trying to rush the churches along too fast. Sullivan instituted security procedures at Board headquarters, which, as in so much else regarding the race issue, relieved some employees and customers and infuriated others.

Sullivan began receiving anonymous threats against himself and his family. Eventually they became so frequent and ominous that he moved his wife and children out of their home in Hillwood, an exclusive West Nashville suburb, to a secluded neighborhood near Old Hickory Lake.

As the Civil Rights Act of 1964 brought yet another wave of change in American race relations, the Sunday School Board published a Training Union youth quarterly dealing with the Christian perspective on race in America. What would in any other time, on any other topic, have been a minor editorial oversight mushroomed into a major crisis that gave the Klan and other detractors an excuse to lash out.

The quarterly for July 4, 1964 contained a reference to James Baldwin, a Harlem-born author who lived in Paris and had written widely on contemporary racial topics in books, plays, and magazines. Quarterlies included a reading list for further study, and one of Baldwin's books was on the July 4 list. The SSB staff writer who wrote the story listed the book, which he'd never read, based on someone else's recommendation. It was the editor's responsibility to make sure the book was appropriate. But the editor in charge had just resigned, and various people were splitting up his duties until a new editor arrived. So the Baldwin book stayed in the reading list.

Unfortunately for the Board, Baldwin's book was in the style that had made him a star in some literary circles: edgy, raw, and peppered with profanities and vulgar references. People surprised that the Board would list a black author in its reading list were outraged when they read his work. Some churches shipped their quarterlies back, and the anti-desegregation radicals had a field day. Eventually the Board received more than a thousand letters objecting to the Baldwin reference.

From the writer of the article on down, everyone involved in the Baldwin quarterly was horrified that the reference had slipped in. The Board released a complete explanation of what had happened as soon as possible. Some people recognized it as the simple mistake that it was while others used it to advance their case that the Board was forcing integration on

Southern Baptist churches and this was the result. Extremists demanded that Baptist Book Stores carry their virulently antiblack materials. An ad hoc group calling themselves the Circuit Riders copied filth-laced pages from the Baldwin book and wrapped them in a copy of the Training Union quarterly cover, then distributed them implying they were published by the Board.

In the wake of the Baldwin crisis, the Board reviewed its editorial and work-flow policies. The procedures were fine; it was merely a matter of innocent human error. It was a sign of how polarized some congregations and individuals had become that they refused to accept a simple and fully documented explanation for what happened. Dr. Sullivan frequently reminded himself that "there is a lot of difference between appearance and reality" and that if people didn't bother to collect the facts, they'd decide based on appearances that were "woefully inadequate."

In walking the desegregation tightrope as best it could, the Board continued coming under fire from blacks as well as whites. In October 1971 the Board produced the January-March 1972 issue of *Becoming*, a publication for fourteen- and fifteen-year-olds. This time Sullivan had seen a potential problem in advance and personally pulled a section from the issue before it was mailed.

The problem was a lesson on racial reconciliation. Sullivan thought it "tended to coerce the churches" to push for integration; the writer's approach was too confrontational. He also disliked a photograph showing a black boy and two white girls standing in a school library hallway. Sullivan's objection had nothing to do with mixing races. Photos of blacks and whites together had appeared by then, according to Sullivan, "hundreds of times before in our publications without difficulty." Sullivan's problem with the picture was that the people in it were too old. They were in fact college students, when the target of the publication was late middle school or early high school age. In addition there were what he called "other visual problems."

Dr. Sullivan recalled a meeting where Board officials discussed "potential misinterpretation of a combination of elements: photographic content, photographic technical quality, and textual material. Any of these elements alone would probably not have been seriously subject to misunderstanding, but taken together they created what we considered an intolerable situation."

Sullivan authorized the same lesson on the same topic for a later edition of *Becoming* with the changes as discussed. "My personal suggestion," he said, "was that the picture used should show fourteen- and fifteen-year-old black and white boys and girls seated around a table. Such would be far more understandable and would fit into the nature of the lesson written." With extra effort the revised feature was completed in time to replace the unsatisfactory one in the same issue.

In spite of catching the errors early, and regardless of the Board's best intentions, changing the first *Becoming* issue of 1972 became what Leon McBeth termed "one of the most widely publicized events in the history of the Sunday School Board." Sullivan had pulled the original story on Friday, October 22, 1971. By the next Tuesday, Religious News Service in New York had somehow gotten a copy of the article and put it on the newswire. *Newsweek* published the problematic photo, captioned "Threatening Photograph," and a brief story. Both the picture and the notion that the Board had squelched it were in the national news for days. The media implied, or reported outright, that the Board was working against desegregation.

Seventeen years after *Brown vs. Board of Education* the public was still wary of the Southern Baptist commitment to racial equality, and many Baptists continued taking potshots at the SSB on the issue. Hundreds of letters flooded in, condemning the Board for impeding racial harmony. Baptist state papers published critical editorials and letters by the dozens. On December 15, the Board tried to explain its position, which was that the Board's responsibility to the SBC was to educate, not to promote one point of view over another. They affirmed, according to McBeth, that the Board "had taken every opportunity to teach the biblical message on race, but its assignment did not call for it to actively promote integration in the churches."

McBeth continued, "The public perception was that the Board had backed down in order to placate segregationist churches who otherwise would have returned the literature. Baptists were embarrassed by the incident, some because they were not segregationists and others because they did not want their segregationist views so publicly exposed." He added that in his view, the Board's biggest mistake was that it "missed its opportunity to put accurate information before the public immediately."

Sullivan was disturbed by how quickly misinformation was picked up in the national media and how impossible it was to set the facts straight once rumors became widespread. "We do not have access to the names of all the publications which printed incorrect information, and attempts at correction are usually separated such a long time from the original story and run in such inconspicuous places that readers of the original seldom see the corrected facts."

He went on to add:

> I have evidence satisfactory to my own mind that not only did one local newspaper writer [with access to national newswires] make this a matter of personal crusade, but that the interests of one of the publishing houses producing materials for black churches were involved.
>
> This publishing house, privately owned, issued a public statement condemning our administrative

action. The statement did not reveal that the same publisher had been using our manuscripts in their publications for decades. Nor did it reveal that their own interests would be best served at this time by a resegregation psychology which would have resulted in greater use by black churches of their literature rather than ours.

When they happened, the Baldwin and *Becoming* controversies generated a lot of emotion and a lot of ink. Eventually, however, they faded into the historical background as racial equality became not only a legal mandate but part of the cultural mainstream as well. Another type of crisis during the Sullivan years opened wounds among Southern Baptists that have never fully healed.

CHAPTER 18

The Message of Genesis

D r. Sullivan walked the race relations tightrope through a season of serious cultural and denominational discord with honor and a fair measure of success. Holding fast to a middle ground true to Southern Baptist teaching and tradition as extremists pressured the Board from both sides, the secretary outlasted his critics. Eventually the Board and the Convention established an equilibrium on the matter, encouraging reconciliation and affirming all people equal in the sight of God, but not forcing change.

Theological conflicts proved more intense and longer lasting than the integration debate ever was. A big debate over interpreting the Bible started after the desegregation movement began but before the Civil Rights Act and the Baldwin controversy. Overlapping the black-white conflict, this biblical interpretation crisis soon overshadowed it as well and has outlived it by decades.

In 1961 Broadman Press published *The Message of Genesis: A Theological Commentary* by Dr. Ralph H. Elliott, a graduate and former faculty member at Southern Seminary who was elected to the original faculty of Midwestern Baptist Theological Seminary in Kansas City when it opened in 1958. Sullivan described Elliott as "one of the most evangelistic professors in the entire Southern Baptist seminary system . . . considered by the religious world to be basically a conservative theologian." However, some of his Genesis commentary, Sullivan admitted, "was to many of the readers new and a bit foreign."

What would become the bone of fierce contention was Elliott's assertion that some of the Old Testament was "parabolic and symbolic" and not necessarily historical fact. For example, on the matter of the ages of Old Testament figures, some of whom lived to be hundreds of years old, Elliott wrote, "In all probability, the Priestly writer simply exaggerated the ages in order to show the glory of an ancient civilization."

Sullivan and others realized even before Elliott's book went to press that it might raise Southern Baptist hackles. The prepublication committee reviewing the manuscript saw problems with it but couldn't reach a consensus on whether to recommend changes. In Sullivan's view they had three options, none of them ideal.

The Board's choices were limited by the Branch Committee, formed by the SBC in 1956 to coordinate various Southern Baptist boards and groups and help them work together more efficiently (the Convention by then had been trying to set up a coordinating authority for more than thirty years). One of the Branch Committee's directives was that the SSB should produce whatever printed materials the other Convention organizations needed to do their work. This meant the Board didn't have full editorial control over its own publications since these other Baptist organizations could call the shots on materials produced for them.

While in theory the Branch Committee mandate kept Southern Baptist seminaries from going to other publishers or forming their own imprint, in this case it tied the Board's hands. As Sullivan later explained, it

> fixed us with responsibility without control of content. Under Baptist polity one agency cannot make decisions about internal operations of another agency. If we sought to force revision of the book at the Sunday School Board we would have been tampering with curriculum material for a theological school. If we refused to publish the book desired by another agency we would be violating a Convention directive.

Our only other option was to produce the manuscript submitted. All three options were dead-end streets.

After lengthy discussion the Board decided to print *The Message of Genesis* as it was, making clear that though it was a Sunday School Board product, it was for seminary teaching and not for use in Sunday school lessons.

Within weeks of its release, the book was excoriated by Southern Baptists who thought its theological position veered too far from Southern Baptist teaching in general and The Baptist Faith and Message in particular, a 1925 statement that proclaimed the Bible "truth without any mixture of error." Leading the charge was K. Owen White, pastor of First Baptist Church, Houston, Texas, who wrote an article titled "Death in the Pot" for the Texas *Baptist Standard* that other state papers quickly picked up. The title comes from a passage in 2 Kings 4:40: During a time of famine, Elisha was about to feed his sons stew that included poisonous gourds. The men couldn't eat because they discovered there was "death in the pot." After Elisha threw meal into the pot, the stew was safe to eat.

White took some isolated quotations from Elliott's book, then declared, "The book from which I have quoted is liberalism, pure and simple. . . . The book in question is 'poison.' This sort of rationalistic criticism can lead only to [our] further confusion, unbelief, deterioration, and ultimate disintegration as a great New Testament denomination." He advised the author and other like-minded people to "find a place of service with groups or denominations of like theological inclinations." Elliott had his defenders, who insisted that his overall views were generally in line with accepted Southern Baptist thought and that discussing diverse viewpoints was essential to a complete seminary education and important for safeguarding academic freedom. But they struggled to make themselves heard above the roar of protest.

The SSB released a statement which said in part, "In accepting [*The Message of Genesis*] for publication, Broadman Press recognized that the point of view expressed in the book would not be coincident with the thinking of all Baptists. It was considered, however, to be representative of a segment of Southern Baptist life and thought."

It was also true that Broadman was under pressure to do a better job meeting the demand for textbooks at the six Southern Baptist seminaries. Publishing Elliott's work was one way the publisher could show it was meeting the schools' needs, even as representatives from other publishers visited seminary campuses to push their own catalogs. But what Broadman and the Board saw as a textbook meeting a legitimate need, many others saw as a book for general readers from a Southern Baptist press saying the Bible wasn't necessarily true from cover to cover.

In January 1962, SSB trustees passed a resolution stating, "The elected Sunday School Board hereby reaffirms its approval of the principles and policies under which

Broadman Press is functioning." The statement added that the Board "further encourages Broadman Press to continue to publish books which will represent more than one point of view and which will undergird faith and contribute to the Christian growth and development of those who read them." The same month, trustees at Midwestern Seminary resolved regarding Dr. Elliott that "we do affirm our confidence in him as a consecrated Christian, a promising scholar and teacher, a loyal servant of Southern Baptists, and a dedicated and warm evangelic preacher of the Gospel."

But all these affirmative resolutions notwithstanding, the Elliott firestorm was just beginning. At the annual convention that year in San Francisco, the controversial book was the main attraction. K. Owen White introduced two resolutions of his own, both of which passed easily. The first was, "That the messengers to this Convention by standing vote, reaffirm their faith in the *entire* Bible as the authoritative, authentic, infallible Word of God." The second declared, "That we express our abiding and unchanging objection to the dissemination of theological views in any of our seminaries which would undermine such faith in the historical accuracy and doctrinal integrity of the Bible, and that we courteously request the trustees and administrative officers of our institutions and other agencies to take such steps as shall be necessary to remedy at once those situations where such views are now threatening our historic position." Many read this as a suggestion or demand that Elliott be fired from his seminary professorship. However, even Elliott's critics opposed a motion to "cease publishing and to recall from all distribution channels" the book in question.

One of the voices raised in Elliott's defense was in the Kentucky state Baptist paper: "Elliott does not deserve a medal for extreme views compared with his fellow Southern Baptists. If he deserves a medal, it is for his courage in writing a book in which he honestly expresses his views. Some teachers who would share his approach to the Bible, though not necessarily his conclusions, feel his only mistake was to write down his conclusions at this time."

All the publicity helped sales of Elliott's book, and when the printing was sold out, the Board decided not to reprint. Publication rights then reverted back to Dr. Elliott, who fielded calls from several other publishers interested in picking it up. A subcommittee of the trustees at Midwestern instructed Elliott not to republish the book. Elliott believed that only the trustees could make such a demand and that the subcommittee's directive was invalid. When he sold the rights to Bethany Press, associated with the Disciples of Christ, and they released the book in February 1963, Elliott was fired by his trustees on a vote of twenty-two to seven.

Hounded for his now notorious theology—a bomb was planted on his doorstep in Kansas City—Dr. Elliott left the SBC shortly after his dismissal from Midwestern and became a seminary professor and pastor in the American Baptist Convention. In summing up the whole situation, *Christian*

Century editorialized that "the issue is not heresy or the right of a professor to teach such mild biblical criticism. The issue is a much more vast one: control of the Southern Baptist Convention's academic institutions and, through this, of the training of the ministry."

Many Southern Baptists would disagree that Elliott's criticism was "mild," but most would concur that *Christian Century* had accurately framed the argument. Under the banner of institutional independence and academic freedom, some seminary professors and others in positions of leadership had become separated from the historic core of Southern Baptist doctrine. Depending on the viewer's perspective, either the church was drifting toward a modernist, relativistic interpretation of the Bible and away from its traditional beliefs, or it was under attack from close-minded reactionaries determined to conform everybody to their way of thinking.

In 1961, the same year *The Message of Genesis* was published, I graduated from Southwestern Seminary in Fort Worth and was serving my first full-time pastorate in the town of Iredell, Texas. I moved with my family a few months later to Tyler, Texas, and a year after that to a wonderful church in San Antonio. I was in Texas when the Texans came out so strongly against Ralph Elliott. Even then I could see how much power this theological divide had and how much momentum it was building.

My friend and former seminary professor Leon McBeth, whose work I've quoted so often, wrote me then that pastors more than anyone else could help Southern Baptists "recover their spiritual equilibrium." But our friendship, which has lasted to this day, couldn't hide the honest fact that we were going our separate ways on the issue of Southern Baptist theology. The best thing about it, and the aspect I wish we had been able to clone, was that in spite of our emerging differences and perspectives, we remained friends who respected and loved each other.

In a letter he wrote to me on July 9, 1963, which I still have, Leon observed: "Jimmy, I have gathered from your correspondence that you are growing more conservative. Fine. Just don't lose your sweet Christian spirit—as so many have. Keep *perspective*, and respect those who may not be quite so conservative as you are, and yet hold on to the basic biblical faith also. Boy, all of a sudden I'm preaching to you! But I think you know what I mean, and if I remember you, you will remain a Christian in spirit and attitude at all times."

This one paragraph contains a miniature version of the whole Elliott controversy and the battles that were to follow. Leon said I was growing more conservative. I didn't see it that way. I believed what I always had, what I still believe, and yet to my mind there were Southern Baptists who were drifting farther and farther from historic Baptist positions and being more and more public about it. They were moving, not I. But he also talked about perspective and respect. If both sides had been able to hold on to those two ideals, the next thirty years would have been a whole lot easier.

McBeth was consistent in his views, then, when he wrote years later that Professor Elliott's firing and Broadman's decision not to reprint his book "indicated the growing influence of a conservative movement which was beginning to take form in the SBC." I would say rather that it indicated the liberal drift in the Convention had gone far enough, and it was time to refresh and reaffirm what it was that Southern Baptists stood for.

One historic comment of Dr. McBeth's I agree wholeheartedly with is his description of the next theological controversy that arose as "the most severe crisis the Sunday School Board has faced in a century of service." The Elliott book was only a warm-up for the debate that raged over the first volume of the *Broadman Bible Commentary*, published in 1969, which also centered around an interpretation in Genesis.

According to Broadman Press editor William J. Fallis, the idea of a Bible commentary had been floating around since 1950. Eight years later, with James Sullivan's reorganization in place and a new emphasis on responsiveness to the textbook and general markets alike, Fallis revisited the idea with the book committee and received Sullivan's endorsement. In fact, Sullivan hoped a Southern Baptist commentary would head off what he called "an increasing polarization of Southern Baptists toward the two theological extremes of liberalism and fundamentalism."

Warming to the idea, Sullivan wanted to produce three separate products: a one-volume commentary for Sunday school teachers, an eight- to ten-volume commentary based on the King James translation for laymen and bivocational pastors, and an academic set based on original Hebrew and Greek biblical texts. Originally he planned to release them in that order, but actually published them in reverse order, with the academic commentaries first.

Along with Broadman's editorial secretary, Clifton J. Allen, Fallis gathered a group of Southern Baptist pastors and scholars in Nashville in November 1958 and again in March 1959 to lay the groundwork for the project. Participants were wary of the whole idea, claiming it would be impossible to please all Southern Baptists no matter what they wrote. Eventually, though, they supported the commentary, and the trustees authorized the project in 1961, the year the Elliott controversy began. The Genesis blowup made the SSB begin second-guessing itself about the wisdom of a commentary that, despite Sullivan's hope to the contrary, might drive the wedge even deeper between conservatives and moderates.

Finally in 1966 work began in earnest. Fallis and Allen, plus another Broadman editor named Joseph F. Green, along with four Southern Baptist seminary professors—John I. Durham, Southeastern; Roy L. Honeycutt, Midwestern; Jack MacGorman, Southwestern; and Frank Stagg, Southern—began defining the shape of the work. There would be twelve volumes, seven on the Old Testament and five on the New, based on the Revised Standard Version translation. They suggested, and Sullivan approved, sixty-four writers for the various sections of text. Most of them were Southern Baptists, with a few American Baptists and British Baptists in the mix as well.

Of his decision to move ahead, Sullivan later wrote that the Board "felt our Baptist people ought to be aware of what was being said and done by scholars in the theological world whether they agreed or not. They should make up their minds in the light of their own experiences and personal interpretations regardless of any position a commentary might take in its treatment of any passage." But as the Elliott matter had proven, that was not always the case. It surely would not be the case in this instance.

The committee's original choice to write the commentary on Genesis was Clyde T. Francisco of Southern Seminary, a leading Old Testament scholar. But Dr. Francisco was under exclusive contract to another publisher that was also preparing a multivolume commentary. Next the committee chose G. Henton Davies, principal of Regent's Park College, the Baptist College at Oxford University in England, and a respected British scholar in Old Testament studies.

Sullivan and the commentary editorial committee agreed that on theological points where there were various worthy opinions, "the writer would be thoroughly objective without appearing condescending toward any who might disagree. We also stated that where several viewpoints generally were held, after objective discussion the writer could insert his own personal view at that point if he wished."

Volumes 1 (Genesis/Exodus) and 8 (Matthew) of the *Broadman Bible Commentary* were released in October 1969. Davies's writing drew immediate criticism, divided for the most part among three issues. First, Davies suggested that Genesis was not written by Moses but was pieced together from previously existing documents. Second, he considered the first eleven chapters, including the accounts of creation and the flood, to be symbolic or allegorical rather than literal history. Third and most inflammatory of all, he seemed to his critics to imply that the dramatic episode in Genesis 22 where Abraham is prepared to sacrifice his son Isaac in obedience to God is either allegorical or a figment of Abraham's imagination.

Davies wrote:

> The story has been interpreted as a parable, just as the story of the prodigal son is a parable. The chief interpretation along these lines has been to see in it the divine repudiation of a child sacrifice, and in consequence the substitution of an animal in satisfaction for the divine claim to receive the firstborn of every womb. . . .
>
> The problem of the story is not in its events, but in its motivation. Why did Abraham feel that he had to make the sacrifice? . . . Did God make, would God in fact have made, such a demand upon Abraham or anybody else, except himself? There are those who would accept this command literally.

Our answer however is no. Indeed what
Christian or humane conscience could regard such a
command as coming from God?

Defending Davies, Sullivan wrote:

At no place does he question the historicity
of the experience. In trying to emphasize that this
was an incident which God permitted rather than
decreed—which would be an allowable interpretation by the very nature of the Hebrew language—he
termed Abraham's own impression that God must
have ordered it as "the climax of the psychology of
his life" [quoted from Davies' text]. Therefore certain
critics concluded that Davies was saying that this was
not a historical incident but something that merely
went on in the mind of Abraham.

Too, Dr. Davies used the words "*our* answer"
referring editorially to his own interpretation. Those
who opposed claimed he was attempting to use the
"our" in reference to a Southern Baptist position.

Straining his management skills and powers of communication to the utmost, Sullivan labored valiantly to rescue
the SSB from the hail of theological crossfire that followed.
He might as well have tried to hold back the sea.

CHAPTER 19

Controversial Commentary

Many people who attended the 1970 Convention in Denver said it was the loudest, most raucous SBC gathering they'd ever attended. Leading the critics this time was Gwin Turner, a pastor from California who had already made his position clear with an article in his church paper titled "Why I Cannot Accept the *Broadman Bible Commentary*." In Denver, Turner introduced a motion "that because the new *Broadman Bible Commentary* is out of keeping with the beliefs of the vast majority of Southern Baptist pastors and people this Convention requests the Sunday School Board to withdraw Volume 1 from further distribution and that it be rewritten with due consideration of the conservative viewpoint."

While the Elliott book had been widely condemned, there had never been any broad-based attempt to recall it. This time Southern Baptists felt either that the offense was more egregious or that the stakes were higher.

Clifton Allen, editorial secretary of the SSB for twenty-three years and general editor of the commentary, tried to explain to the restless crowd that Broadman books never assumed to define the Southern Baptist position on anything and that the next generation of seminarians deserved "a heritage of the open mind and open Bible." His words fell on unhearing ears.

Herschel Hobbs, the revered conservative Oklahoma pastor who had chaired a committee to revise the 1925 statement of faith in the wake of the Elliott controversy, was shouted off the platform when he tried to address the Denver gathering. Dr. Sullivan never had the chance to be thus insulted by the audience: according to church historian Jesse C. Fletcher, he was refused time to speak on the topic altogether. Fletcher further contends that a network of conservatives formed originally to oppose the Elliott book sprang into action against the commentary. Chief among the group were Ross Edwards, editor of *Baptist World and Way*, and North Carolina pastor M. O. Owens.

After a rowdy and heated debate, the Convention passed Gwin Turner's motion to recall volume 1 of the commentary by a margin of five to two.

There was more to this resounding defeat than an ideological debate. At least part of it was due to a string of misunderstandings. To their credit the Sunday School Board had seen this storm on the horizon but felt they were duty bound to publish the controversial material. The Board didn't see it as endorsing a particular biblical interpretation on behalf of Southern Baptists, but many Baptists took it that way.

Another confusing point was that in 1965 the Board had been instructed to prepare a one-volume Bible commentary for general and Sunday school use. Some messengers and pastors thought this book was that commentary, not realizing it was part of a much longer scholarly work that had already been in the planning stages for years when the one-volume project began.

Further muddying the waters, at least by Sullivan's reckoning, was a controversial conference of the Christian Life Commission in Atlanta that had also infuriated conservatives. Hoping to tackle the radical cultural forces of the 1960s head-on, the commission had invited a situational ethics professor (promoting the idea that what's right changes with the circumstances) and a representative from *Playboy* magazine to debate them. Sullivan held that "extreme rightist organizations" believed that by giving these people a public forum for their ideas, the SBC was endorsing them. To Dr. Sullivan, ever seeking accommodation and middle ground, this aggressive stance made the Genesis commentary matter all the worse.

In *The Southern Baptist Convention*, Jesse Fletcher identified another point of friction connected with the commentary debate. Two years before Denver, the 1968 Convention
in Houston chose W. A. Criswell as its president. By then
Dr. Criswell, pastor of First Baptist Church in Dallas since
1944, had become a towering figure in the denomination. (A
few years later he would become my boss.) The year he took
the president's gavel, Criswell wrote a book, *Why I Preach
That the Bible Is Literally True*, published by Broadman Press.
Denominational moderates chafed at Criswell's conservative
theology and Broadman's promotion of it. The Association
of Baptist Professors of Religion formally criticized both the
book and its publisher. The next year, at the 1969 Convention
in New Orleans, professors and their supporters backed
a candidate opposing Criswell's reelection as Convention
president, Professor W. C. Smith Jr., of Richmond University.
Criswell received more than 7,000 votes to 450 for Smith.

This should have shown clearly who was in the Southern
Baptist mainstream and who wasn't. But this theological
divide would get worse before the reconciliation and healing
could begin.

Meanwhile Clifton Allen, James Sullivan, and others
had to figure out what to do, and here the confusion continued. Many convention participants, not understanding how
the process works, expected their vote to change matters
immediately, compelling Broadman to withdraw the current volume 1 from the market and get to work on a rewrite.

But the floor vote only authorized the convention-appointed SSB trustees to decide what to do. It wasn't for Sullivan or Broadman Press to decide; they were at the service of the trustees, who were in turn appointed by Convention leadership. For these and other reasons the revision process went on for years.

At their semiannual meeting in August 1970, the trustees of the Baptist Sunday School Board considered their options. The first was to do nothing; the Convention resolution had been a *request* to withdraw and rewrite the commentary volume, not an order, though refusing one would certainly lead to the other. The second option was to abandon the entire commentary project. Not only would this be extremely expensive, it would confirm critics' insistence that Baptists should not produce a Bible commentary at all. Furthermore, with all the contributors' work wasted and their ideology in question (by association if nothing else), top-caliber writers would shun Broadman Press in the future.

The third way was a rewrite, which led to another long list of questions. Volume 1 had eleven writers in all. Was the Convention ordering the whole volume rewritten? Just the commentary sections? Just the commentary on Genesis? Would explanatory footnotes be sufficient? Should the original writers rewrite their work, or should Broadman hire other writers? (Sullivan believed that only the original authors could *rewrite* their own work.) What about contributors whose sections weren't affected; should they have the chance to withdraw from the project?

The trustees decided the original writers should write the new material because hiring new writers would be going beyond the Convention's resolution. After a lengthy discussion they also decided to recall and warehouse all unsold copies of volume 1 and to give Davies first crack at the new text. Davies was coming to America for a speaking tour the following July, eleven months away. Rather than spend the time and money to bring him over before then to discuss the situation in detail, the trustees agreed to meet with him the next summer. Nothing in the Convention resolution indicated any sort of timetable, and as far as the SSB knew they had all the time they wanted. In conversations, according to Sullivan, Davies "had assured us that he would do everything within his power to produce the type volume Southern Baptists wanted. Furthermore, he stated that if he could not conscientiously do what the Convention wanted he would eliminate himself from the project totally."

Just when everything seemed to be getting back on the rails, shortly before the 1971 convention (which in turn was a few weeks ahead of Davies's American visit), the Religious News Service published a story headlined "British Scholar Won't Compromise Major Points on Commentary Withdrawn by Southern Baptists." The lead sentence reported Davies was "unwilling to compromise his conclusions to insure reissue of the volume."

The Board had not asked Davies to "compromise his conclusions," and what they had asked him to change, according to Sullivan, Davies had said he'd do "everything within his power" to accomplish; if he couldn't change it in good conscience, he'd bow out.

Untrue as it was, the article further fanned the flames of disunity. Though Davies himself repudiated its conclusions, the story was timed exactly so that it was far and away the lead topic as the Convention assembled for its 1971 meeting in St. Louis. The article implied that the Board had not taken the previous year's Convention resolution seriously and that Broadman had ignored a directive from its governing body (which, as we've seen, was not the case).

At the convention Kenneth Barnett of Oklahoma "moved that the Sunday School Board be advised that the vote of the 1970 Convention regarding the rewriting of Volume 1 of The Broadman Bible Commentary has not been followed and that the Sunday School Board obtain another writer and proceed with the Commentary according to the vote of the 1970 Convention in Denver." After a lengthy debate this overt condemnation of the Board squeaked through by a vote of 2,672 to 2,298. Not only did it embarrass the SSB; it also created an awkward situation between the SBC and the Baptist World Alliance, which Dr. Davies was serving as president.

Sullivan observed, "It is unfortunate that some who did not understand the delicacy of such a situation felt that we were either dragging our feet intentionally or resisting the

Convention's actions altogether. Instead, we were trying to keep all bases covered so that when things were once settled there would not be lasting scars remaining between Baptist bodies internationally."

A group led by Gwin Turner, who had been in the forefront of the 1970 debate, informed the Board that they were "exceedingly displeased with the overall tone of the set and with many particular details," and wanted the entire multivolume commentary series rewritten.

In August 1971 a special committee of SSB trustees met far into the night to discuss the crisis, then joined with the full board the next day to hammer out a plan for immediate action. Some wanted to report to the Convention that they had "insurmountable problems" with the resolution as it stood and request that it be clarified or rescinded, but the full group voted down that idea.

A briefing paper prepared for Dr. Sullivan indicates the complexity of the problem the trustees were wrestling with:

> Will the Convention insist that book publica-
> tion conform to and support a prescribed theological
> stance or specific theory of biblical inspiration deter-
> mined by a majority vote of the messengers attending
> a given Convention? . . . Will the Convention support
> responsible freedom in the context of the autonomy
> of churches, the freedom of personal conscience, and
> the voluntariness of our denominational fellowship or

seek to impose restrictions on this freedom according
to a majority vote . . . of the Convention?

The briefing paper recommended that Sullivan advise
the trustees that a rewrite would not achieve the Convention's
objectives and that such a rewrite was not feasible. Sullivan
decided against this radical approach. After more long hours
of discussion, the Board formulated a motion to "request and
authorize the administration to seek to secure a new author
for the Commentary on the text of Genesis, that other materials in Volume 1 be used if other authors are agreeable, and
if not, that other contributors be enlisted if this is thought
advisable, and that the administration be authorized to work
out satisfactory legal and financial arrangements with all
parties involved."

Trustees then spoke for and against the motion. Some
agreed with the man who declared:

> I disagree with most of the stuff the Board
> publishes, . . . but I don't insist that it be rewritten to
> conform to my judgment. . . . I will fight for the right
> of this man to stand up and say, "Davies stinks and
> I don't like his commentary and I won't read it and
> it's no good." But I cannot vote for anything that puts
> a publishing house . . . in the position where anyone
> who doesn't agree with anything that's published
> will destroy a method of operation that has proven to
> be very, very successful, and impose upon it a

dictatorship of prejudice any time anyone can persuade any Convention to lift enough hands.

A colleague with the opposing view said, "Unless we follow the Convention mandate to the letter, I think a deaf ear will be turned toward this Board by the great majority of the Convention." But if they followed this mandate, "I think this is one way of taking action that will reestablish the fellowship between this Board and the Convention, and break down some of the hostility that exists." He and other like-minded trustees prevailed.

Another motion was proposed that the Board "record a peril of which we have become acutely aware," which was that the Bible commentary could be used to establish a Baptist creed. "We pledge ourselves to provide leadership in protecting the Baptist belief in the priesthood of the individual believer. . . . [The Board] is keenly aware that if it participates in developing a creedal commentary it will be performing a disservice to Southern Baptists which will be far worse than complete abandonment of the commentary." This motion was deferred.

Despite his willingness to rewrite his contribution, G. Henton Davies was replaced for the revised volume 1 by Clyde Francisco, Broadman's original choice, who had fulfilled his exclusive publishing contract elsewhere and was now available. Critics generally agreed that Francisco's interpretation was not all that different from Davies's. But what a difference the new expression of that viewpoint produced! Two other volume 1 contributors, Robert G. Bratcher and Kyle M. Yates Jr. declined to have their articles appear in the revised text and their contributions were replaced.

The subject came up again at the 1972 Convention in Philadelphia. A motion was presented describing the entire commentary as "out of harmony with the spirit and letter of The Baptist Faith and Message," and requesting that the Board "withdraw from further sale the entire set, seek a new editor, and rewrite the commentary from the point of view that the Bible is 'truth, without any mixture of error.'" The motion was soundly defeated, as was another motion to remove the name Broadman from the title.

Perhaps the best summary of the whole business was an insightful article from Joe T. Odle, editor of the Mississippi *Baptist Record*, who wrote, "What is being said is far deeper than mere discontent with a commentary. Southern Baptists are saying that they are determined to stay with the Bible believing conservatism which has characterized the convention since its beginning, and they are not willing to move toward a more liberal position. . . . We may have seen the last convention where messengers feel compelled to deal with theological issues."

If only it were so.

CHAPTER 20

Facts, Figures, and Fundamentalism

While he presided over a rocky era in the cultural and ideological history of the Sunday School Board, Dr. Sullivan also oversaw a time of tremendous modernization and growth. After assuming office he moved quickly to institute long-needed improvements in the way the Board was organized and the way it did things. He set up a four-man Office of the Executive Secretary-Treasurer to help him formulate and implement changes. He redivided the Board into four divisions and moved various people around to make best use of their gifts and talents.

During the Sullivan years a number of trailblazing men and women retired. One of them was Homer Grice, whose Vacation Bible School had become a summer institution across the country. J. E. Lambdin, the visionary behind Baptist Young People's Union (later Training Union), also completed his career of service in 1959 after thirty years. Miss Ethel Mae Allen, who began work as secretary to Dr. J. M. Frost in 1908, retired as secretary to Dr. Sullivan in December 1953, having served every leader in the history of the Sunday School Board.

Sullivan used this season of reorganization and retirement to bring new blood into the Board and further revamp its operations. Revolutionary as the ideas of Arthur Flake (who had retired in 1937), B. W. Spilman (retired 1941), and others had been in their time, the world had changed dramatically over the decades since; and the Board had to find ways to change with it.

Some programs introduced or revamped near the end of Dr. Holcomb's tenure carried forward under Sullivan with encouraging momentum. The first denomination-wide January Bible Study, in 1948, attracted about 23,000 participants; by 1955 more than 300,000 people purchased the study materials and joined in the program. Since the end of World War II, Sunday school enrollment was up by more than 2 million to almost 5.5 million, Training Union enrollment had more than doubled to almost 1.7 million, and Vacation Bible School had tripled to more than 2 million.

One of Sullivan's strengths was finding the right person for a job, assigning responsibility, then standing back and letting him do the work. An obvious example was J. M. Crowe, who had come with Sullivan from Texas to manage day-to-day operations and implement Sullivan's management directives. Another important hire was William Lewis Howse Jr., who took over the enormous new education division. Of the four divisions of the Board after Sullivan's reorganization, the education division—a combination of the old editorial division plus the education and promotion division—was responsible for every publication the SSB released, from Sunday school quarterlies to hymnals to the entire Broadman catalog.

Howse had been a minister of education at First Baptist Dallas, among other churches, and was also a professor at his alma mater, Southwestern Seminary, before joining the Board in 1954. Of Howse's success in helping bring the Board through its reorganization and managing it until he retired in 1971, Sullivan later said, "I doubt that any man ever did more precisely and flawlessly what he was employed to do as Dr. Howse did in this position, that of fusing two vast divisions into one unified operation moving toward a common objective. The fact is that if Dr. Howse had not accepted our offer, we likely would have been forced to go in another direction organizationally. He was the only man we knew who could do what we felt had to be done."

Part of Sullivan's plan was to simplify the way the Board and the Convention did its work in order to reduce duplicated effort, miscommunication, and wasteful overlap in programs and responsibilities. Over the years various agencies at the SBC were created and developed independently of one another, resulting in an operational patchwork. Individual teaching and training agencies, for example—Sunday school, Training Union, Women's Missionary Union, Church Music, and Brotherhood—had overlapping memberships, overlapping curriculums, and overlapping meetings to discuss the same issues. Each agency had its own plans, schedule, agenda, and little if any coordination with the others.

In 1924 the SBC had gone as far as recommending in a minority report that the Sunday School Board be abolished and its work parceled out to four job-specific boards set up to replace it. In 1937 the Convention appointed a committee to see how they could better correlate and coordinate their work; the "multiplication of organizations" was mechanizing denominational life, they warned, and "there is much overlapping and lost energy as a result of this excessive organization." A committee formed that year met for several years without any concrete results; a new correlation committee appointed in 1946 (which included Howse) chaired by Gaines S. Dobbins, also met over an extended period.

Of the various observations and recommendations the Dobbins committee made, one of them had a major impact on the life of the Board and Southern Baptist churches, though it took years for it to assume its final form. In 1948 the Dobbins committee suggested developing three Sunday school curriculum programs: one for the 15,000 churches having fewer than 150 members; a second for the 7,500 churches with 150 to 400 members; and a third for the relatively small number of churches with more than 400 members. This idea of having parallel but separate lessons for different size congregations lodged in the back of Howse's mind for years until a Board colleague revived it with a drawing on a coffee shop napkin.

In 1959 W. L. Howse had a heart attack. After he recovered, Sullivan hired William O. Thomason to help him manage his massive responsibilities. For the next several years the two worked side by side at the head of the education division, and even coauthored a study course book on program correlation in 1963 titled *A Church Organized and Functioning*. On the way back from a meeting in Texas, Howse, Thomason, and a few others were changing planes in Memphis and went to the coffee shop to wait for their Nashville flight. Talk turned to a discussion of curriculum. Recalling the moment, Howse wrote: "The question of what would be studied within the context of a correlated curriculum came up. I asked what the curriculum framework would cover. Thomason in his characteristic manner pulled a paper napkin from the dispenser on the table and quickly indicated with his pencil that we could get an overview of the biblical revelation first, then have studies on each of the four functions and close the series with a wrap-up of all previous studies under Christian discipleship."

On another trip together, waiting in their hotel room to leave for the airport, Howse and Thomason sketched out a three-year curriculum for what would soon be called the Life and Work Series. The Sunday School Board approved the idea in July 1964, and materials were ready by October 1966 for a three-year trial run. Long before three years were up, the Board decided to make Life and Work a permanent option for Sunday school instruction; it had quickly become the best-selling Sunday school series in Board history.

Some in the denomination warned that having two sets of Sunday school lessons would be confusing and divisive. Concerned SSB workers cautioned about the expense of producing and promoting two products. But soon the two existed peacefully side by side. The traditional Convention Uniform Series, which tended to appeal to smaller or more traditional churches, taught what the Bible said. The Life and Work series emphasized what the Bible meant and how to apply it to life situations.

Bringing up application of biblical principles meant bringing up current events which, in the 1960s, was a surefire recipe for conflict. It was much easier to produce a lesson on what a passage of Scripture said than to write one explaining what it meant and how to use it. Some of the SSB leaders conceded that the new lessons caused more disagreement than they had expected, and "created many hard feelings." Some Baptists wanted only "to know what the Bible says, not what it means." The Life and Work curriculum broke new ground in that it went beyond scriptural exposition to concentrate on application. As one historian notes, the two World Wars were scarcely mentioned in Sunday school literature. Life and Work signaled a completely new approach to Bible study.

The Board's approach to church music changed during these years too, moving beyond the gospel and camp meeting-style hymns of B. B. McKinney and the *Broadman Hymnal* to include a broader musical selection. W. Hines Sims, who had replaced McKinney after his death in 1952, edited the new *Baptist Hymnal* of 1956 to include a balance of McKinney's type of songs with more musically refined selections that appealed to larger urban congregations. Here again the Board was modernizing and broadening its reach to appeal to a wider, more contemporary audience.

Some relatively minor changes produced interesting reactions. One example various historians have noted was a suggestion to change the name of Baptist Training Union. Philip B. Harris, who had taken over leadership of BTU after the legendary J. E. Lambdin retired, wanted to spruce up the program's image, including giving it a trendier name. After several years of rolling the idea around, the department suggested the new name "Quest," intended to convey "the dynamic search for excellence in the Christian life."

Representatives of the Board unveiled the new name at the 1969 Convention at New Orleans, where the messengers were generally out of sorts because the temperature inside the meeting venue was roasting hot. "Almost every Convention report faced a hostile reception," Leon McBeth reported, "and observers said the messengers were in no mood to approve anything." Attendees knew that Training Union was going to propose a makeover; but in order to heighten the excitement, the name had been kept top secret. When Quest was revealed, response was tepid. Some in the audience resented the lack of advance notice; some just didn't like the new suggestion. Some were flatly embarrassed: a new line of Quest feminine hygiene products had recently been introduced nationwide. Ultimately the new name was unceremoniously torpedoed.

Between 1920 and 1960 the number of Southern Baptists more than doubled to 9.7 million (though the "Million More in '54" campaign fell short of its ambitious goal, it had still added 600,000 new members). To serve this growing constituency, the Sunday School Board had steadily expanded its programs and personnel to the point where employees were once more cramped by the limited space at the Nashville headquarters.

Sullivan and other Board leaders had expected the Million More campaign to increase demand for their services gradually, first in Sunday school materials, then evangelism training, and so forth. "Surprisingly," Sullivan wrote, "all areas expanded simultaneously. That produced delightful problems, even acute ones, and we simply had to expand our physical properties to meet the rapidly growing demands being received from the churches, associations, and state

conventions. This could not be done with the present allowable space."

When his friend Marvin Crowe joined him from Abilene
in 1953, he had to make do with a cordoned-off section of
hallway for an office. Despite the expense of buying property and building new buildings, Sullivan looked around
Nashville for expansion room. All of the existing SSB buildings were filled to the brim, and some needed replacing even
if there weren't a space shortage. Shipping materials out of
the multi-story Shipping Building was an ordeal because pal-
lets of materials had to be handled several times to get them
from upper floors to the shipping docks. The building where
inventory was stored and mail processed had only one loading dock, which meant delivery trucks would wait as long as
three hours to drop their loads. What had been state-of-the-
art operations in the 1920s was inadequate to serve a denomination now twice as large in the age of jet travel and instant
communication.

Sullivan's first serious effort at buying new property was
to approach the Louisville & Nashville and North Carolina &
St. Louis railroads about buying a big warehouse on five acres
that the two lines jointly owned in the blocks behind the
Administration Building. The owners weren't interested at first;
but later when the two railroads merged and faced a cash shortage, they accepted the Board's offer. In the meantime Sullivan
had taken an option on 120 acres on the outskirts of Nashville

where an old plantation, Hundred Oaks, was being sold off for development. When the railroads changed their minds and sold their warehouse, the Board released its option on Hundred Oaks. (A shopping mall eventually occupied the site.)

In 1959 Sullivan helped lay a cornerstone at the old warehouse site for an enormous Operations Building more than five hundred feet long with everything on two floors and plenty of loading docks. A parking deck on the roof solved another nagging problem by providing plenty of convenient free parking for employees and visitors. This building revolutionized the way the Board ran its business and served as the warehousing and shipping hub of the SSB for decades (until the Board outgrew it and built a new distribution center out of town). Delivery, shipping, storage, and inventory management were all vastly improved. The Board also instituted an automated punch-card system, a mechanical predecessor of computerized inventory control, for tracking orders. The first floor handled all church publications, training materials, and supplies, with orders coming in at one end and products going out the other. The second floor held inventory for Baptist Book Stores and processed their orders. The days of hauling orders up and down elevators on electric carts in the old Shipping Building were over at last.

The mail remained a bottleneck. The Board sent and received huge volumes of mail every day, collecting orders and sending out products and invoices. All the mail had to be loaded into bags, weighed, trucked two blocks to the main post office, and unloaded. In 1963 the post office replaced its old sorting system based on one- or two-digit postal zones with an automated five-digit system called the Zone Improvement Plan code, or ZIP code. The Board's labor-intensive methods made it hard for them to take full advantage of this new efficiency.

In the spirit of expanding and modernizing their operation, the Board came up with the ingenious idea of running a conveyer system from the Operations Building to the post office. Nashville's main downtown thoroughfare, Broadway, separated the two buildings and ran at that point on a viaduct that carried the street across a wide ravine. If they could attach a conveyer under the viaduct, they could send bags of mail directly to the post office, saving enormous amounts of time and labor.

The problem was that the city, county, state, and federal government all had some degree of control over the viaduct, and the Board would have to get permission separately from all four. Sullivan asked the Board's attorneys what they should do. They advised that "it would be 20 years before the federal government would find out that he had attached a conveyor system, and would take another 20 years for them to decide what to do about it." The Board built its conveyer without asking anyone's permission. No question was ever raised about it, and the conveyer remained in service until years later when the main post office moved to a new building near the airport.

As soon as building materials had become available after World War II, the Board had also started building the office tower atop the center portion of the Administration Building, which had been designed with this addition in mind. The nine new floors atop the two-story base were occupied as they were completed, so that by the time the Operations Building was finished the new administration offices were filled as well. About the same time, in 1960, the Shipping Building was renovated inside and out, its brick exterior, stone sills, and big multipaned windows sheathed in limestone and windows reduced to a fraction of their original size to better match the Administration Building beside it. The two were joined together and the Shipping Building renamed the North Wing.

Sullivan led the way in buying up the rest of the block these two buildings stood on for further expansion, and to give the Board an unbroken plot of property from Eighth Avenue North, where the original 1913 headquarters (by then named the Frost Building) was, to the Administration Building and North Wing on Ninth, and the Operations Building on Tenth. The Board bought additional property near the old Printing Building on Commerce Street, which ran perpendicular to the others and connected them. Over time the SSB had real estate negotiations with various private residences, including one once used by a former Tennessee governor, a funeral home, a brewery, a gas station, a hamburger stand, and a rumored house of ill repute. To offset the negative publicity of closing down the popular hamburger stand, the Board opened its company cafeteria to the public.

During these expansionary years the Board revisited its long-standing policy of allowing other Convention organizations office space rent-free. In the course of planning for the future, the Board offered to refurbish the Frost Building and give it to the Convention or give the Convention the money to build its own building. The Executive Committee decided to build a new building, and soon the Convention had its own home on James Robertson Parkway near the state capitol, about a dozen blocks from the Frost Building.

The Board eventually renovated the Frost Building for its own use. But for a couple of years beginning in 1963, the Board leased most of it to the local metropolitan government. Nashville was building a new public library on the site of the old one, which was being demolished. The city needed a temporary home for its books and leased the Frost Building to serve as the main downtown library until the new building was finished.

As part of the Southern Baptist denomination, land and buildings owned by the Board are supposedly exempt from taxation as church property. However, legal precedent allows portions of the property used for nonreligious purposes to be taxed. The Board's land purchases in the 1950s attracted the attention of Nashville's tax assessors, who were alarmed at seeing so much property going off the tax rolls.

Dr. Sullivan thought he had avoided a showdown with the local government when he turned down an offer that seemed too good to be true. The city had criticized the railroad for selling its property to the SSB and taking so much valuable land off the tax rolls; in retaliation for selling, the city raised the taxes on the remaining railroad property. Angered by the city's actions, the railroad president called Dr. Sullivan and offered to sell the Board another valuable tract of land, adjacent to what they had recently bought, for a dollar. Doing so would get it off the tax rolls too and give the railroad the last laugh.

Tempting as the offer was, Sullivan hesitated. "The unusualness of the offer made me suspicious," he said. "I anticipated that we could be subjecting ourselves to extreme struggles with the city if we got caught in the fight between City Hall and the L&N Railroad." He feared accepting the deal would put the Board in the tax man's crosshairs. "As it turned out, perhaps it was the worst business decision I made while I was at the Board, but it seemed to be the best one at the time."

Unfortunately city hall came after the Sunday School Board anyway. The Board had always paid property tax on property it rented or leased to other firms, such as the Printing Building. But in 1960 the city claimed the Board's employee parking lot was taxable. The Board paid the assessment under protest and filed a lawsuit to test the legality of the city's action. In 1961 the assessor placed all the Board's property on the tax rolls, claiming the Sunday School Board was not actually a church and therefore was not entitled to an exemption. When the city board of equalization ruled in favor of the SSB, the tax assessor appealed to the state supreme court, which held that the Board's parking area and cafeteria were taxable but the rest of the property was exempt.

Expensive as all this expansion was, Sullivan believed it was essential for the future of the Board and also believed new buildings ought to be pleasant, safe places employees could be proud to work in. The Operations Building cost $4.7 million not counting the land; remodeling the old Shipping Building cost $1.2 million; other remodeling took $1.6 million, including more than $300,000 for renovating the Frost Building. The Board bought land on the edge of town for a new printing operation. Every building and renovation project was debt-free by the time it was finished, and every piece of property appreciated over the years to many times its original cost. Sullivan had building in his blood—his father was a contractor—and he no doubt felt confident as he initiated all this new construction and shared a sense of genuine accomplishment as the work was finished.

The Board also invested in expanding Baptist Book Stores. Originally stores had been sited at state convention offices. As shoppers began migrating away from downtown toward suburban malls, downtown stores lost business. New stores were built in response to the changed shopping habits. Like every other change, relocating the stores pleased some customers but irritated or offended others.

Another area where Sullivan oversaw tremendous expansion was at the two retreat centers, Ridgecrest, North Carolina, and Glorieta, New Mexico. The original buildings at Ridgecrest were dated and inadequate for the thirty thousand people who used them every summer. At Ridgecrest, Spilman Auditorium and other old structures were replaced and more dormitories built. At Glorieta, which was a collection of tents and prefab buildings when Sullivan took up his post, an extensive building program starting with roads and water mains had added Holcomb Auditorium with its distinctive multisided steeple, dining hall space, meeting areas, and dormitories. Where many Baptists assumed that Glorieta, isolated and undeveloped as it was, would develop slowly over time, the Board broke ground there for seven new buildings simultaneously.

James Sullivan took control of the Sunday School Board when he was only forty-three and managed it through more than twenty years of incredible change. He was a strong and capable man who could have gone on years longer but perhaps wearied at last of the endless challenges to his leadership by people who seemed to have no idea what they were talking about. He wrote of the "speed with which certain organizations" passed "resolutions of condemnation" without ever bothering to check the facts. He no doubt often recalled the comparison a professor at Hardin-Simmons made that leading was like building a house with warped boards. When you nailed down one end, the other snapped up; but when you secured that end, then the other one popped out of place. And often you'd go to bed with both ends flapping at once.

It was an unprecedented situation, but one his successors would know well, for the executive secretary of the Board to be personally attacked by enemies who disagreed with his leadership or views. He had already moved his family out of town and gotten an unlisted phone number, but even on SSB turf he wasn't safe. His assigned parking space was a highly prized one under a tree. When he reprimanded a temporary employee for parking there repeatedly, the employee cut the tree down.

Vowing not to repeat the history of earlier leaders and stay beyond his time, Sullivan decided to retire at a youthful sixty-five, still healthy, vigorous, and full of ideas. His legacy was a modern, vibrant, solvent organization that was fully up with the times. He had reorganized the Board again in 1971 to make further improvements and refinements. He started a full-fledged public relations department, a first for the Board. In addition to an annual output of more than 100 million periodicals, he oversaw Broadman books, written for a wider religious audience, and those from a new imprint, Convention Press, written specifically for Southern Baptist audiences.

Looking forward near the end of his tenure, Sullivan reflected on the challenges he saw ahead for Southern Baptists:

As we face the future, it is my hope that we can manifest more maturity now that our Convention is coming of age in years and size. Some things that have "rocked the boat" in the past should not be experienced by my successor in office.

One of the more difficult things to face is extremism. There is a certain degree of tolerance beyond which an institution cannot go. The moment an administrative officer begins to level off the swing of an institution and say that we can go no further in a certain direction, he brings upon himself the hostilities of passionate extremists who feel that they are in the middle of the road and everybody else is an extremist. Actually these critics are so often on the fringe of the whole denominational structure and are unaware of it.

Fundamentalism with a capital *F* has always been a problem in Southern Baptist life even though most all of us are fundamentalists with a little *f*. We are justifiably proud of that position. Actually there are few "modernists" in Southern Baptist life. If anyone seems so inclined, he usually eliminates himself before he becomes a problem to the denomination. . . . Fear of modernism in the Southern Baptist Convention is a false fear. Usually such is drummed

up by certain people who are trying to foster an
extremism at the other end of the line. . . .

It is not the theological position of
Fundamentalism which is hurtful. It is the pharisa-
ical spirit. Legalism is as deadly as modernism and
should be resisted to the same degree. Many times
those holding extremely Fundamentalistic positions
have emotional problems of their own. Sometimes
they are spiritual problems of a deep nature. In fleeing modernism we cannot run into the fold of crass
Fundamentalism. In fleeing Fundamentalism we
cannot run into modernism. We must take a solid
middle, conservative stance. There we will stand
fast because there our people are. We must do this
unapologetically.

These are the words of a man admirably unshaken in
his beliefs after twenty-one years of tumultuous leadership.
He was also unshaken in his resolve to make sure the man
who replaced him was better trained and equipped than he
had been. Though I admired Dr. Sullivan's accomplishments
and respect his views, I believe there is a time when taking a
"middle" stance is no longer enough. We can argue as brother
and sister in Christ about what the Bible means, but there is
no room at the Southern Baptist table for people who question the Bible as a Christian's ultimate authority. Dr. Sullivan

wrote that "fear of modernism" was "a false fear." The history of the Board since then has proven otherwise. We can love other people even when we disagree with them. But we can never accept any question or dilution of the fact that Christianity is built on the solid rock of Scripture and nothing else.

CHAPTER 21

"What We Ought to Do"

James Sullivan gave his board of trustees better than a year's notice that he wanted to retire. He had led the Sunday School Board through a period of remarkable growth. During 1953 the Board took in about $12.5 million from all sources, including book and music publishing, church publications and supplies, audiovisual products, and bookstore operations. His last year in office the total was $60 million. He spearheaded a massive building program in Nashville, at the two conference centers, and among the Baptist Book Stores. By his own estimate he built or replaced fifty buildings in total, all of them debt-free by the time they were finished.

Besides the buildings, another great source of satisfaction for Sullivan at his retirement came from keeping Southern Baptists praying and working together despite the increased polarization over theological issues such as the definition of inerrancy and cultural issues such as abortion. The great social upheavals of the 1960s and 1970s highlighted and intensified these differences. Sullivan considered himself a traditional conservative who did all he could to build consensus and maintain a sense of harmony among all views.

His chief disappointment, and one his successor would have to face, was that Southern Baptists had almost stopped growing in numbers. One reason, some thought, was competition from television on Wednesday and Sunday nights. In 1950 television was a rare and expensive curiosity. Nashville got its first TV station in 1953, the year Sullivan came to town. By 1960 it was commonplace, and by 1970 it was an institution. In the mid-1960s, Training Union enrollment took a serious tumble, which was blamed in part on people staying home Sunday nights to watch *The Wonderful World of Disney* and *The Ed Sullivan Show.* Also through the 1950s and 1960s families began owning two cars, and more mothers started working outside the home. This meant less time for "extra" activities like church programs other than Sunday morning.

Even more important was the widespread antiestablishment feeling of the times that marginalized institutions in general and churches in particular. Socially conservative as they were, Southern Baptist traditions and standards seemed old-fashioned, straight-laced, and irrelevant to members of a skeptical and morally drifting generation. The civil rights movement followed by protests against the Vietnam War fed the flames of discontent. Then came the Watergate scandal.

While Sunday School Board trustees were deciding whom to nominate as their next executive secretary, the US Senate was considering impeachment proceedings against President Richard Nixon for lying about what he knew of a break-in at Democratic National Committee headquarters in Washington's Watergate Hotel. A clandestine team with ties to the White House was caught by a security guard planting listening bugs in DNC telephones. On August 9, three months after the new SSB executive secretary reported for work, Nixon became the only president in American history to resign his office. Morally and spiritually it was an unsettling time.

Early in Sullivan's tenure, the Million More in '54 campaign had registered 600,000 new Southern Baptists. Beginning in 1959, the Baptist Jubilee Advance made strides toward establishing 30,000 new missions and preaching stations by 1964. The Board's Training Union, Church Music, and Church Architecture departments all geared up to assist in the effort and even added a new administrative position, superintendent of new work, and a new vocational guidance service. But between 1965 and the end of the Sullivan era,

Southern Baptist church membership inched up only slightly, struggling against a culture that was suspicious and confused and uncertain about what it stood for.

With these events and movements as background, in February 1974 the SSB trustees chose Grady Coulter Cothen to succeed Sullivan effective February 1975. Arriving at the Board in May, Cothen had almost nine months, the longest in Board history up to that time, to learn from Sullivan on the job. It was the training experience Sullivan himself had wanted but never got, and his wise decision to mentor his replacement was something I copied years later. Cothen was also the first leader of the board to start out with the title of "president." The old and by now rather quaint "executive secretary-treasurer" had come to confuse outsiders. Some of Sullivan's correspondents, seeing his title on a letter, thought he was an office administrator; the change to president was made in 1972. Cothen set another precedent by taking a battery of psychological tests to assess his aptitude for the job. Sullivan had had all his senior staff take a similar exam.

Grady Cothen was born in Poplarville, Mississippi, about seventy-five miles from New Orleans, in 1920. His father was a Baptist preacher, and Grady and his three brothers (two older, one younger) all followed him into the ministry. The family moved to Chattanooga for a few years during the Depression, then back south to Hattiesburg, Mississippi, only a county away from his hometown. After he graduated from high school in Hattiesburg, Grady entered Mississippi College in 1938, ten years after James Sullivan had started there. Like his predecessor, young Cothen paid some of his expenses with part-time office work. Cothen landed a job typing and taking shorthand in the college church office. Where Sullivan had been a star football player, Cothen became a leader of the debate team, which was coached by his favorite professor. Cothen later called debate the most important subject he ever took in college.

Two months before Pearl Harbor, in September 1941, Cothen enrolled in New Orleans Baptist Theological Seminary, then called the Baptist Bible Institute. Following his graduation in 1944 with a master's degree in Christian training, he left his wife, Bettye, behind to join the navy. He went to chaplain school in Virginia, then served two years as a chaplain in California and in the Pacific Theater. He believed the experience strengthened his faith:

> I discovered all over again that a theology that does not tie to reality, and a theology that does not deal with evil, and a theology that does not deal with redemption, is no theology at all. So I came out of the war experience more firmly convinced in my conservative biblical theology than I had ever been. It had been tried in the crucible and it was adequate, and that's a glorious experience.

After the war Cothen pastored churches in Chattanooga, Oklahoma City (where he served eleven years at Olivet Baptist), and at First Baptist, Birmingham, Alabama. He moved west in 1961 to become executive secretary of the Southern Baptist Convention of California. Five years later, even though he didn't have an earned doctorate, he was tapped for the presidency of Oklahoma Baptist University (OBU) in Shawnee. His proven administrative ability and take-charge attitude evidently balanced out any reservation the OBU search committee may have had about his academic credentials. From there he moved on a few years later to accept the presidency of his alma mater in New Orleans.

Grady Cothen was not as well-known in the SBC as other prospects the Board trustees might have chosen. But the search committee was impressed by his administrative skills, which Sullivan held in high regard, and by his work leading a state convention, a college and a seminary successfully through such contentious times. Here was a man who could pick up where Sullivan had left off, a leader with modern management ability and a knack for bringing opposing sides to an agreeable compromise.

Though both the seven-member search committee and the full board of trustees voted unanimously to recommend Cothen, it looked for a while as if he would be the first nominee to head the SSB whose election might be contested. Up to this time, every Board leader who was also a seminary graduate had a degree from Southern Baptist Theological Seminary in Louisville. In an interview with church historian Leon McBeth years later, Cothen confided: "I got a telephone call from a friend of mine who said, 'The graduates of [Southern Seminary] have agreed among themselves that this is too big a plum for a New Orleans Seminary graduate to get, and a group of them from Florida are going to nominate another candidate from the floor after you are nominated.'"

He told his informer that "if they wish to nominate from the floor, tell them to have at it." But there was no challenge to his nomination and he never heard any more about it.

One of the first steps Cothen took when he arrived in Nashville, and one of his chief tasks during his preparation period in 1974, was to go on listening tours, learning what state conventions, seminaries, and other Southern Baptist entities wanted and needed from the Sunday School Board and how the Board could serve them better. In six months he made fifty-five trips, pencil and pad in hand, saying: "Tell me what we're doing we ought not to do. Tell me what we ought to be doing that we aren't doing, and tell me what you'd change if you could change it. And if that doesn't cover what you want to say, what do you want to say?"

Years of growth and change had strained some of the ties between the Board and these varied groups, as had the Elliott controversy and the *Broadman Commentary* debate. There was probably some sensitivity to the fact that even as church and Sunday school enrollment leveled off in the 1960s and 1970s, the Board's income and surpluses kept growing. The Board gave away huge amounts of money to all sorts of

Southern Baptist groups, including some informal gifts that were not part of the official record.

After he took office, Cothen announced four priorities that would guide him as president. Because he wrote and spoke about them so often in the years that followed, it's worth a moment to look at them.

First was what he called "in-depth Bible study for the masses." Fully committed to maintaining the highest standards in quarterlies and study materials, he wanted to reach beyond them to attract the millions of Americans who didn't go to church and didn't study the Bible. He believed that the simple message of the gospel would convert large numbers of these people. He often repeated his conviction that Southern Baptists were "a people of the Book" and that their duty was not to argue over it but "to expound it, to expose it, to exegete it, to teach it, to preach it, to proclaim it."

Cothen's second emphasis was "equipping the saints," revitalizing the task of discipling converts. With the total membership of Southern Baptists stagnant and Training Union participation sinking, Cothen feared the churches were neglecting discipleship training, stunting their spiritual growth. He wanted to find new ways to attract new church members and help them mature in their Christian development.

The third goal was "supporting and enriching family life" in the midst of all the societal changes that distracted and threatened traditional family values. He resolved to "challenge and support our churches in bold efforts to halt the hurt and destruction taking place and to establish families on a Christian foundation that can weather storms." (One readily visible result of this goal was the series of new publications the Board published, including *Living with Children*, *Living with Teenagers*, *Christian Single*, and *Mature Living*. These joined the long-popular *HomeLife*.)

Fourth was a commitment to help and encourage pastors and church staff. As head of the California state convention and on his listening tours, he frequently heard stories of pastors laboring under the dual strains of denominational tension and drastic cultural change. Job burnout and forced terminations were escalating problems. In California, Cothen had initiated an annual pastors' conference to train, motivate, and encourage this dedicated but besieged group. Ministers, he insisted, "need sources of training, equipping, and encouragement for the task. The Sunday School Board must shoulder its portion of the task in providing this aid and encouragement."

For all his good intentions, Cothen found ready opposition from Baptists who thought he wasn't doing enough and others who thought he was sticking the Board's nose into places where it didn't belong. There were also some rumblings from within the SSB about how Cothen developed and announced these goals, which would in theory be at the core of everything the Board did for years to come. In the past a president would have come up with such a list after plenty of discussion and consultation with various Board executives and groups. That wasn't Grady Cothen's style. To him the old way of doing things was too slow. In some quarters he had a reputation as a "shoot from the hip" manager, a reputation that grew steadily during his years at the Board.

He explained, "I decided rather than go through all that kind of process at the Sunday School Board, creating committees and doing another five years of study, that I would simply out of my own experience set forth some priorities. I figured I knew what those priorities ought to be."

Like Dr. Sullivan, Cothen set about reorganizing the Board soon after taking office; and like Sullivan, he hired a strong second-in-command to handle day-to-day operations. Where Sullivan had made tremendous strides in wringing out the vestiges of horse and buggy days from the Board's business practices, Cothen saw the need for another big leap. "We had to modernize the organization," he said. "There simply had to be some rather dramatic changes made to keep up with the main stream of financial life, for example. The institution had never had a chief financial officer before I came."

Cothen moved William O. Thomason, a longtime Board employee whom Sullivan had been grooming for an executive spot, into the position of executive vice president, then appointed a series of vice presidents who reported to Thomason. He also made DeVaughn Woods vice president of financial affairs, with specific responsibility for managing the Board's large holdings of ready cash. (This fund was about

$8 million when DeVaughn took over and grew to $31 million by the time Cothen left the Board.)

Health problems forced Cothen to take medical retirement after only nine years on the job. But it was an action-packed and historic season in Southern Baptist life. Working toward his four priorities, he led the Board in developing several major new products, at least two of which were resounding successes and one that wasn't. He was also at the helm when all the ideological tension that had been simmering in the Southern Baptist Convention for fifteen years since the Elliott controversy finally boiled over. And that was when the direction of the Convention and the Sunday School Board were, depending on your point of view, reclaimed by traditional conservatives or hijacked by devious fundamentalists.

CHAPTER 22

Bibles and Broadcasting

One enduring result of the listening sessions Grady Cothen set up early in his time at the Board was a third line of Sunday School study materials to go along with the Convention Uniform Series and the newer Life and Work curriculum. What he heard in Southern Baptist churches across the country confirmed his own belief that the two existing study programs took too much of a "hop, skip, and jump" approach, considering the Bible in little fragments according to the lesson topic. Cothen wanted to see a lesson series that covered the Bible in depth.

The January Bible Study had proven extremely popular since it started in 1948 thanks to its systematic study of one entire book of Scripture. That success made Cothen confident that a Bible book-focused Sunday school series would be welcomed. According to Cothen, it was Robert Naylor, president of Southwestern Seminary, who first specifically suggested "a curriculum that would allow a person to study through the Bible and complete the study sometime before Jesus returns."

Cothen believed a new series would satisfy criticism from Baptist congregations that existing lessons were too helterskelter and lacked continuity. Some at the Board also thought a new series would satisfy churches that criticized some of the existing material as too ecumenical. There were also churches that disliked straying in any way from the King James translation.

The Convention Uniform Series had been published since 1872, nineteen years before the Sunday School Board existed. It started with a group of Sunday school leaders from various denominations working jointly on a lesson series, and the Board began using these lessons as soon as it was operational in 1891. As the Board grew and prospered over the years, it came to dominate the process. While all denominations studied the same Scripture passages and topics at the same time (this being a "uniform" series), each denomination selected its own writers for its lessons. So while the lack of continuity was a fair criticism, the charge of ecumenicalism was not.

The Life and Work series had come along in 1966 and ten years later was outselling the Uniform Series; by the time Cothen took office, more than half of Southern Baptist churches were using the more topical, more contemporary, application-based lessons. In considering a new Sunday school series, Cothen planned originally to discontinue one of the others. But as Dr. Sullivan had discovered when he suggested replacing an old series with a new one, existing lesson series had plenty of supporters. Some churches had used the Uniform Series for generations and wanted to continue the tradition indefinitely. Even more churches liked the Life and Work lessons.

Walking in his predecessor's footsteps, Cothen revisited the question of adding a new series and keeping both existing ones, for a total of three. Again there was the problem of cost and resource allocation. Adding a third option wouldn't increase the size of the market, but it would increase the Board's production cost and require more workers and more space. It would add to the confusion for church Sunday school planners who had to consider three independent programs of study rather than two. Some thought one set was better for youth and another for adults; others ordered two different kinds, or all three, because some teachers liked this one and some liked that one.

As had happened with Cothen's points of interest, there were rumblings in the ranks that the president hadn't consulted enough on the idea of a third lesson series with those who would have to make it happen. Historian Leon McBeth reported, "A. V. Washburn, then head of the Sunday School

Department, supported this move only after a period of resistance. . . . Some felt the Board tried to bring out the Bible Book Series without enough preparation and planning."

Over time the Bible Book Series took about one-fourth of the market, the Uniform Series roughly the same, and Life and Work remained the choice of about half of the Board's customers.

One of Grady Cothen's greatest achievements as president of the Board was spearheading the purchase of the Holman Bible Publishing Company in 1979. In the long term Holman has been a tremendous evangelism tool and an important financial component of the SSB. This step also started with one of Cothen's listening sessions. McBeth tells the story of the new president's first meeting with his administrative staff in 1975. One way Cothen got the group to think long-term was to go around the circle and ask each person what he would do if he could spend a million dollars on his work. James W. Clark, then head of the large Broadman publishing operation, said he would buy or develop a Bible publishing company.

To Cothen and others, this suggestion may have come like a bolt out of the blue. What could be more natural and logical and true to its mission than for the Board to publish Bibles? Of course they should! But what seemed perhaps like an obvious answer was actually not so clear-cut. Printing plates belonged to established companies unlikely to lend or lease them to new competitors. Most Bible translations were copyrighted, which meant negotiating usage fees and paying royalties. Building a Bible publishing operation from scratch was possible, but it was an expensive process that would take years to complete, then years more to pay back the investment.

In 1978 James Clark was promoted to executive vice president, Cothen's second-in-command, succeeding William Thomason who resigned on account of personal problems that had made it unfeasible for him to continue at the Board. That same year Clark learned that the A. J. Holman Company of Philadelphia, the oldest Bible publisher in America, was for sale. The New York publisher Harper & Row was acquiring the venerable J. B. Lippincott & Co., of which Holman was a subsidiary. But because Harper & Row already published Bibles under its own imprint, they felt Holman was too much duplication of existing lines and wanted to spin it off as part of the Lippincott transaction.

Holman was founded in Germantown, near Philadelphia, by an immigrant German preacher named Christopher Sauer (also written as Saur), who settled there in 1724. Trained as a tailor in Europe, Sauer learned the printing trade in his adopted country; his devotion to Scripture inspired him to publish a Bible. He finished his first edition of one thousand copies, in the German translation by Martin Luther, in 1743 and sold them for eighteen shillings a copy. By then Philadelphia was becoming a center of printing in the New World. During the same period Benjamin Franklin was making a name for himself in the city and beyond with his popular book *Poor Richard's Almanac.* Sauer's son Christopher, who anglicized the family name to Sower, produced a second edition in 1763. He stored the third edition of three thousand, printed in 1776, as loose pages, planning to bind them as orders came in. Unfortunately, only fifteen copies were bound before the Revolutionary War began, and the rest of the pages were used for gun wadding.

In 1801, Christopher Sower and his son Samuel moved the business to Philadelphia only a few blocks from Independence Hall. There they printed their first Bible in English. Andrew Jackson Holman joined the company as plant superintendent in 1839. Over time he acquired a controlling interest from the Sower family and, in 1869, renamed the business the A. J. Holman Company. From their prominent Arch Street headquarters, Holman produced and distributed a comprehensive selection of Bibles in every price range, as well as other large-format specialty products such as photo albums. Holman descendents owned the company for nearly a century, making the transition from steam power to electric presses, binding machines and other modern equipment. But as the pace of change and innovation accelerated and offset printing began to replace traditional metal type letterpresses, the family realized they would not have the capital to stay competitive. In 1961 they sold the company to Lippincott.

Holman was a well-respected and well-known business, and several companies were interested in bidding for it. Cothen and vice president for finance DeVaughn Woods were authorized by the SSB trustees to negotiate the purchase, which would include all licensing rights, printing plates, and stock on hand. The Board's advantage was that Harper wanted a quick sale for cash, and none of the other bidders could make an all-cash offer. Cothen later recalled, "We went to New York by appointment one day and signed a check for $2.3 million and we bought Holman." (After a stock inventory, the Board received about a $100,000 refund.)

Between the day the purchase was finalized, April 30, 1979, and the end of Cothan's presidency, Holman published both New American Standard and King James translations of the *Master Study Bible*, the *New American Standard Exhaustive Concordance*, and other new products. Where Lippincott had seen Holman only as a business, the Board saw it also as a ministry, working to improve existing lines, develop new ones, and market them effectively with missionary zeal. Yet this commitment to ministry produced handsome financial results: by 1984 Holman had earned back its entire purchase price.

Holman Bible Publishers has been a tremendous benefit to the Board and the Convention down through the years. Another project that was also important historically but less successful over the long haul was the Board's lengthy and expensive foray into running a television network. It seemed like a good idea at the time, but various problems kept it from being what its proponents insisted it could have been.

As a pastor in Oklahoma in the 1950s, Cothen had written, produced, and appeared in a local Tuesday night television show preaching to the general public. As president of the SSB, he saw what an impact the Arab oil embargo had on attendance at the Ridgecrest and Glorieta conference centers. The jump in gas prices convinced many people to stay home. And even in years when the conferences were packed, the Board could still only teach and exhort so many thousands of people a year. Based in part on his Oklahoma experience, Cothen believed television could be the way to reach more people.

In 1978 the Board, working with the Convention's Radio and Television Commission, launched a thirty-minute program called *At Home with the Bible*, hosted by Frank Pollard, pastor of First Baptist Church, Jackson, Mississippi. Each program included a Bible lesson, interviews with guests who had experience or insights relevant to the topic, and music from the husband and wife team of Bill and Jeanine Walker. Viewers could request any of four free study guides to follow along, depending on their depth of interest: learner, apprentice, intermediate, or senior. The idea was to bring Bible study into the homes of people who didn't or couldn't come to church. It was a way of meeting Cothen's goal of bringing Bible study to the masses.

The Board produced ninety-eight programs before the project was shelved. Some Southern Baptists thought television production belonged under the Radio and Television Commission exclusively or under the Home Missions Board and that this effort was more evidence of the SSB throwing its weight around. Viewers and critics gave the show generally good marks for quality, but surveys showed that people who watched it already went to church. In Leon McBeth's words, "So the programs were not really bringing Bible study to the masses as all, but bringing very expensive programs to people who already attended church."

The Board's next TV project was far more ambitious. Eager to branch out into the world of modern communications, Cothen had a strong desire to integrate television somehow into the ministry and outreach of the Sunday School Board. Historically, the Board developed products and services in response to demonstrated needs or requests from churches or Convention leadership. In this case there was no demand for action, no groundswell of support. In what some would consider the prime example of a shoot-from-the-hip management style, Cothen formed the idea of a Sunday School Board television network and set about bringing it to life.

Cothen envisioned the Baptist Telecommunication Network not as a competitor to the Radio and Television Commission's American Christian Television System. ACTS was aimed at a general audience and broadcast what one assessment called "entertainment" with the purpose of evangelism. BTN was aimed at Southern Baptist congregations and would broadcast Bible study, teacher training, and Sunday school lesson preparation: it would bring Ridgecrest and Glorieta sessions to the masses at home.

BTN was a private satellite broadcast service. The Board bought the necessary hardware, leased time on a satellite, and offered receivers to churches and interested individuals for a fee. Once the system was set up, Southern Baptist groups of every sort could use it to communicate across the denomination, set up teleconferences, and conduct classes. It was not, however, an electronic church. It was for internal "wholesale" church training and discussion, not for preaching to an audience. It was never intended to appeal to home subscribers but to churches.

From the beginning the network met stiff resistance. No church had ever done anything like it before, so there was no precedent to study. Before approving the idea, the Board trustees hired Edutel, a California consulting firm, to assess as best they could the costs and benefits to Southern Baptists. After months of study they advised against it. Nevertheless the Board approved BTN at Cothen's insistence in 1980, with the goal of having the network up and running by the 1984 Southern Baptist Convention in Kansas City.

As the project unfolded, the Board began to realize they didn't have nearly enough programming to support a network and no way to produce it. Churches balked at the cost of installing the receiving equipment, which originally was $15,000 per church though the cost soon plummeted to $3,000. (Even when the price fell to $1,500, the Board signed up only a small fraction of Southern Baptist churches, some of which cancelled their contract or stopped paying usage fees but kept getting the programs anyway. The Board had no way to monitor who was using the network without paying for it.)

Told by his own staff that the June 1984 deadline was impossible, Cothen forged on all the more resolutely. In a 1983 interview he remained confident that the future potential of BTN was worth the short-term trauma:

> I see, for example, a regular weekly program on each of the Sunday School lesson series in which an expert teacher, biblical scholar, will lead teachers all over America for twenty minutes at whatever time they can get to it during the week in preparation for next Sunday's lesson. . . . I see an expert in Nashville working with a small choir as he helps those unpaid church music workers all over America in getting their music ready for Sunday. . . . I see it as a means of conducting a national pastors' conference that will help pastors come to understand what's going on in the denomination. . . . I see it as a means of steward-ship education. I can see the Baptist Joint Committee on Public Affairs dealing with church-state issues in a public way that will get direct information to pas-tors and churches. . . . We haven't begun to explore yet what it can do. A child could get excited about that.

BTN made its debut broadcasting some of the sessions from the 1984 Convention in Kansas City to considerable fanfare in the denomination, but it couldn't seem to catch hold. Despite a publicity blitz few churches signed up to receive the satellite transmissions, and many had never heard of them. Learning of BTN, Southern Baptists tended to confuse it with ACTS or Radio and Television Commission programming.

It didn't take long to reveal that a teaching seminar on television would never duplicate the experience of going to one of the conference centers, where the fellowship, informal after-hours meetings, and fresh air were all part of the process. In spite of the stated focus on training and teaching, churches complained that BTN programs were boring. T. L. Holcomb had dreamed of reaching "the last church" with resources of the Board. But now that the means were at hand, the message was, depending on your viewpoint, misunderstood, inadequate, or ignored.

Of course along with these big projects, Grady Cothen oversaw scores of smaller ones. One highlight (though for the most part complete before his arrival) was a new edition of the *Baptist Hymnal*, published in 1975, which produced a wave of sales in the millions. Some churches had been upset that the original 1956 edition had deleted so many old favorites from the classic *Broadman Hymnal*. The new edition, edited by William J. Reynolds, head of the Church Music Department, restored some of them and added other material. It was introduced with a four-day celebration called PraiSing featuring George Beverly Shea, the Nashville Symphony, the

Fisk Jubilee Singers, and ten thousand attendees. Over thirty hours, fifty choral groups working in shifts sang every verse of every hymn from cover to cover.

Cothen also made a change affecting Broadman in the way Baptist Book Stores stocked their shelves. He was disturbed to walk into stores while he was traveling and see that they had few or no Broadman books on display. Solving the problem in his customary no-nonsense way, he issued a directive that Baptist Book Stores would carry and display Broadman stock. During Cothen's years as president, Baptist Book Store sales nearly doubled from $28.7 million to $52.5 million.

It was also Cothen's idea to initiate a program for children of people who came to training at the conference centers. As attendance grew, the number of children and teenagers who had traveled with their parents and had nothing to do during the sessions became a real challenge. Cothen wanted to put the kids in old overflow dormitory-style housing the adults didn't like anyway and give them a program of their own. The Church Recreation Department of the Board agreed to take it on. They came up with Centrifuge, a combination of group play, Bible study, mission outreach, and discipleship that was enormously popular from the first and became a major evangelistic event in its own right.

Cothen's fertile mind produced a number of other good programs. To help the board keep in touch with the six Southern Baptist seminaries, this former seminary president offered to fund a "liaison professor" at each seminary, who would be chosen and his duties defined by the individual school. Each in this group of six would have the responsibility of keeping the lines of communication open and clear between the Board and his institution. To support pastors overseas, Cothen implemented a "mini-library project," assembling a collection of a dozen or so books for Baptist pastors in distant places. Working with Baptist World Alliance, the Board provided $200,000 to send more than sixty-six thousand books to seventy-three countries.

His management style made Grady Cothen a demanding taskmaster. While this produced results, it also produced some choppy seas regarding employee relations. McBeth said only that Cothen "faced more than his share of serious personnel problems during his decade (sic) at the helm of the Board. Some of these problems involved high ranking officials, leading to widely publicized terminations." In *The Southern Baptist Convention*, Jesse C. Fletcher writes that Cothen's position in the SBC "was increasingly undermined by personnel problems." One story that comes to light involved a handpicked executive vice president who left in 1978 amidst a swirl of accusations that he was having an affair. Another employee was so incensed at the matter that he eventually sued the SSB.

Beginning in 1980, Cothen developed ulcers, and his condition deteriorated over the next few years. The trustees gave Executive Vice President James Clark more and more to do. As his condition worsened, Cothen moved his office to the eleventh floor for more quiet and privacy. His hospital stays grew longer, and Clark took charge for extended periods. In 1982 Cothen requested medical retirement, and the trustees began looking for his replacement.

Certainly his operational style and the personnel crises he had to manage contributed to his ill health. But there was much more going on outside of Nashville during these years that would probably have given anybody ulcers. The Southern Baptist Convention was in danger of falling apart, and Grady Cothen was right in the middle of it.

And so was I.

CHAPTER 23

What Happened in Houston

The same year Grady Cothen left New Orleans for Nashville to take charge of the Sunday School Board, another Southern Baptist raised in the south, trained as preacher and the son of a preacher, also moved from one city to another to start a new job. The difference was that while Cothen went from one important and high profile position in the SBC to another—from seminary president to president of the SSB— I went from one of the largest, highest profile churches in the Convention to one that most people had never heard of. The first time I visited there I had to stop at a 7-Eleven and ask directions. It was during the Cothen years that your narrator in this story first turned up as part of the story himself.

In 1975 I ended a whirlwind twenty-six-month period as assistant pastor to W. A. Criswell at First Baptist Church in Dallas. Dr. Criswell had led the congregation there for more than thirty years, building it into a megachurch; some called it the biggest and most influential church in the SBC. Its buildings covered three city blocks downtown; its members included some of the wealthiest and most influential businessmen in the nation; its ministry reached out to tens of thousands of people weekly through church services, broadcasts, and a long list of outreach efforts.

I've known I would be a preacher like my father and grandfather since I was fourteen, and at seventeen I preached my first revival in Houston with my friends Chuck Swindoll and Charles Dan Oglesby. I graduated from Baylor and Southwestern Seminary and served some wonderful churches in Texas and Missouri before being called to the pulpit in Del City, Oklahoma, in 1970. The pastor there, John Bisagno, had accepted a call to First Baptist Church in Houston, and I was honored to follow him at Del City. The three years and seven months I spent at Del City were some of the most challenging, satisfying, and rewarding of my life. My wife, Carol Ann, and our three children, Randy, Bailey, and Terri, loved the community and the church, and the people loved us in return.

In 1973 I preached for a young adult retreat at First Baptist Dallas. It was a time when Dr. Criswell and others had started thinking about who would come after him in the pulpit once he retired. For whatever reason, my preaching that weekend caught Dr. Criswell's eye. One thing led to another; and before I knew it, I had an invitation to come to First Baptist Dallas as Criswell's associate. The perception was that I was Criswell's choice to succeed him upon his retirement.

In my wildest dreams I never thought anything could pry my family and me away from Del City; but after lots of thought, prayer, and discussion, we decided God had called us to make the move. However, as I told my brother before I left Oklahoma, I believed even then that I would never take Criswell's place in Dallas. I was going there in service to God to help Dr. Criswell as the associate pastor but felt somehow that, despite what everybody else was saying, I would not ultimately lead that magnificent church.

In the end I was right. My family and I were blessed many ways during our years in Dallas. Along with serving at First Baptist, I had the honor of being appointed to the SBC Annunity Board and the Baylor board of trustees. But Dr. Criswell's approaching retirement raised a host of conflicts that led me to resign my position as his associate.

I was glad when I went to Dallas. And I was glad when I left.

From there I was called to pastor the First Baptist Church in Euless, Texas. After the pressure-cooker atmosphere and all the challenges of Dallas, the new pulpit felt like an oasis of calm. From a church with a weekly attendance of six thousand, I transitioned to a congregation with an attendance of nine hundred and settled in to work.

In the years following the *Broadman Commentary* controversy, I watched as Southern Baptists began choosing up sides in ever greater numbers. Dr. Criswell, who was president of the SBC when the commentary conflict developed, spoke for many in the denomination when he said that liberals were "termites who would destroy the church." This and other similar comments he made were published and repeated many times over. But people who disagreed with him bristled at the suggestion that unless they embraced an exact, specific set of beliefs they weren't good Southern Baptists.

Grady Cothen identified himself as a conservative, traditional Southern Baptist. But he believed the changes beginning to take place in the SBC were stirred up by an "inerrantist faction" that threatened the Baptist traditions against creedalism and any sort of priestly hierarchy. Not only did he believe that inerrantists were taking over the Convention, but he also felt certain that the conservative wave breaking on the shores of the SBC in 1979 derailed one of the most promising Sunday School Board programs of recent times. Between 1960 and 1980, Southern Baptist church enrollment had increased less than 2 percent per year. A bold new interagency push was poised to recapture the growth rates of decades past; but according to some views, including Cothen's, it was robbed of its potential by the attention and energy that was diverted into the theology controversy.

But another way to look at it was that if we couldn't get our spiritual house in order first, we would never be able to convince a new generation of people to join us.

All the various threads of this chapter in SSB history—my involvement (I had the honor of being elected chairman of the SBC Pastors' Conference that year), the conservative/moderate controversy, the new SSB outreach effort, and the presidency of Grady Cothen—came together at the 1979 Southern Baptist Convention in Houston. Some historians later described it as a showdown. Whatever it was, it was precipitated by a Texas layman who had done his homework carefully and wasn't afraid to ask hard questions.

Paul Pressler was an appeals court judge in Houston who was concerned about what he saw as a liberal drift in the Southern Baptist Convention and decided to do something about it. His family had been lawyers, Texans, and Southern Baptists for generations. He was a member of Second Baptist Church in Houston when the Elliott controversy unfolded and was alarmed to learn that his pastor, James Riley, supported Elliott and spoke on his behalf. In 1963 Pressler convinced the deacons to form a committee to study the Elliott matter, and after a year and a half each member of the committee wrote his own report. Pressler's was fifty pages long, and it fired the opening conservative volley:

> Something is tragically wrong in the Southern Baptist Convention. We must recognize this fact and face up to it. As Billy Graham stated at the Texas Baptist World Evangelical Conference in Dallas a short time ago, "Southern Baptist statistics are declining. I am convinced the two greatest causes of the decline are lack of men and women filled with the Holy Spirit and lack of faith in the Bible as the infallible Word of God."
>
> The doubt cast upon the authority of Scripture by professors in our seminaries is a cancer which is eating out the life of our denomination. It is not known whether it is too late to adequately eradicate this infection which has spread in such a way that it is detrimentally affecting the whole of our Convention. Positive action must be taken in the immediate future if we are to save our Convention from becoming a useless and lifeless group which, although having the form of religion, does not have the power that God seeks to give through His Holy Spirit. . . .
>
> Very little time remains in which effective action can be taken. Elliott's supporters hope to train a new generation of preachers who are in agreement with their theological position. They

are content to let the opposition pass all the resolutions they wish as long as nothing is done to disturb their positions in seminaries. We cannot fail in our responsibility to act.

Pressler discovered the key to acting on that responsibility ten years later during a drive from Lenoir City, Tennessee, to Atlanta with William Powell, former member of the SBC Home Mission Board and head of a new ministry called the Baptist Faith and Message Fellowship. While they were driving, Powell explained what he had learned about how the SBC was structured. The Convention president is elected by the messengers and then appoints a committee on committees in conference with the vice presidents. The term "in conference" isn't defined in Convention bylaws. The committee on committees then appoints a committee on nominations (formerly called the committee on boards), which in turn nominates candidates for election to all the boards, agencies, and commissions of the Convention.

By appointing conservative members to the committee on committees, the Convention president could increase the chance that more conservatives would eventually be appointed to these managing boards and commissions. It would take up to ten years for all the old members to roll off, but eventually, if conservative presidents were elected for several terms, the population of the boards would be conservative as well.

To help him, Pressler consulted with Paige Patterson, whom I had become friends with after I hired him to head the Criswell Bible Institute of First Baptist Dallas. Judge Pressler had met Patterson when Patterson was a student at New Orleans Seminary. A deacon at Pressler's church who had read his notorious Elliott committee report suggested he look Patterson up. Pressler said he was willing to devote time and resources to correcting what he considered a dangerous theological drift at the seminaries.

Though we hadn't been well acquainted over the years, Paul and I had actually known each other for two decades. In 1957, when he was finishing his last semester of law school and I was a newlywed attending Baylor, I had supported him as a candidate for the Texas state legislature (he won).

By the time of the 1979 Convention in Houston, Pressler had talked with many Southern Baptists about how to redirect the SBC by electing a conservative president who knew how to make appointments to the committee on committees. Seminary presidents, trustees, and professors felt their independence was at stake. Those in town for the convention from Southwestern Seminary had an ad hoc meeting where the seminary president, Russell Dilday, warned that "the Convention wants to turn the seminaries into Bible schools." As I was walking into the convention hall with my brother Charlie, my longtime friend and former professor Leon McBeth, who taught church history at Southwestern, ran up to me on the plaza outside, grabbed me by the lapels and said, "Don't let them destroy our Convention!"

One of the first casualties in any conflict is the truth, and this time was no exception as one small but representative example will show. Grady Cothen's account of the 1979 convention says that Judge Pressler "reportedly sat high in a sky-box overlooking the convention floor calling the signals for his organization." In *The Southern Baptist Convention* Jesse Fletcher agreed: "By the time the Convention convened in Houston the great sky boxes in the Astrodome were under Pressler's control, and floor lieutenants had been organized to be in direct contact with leaders high in the boxes."

First of all, the SBC Convention wasn't anywhere near the Astrodome, where the 12,500 messengers would have been lost in a vast space that holds 60,000. It was at the Summit, an arena closer to downtown where the Houston Rockets played basketball. Second and more important, Pressler didn't reserve the skyboxes and didn't pay for them. Because there were few restaurants near the Summit, he had asked a friend who worked in a building nearby if he and others could eat their meals in the company cafeteria. The friend suggested instead that Pressler use his company's skybox and bring in sandwiches.

Visiting the skybox, Pressler saw signs on the doors of adjacent boxes with names of other companies where he had friends. He called several of them, who obviously wouldn't be using the space during the convention, and got permission to use those as well. One reason he spent as much time up there as he did was that his son, who suffered severe physical handicaps, was subject to mysterious convulsions and headaches and the box offered him a quiet place to lie down.

Many other groundless charges were leveled against Pressler. One was that he orchestrated action on the floor from his skybox. In fact he never maintained close contact with convention proceedings from there and would have been far more effective in that role on the floor. Another charge was that the skybox was closed to visitors or ideological opponents. Yet Presnell Wood and various state editors were welcomed there. No one made any effort to keep them out; Pressler's skybox was open to all.

Critics also claimed that the judge sent busloads of sympathetic messengers to Houston and commandeered parking spaces at the Summit. In fact he helped arrange one bus from Austin and copied and distributed the Convention's own information about parking to people he thought might find it useful. Fleets of buses are common at SBC conventions, typically carrying messengers from churches within driving distance of the venue.

Challenges also came up later about Pressler's credentials as a messenger. Questioned about the matter, Pressler volunteered to give up his credentials before the vote was taken. His offer was refused; it was also overlooked in most of the press reports.

Largely on account of Pressler and Patterson, SBC messengers had a new understanding of how their Convention worked and how, if they wanted to, they could produce a slate of conservative trustees and boards over time for the various denominational entities. Adrian Rogers was elected president of the Convention on the first ballot in a six-way race. I've never seen any evidence that Judge Pressler tried to strong-arm anybody or coerce any votes. I believe all he did was make sure people knew what was at stake in the election and how they could make a difference in the outcome.

Of Rogers's election Grady Cothen later wrote, "Some thought there was simply a swing of the pendulum. Others thought it was serious but there was not much the Pressler group could do. Others thought discerning people would see the light pretty soon and the ship would return to a straight course. No one was aware that this was the beginning of a major fundamentalist movement. They had never seen such a movement before, did not believe that it was serious, and were unprepared to deal with it."

Porter Routh, who had been head of the Executive Committee of the Convention for more than a quarter of a century, believed the Convention should consider the disagreements over the direction the seminaries were taking: "I am concerned about the methodology of a secular political machine used at the convention this year. I don't believe this is the way God would have us move in the future."

Many of us felt that we had to act to preserve the theological integrity of Southern Baptist seminaries and that the proper way to change things was by using the system that had been in place for many years. That was what we did. Pressler believed the conflict could have been stopped after Adrian was elected if the seminaries and their moderate supporters had taken two steps to accommodate the views of the conservative majority: "The first was to add to their faculties professors who personally held a traditional, conservative position and would have taught the traditional Southern Baptist belief that the Bible is completely true. The other was to halt the ridicule and attacks on students who defended the belief that the Bible was completely true. However, neither was done."

Cothen believed that the moderates' big misstep at this stage was labeling the actions of Pressler, Patterson, Rogers, and the rest as a power grab. In his book *What Happened to the Southern Baptist Convention?* he wrote, "The fundamentalists insisted that the conflict was over theology. Others saw it as a struggle for power. A major mistake of the moderates was the failure to see that for the fundamentalists the issue was really theological."

Cothen also expressed his belief that the biggest new evangelism outreach to come along for the denomination in years was sidelined by the inerrancy debate. The Sunday School Board, along with the Women's Missionary Union, the Radio and Television Commission, both mission boards, and a host of other SBC entities, had spent years developing what became Bold Mission Thrust, a campaign to take the gospel of Christ to everyone in the world by the year 2000. From a seed planted by the SBC Executive Committee in 1970, a planning committee produced an ambitious list of goals, approved by the Convention in 1977, to reach the world for Christ with (among other resources) five thousand new missionaries and a hundred thousand new short-term missionary volunteers. Bold Mission Thrust set its sights on tripling the combined receipts of all state conventions and the Cooperative Program, personal giving of a double tithe by 2000, and a total of fifty thousand Southern Baptist congregations.

The kickoff for Bold Mission Thrust, at the Houston Astrodome during the 1979 Convention, featured Billy Graham, an eight-thousand-voice choir, and fifty thousand enthusiastic Southern Baptists ready to put the long-awaited plan into action. The Sunday School Board had been busily writing and producing materials about BMT, and other boards and commissions had been equally committed. Cothen and others later claimed that the inerrancy debate compromised BMT's momentum and hindered its chances for success. These statements were made in spite of the fact that Adrian Rogers expressed strong support for BMT and subsequent Convention presidents did likewise. Some of the goals, including having ten thousand volunteers a year and a missionary presence in 125 countries, were achieved well ahead of schedule. Others were inspirational mountaintops that seemed unreachable from the beginning.

Bold Mission Thrust was an exciting and fruitful evangelism outreach, though it didn't accomplish everything by 2000 its originators had dreamed about in 1977. The importance of BMT was one of the few points every Southern Baptist could agree on as the controversy continued.

CHAPTER 24

President's Perspective

Only willful ignorance or intellectual dishonesty can account for the claim that the Bible is inerrant and infallible. . . . No truth-loving, God-respecting, Christ-honoring believer should be guilty of such heresy. To invest the Bible with the qualities of inerrancy and infallibility is to idolatrize it, to transform it into a false god. . . . We are not bound by the letter of scripture, but by the spirit. Even words spoken by Jesus in Aramaic in the thirties of the first century and preserved in writing in Greek, 35 to 50 years later, do not necessarily wield compelling or authentic authority over us today."

This statement, reported by the Baptist Press on March 25, 1981, was from Robert Bratcher, a Southern Seminary graduate, former Baptist missionary, and translator of *Good News for Modern Man*. It was an extreme view, but it illustrates some of the contours of the controversy Southern Baptists found themselves facing as the 1980s began.

Adrian Rogers opted not to run for reelection. This was partly because if he served the customary two terms, the conservatives would have to field a new candidate at the 1981 Convention. Since the meeting that year was scheduled for far-off Los Angeles, attendance would be down, especially from churches in the South that knew and understood what was at stake. The conservatives would stand a better chance electing a new man in 1980 at St. Louis, who could then run for reelection in 1981. Also gall bladder surgery earlier in the year slowed Adrian down in the months leading up to the convention in St. Louis.

A number of people encouraged me to run for Convention president in 1980. However I had already promised my good friend Bailey Smith, who followed me as pastor at Del City, that I would nominate him. I met with Bailey, John Bisagno, and a few others in John's hotel room before the 1980 election as we prayed and discussed what we should do. I nominated Bailey as I had said I would, and he won a six-way race with almost 52 percent of the vote on the first ballot. This, even more than Adrian's election the year before, was a signal that the Convention was changing. People who didn't take the conservative groundswell seriously then were beginning to do so now.

During the two years of Bailey's SBC presidency, the moderate forces undertook a serious effort to regain the upper hand in the denomination. Though no incumbent had been opposed for reelection since W. A. Criswell won a second term in 1969 with more than 90 percent of the vote, the moderates decided to field a candidate to challenge Smith in 1981. They chose Abner McCall, president of Baylor University, who had come in fourth with just over 5 percent of the vote against Adrian Rogers in 1979. Bailey won the race with 60 percent of the vote.

At the 1982 Convention in New Orleans, I again received a lot of encouragement to run for president. This time I agreed to do it. The opposition convinced Duke McCall (no relation to Abner), who had been president both of New Orleans Seminary and of Southern Seminary in Louisville, to run against me. I had breakfast with Grady Cothen the day of the election, and he told me he was going to nominate Dr. McCall. I appreciated his honesty, but I can't recall a time when any other SSB president ever did anything so publicly partisan. Two Louisiana pastors also ran. On the first ballot I received 46 percent of the vote to 35 percent for Dr. McCall, with the rest split between the other candidates. On the run-off I polled 57 percent of the votes.

In spite of his opposition, I wanted Cothen to know that I held nothing against him personally and that I would do all I could to remain on cordial terms with him. I wanted to reach out to both sides in the conflict, particularly to the moderates who saw me as the enemy. One of my first speaking engagements as Convention president was at Southwestern Seminary in Fort Worth. Fortunately I received a warm, genuinely friendly welcome there. After the message the students gave me a standing ovation. Even the campus paper reported that I was "fast acquiring a reputation as a healer in the Southern Baptist Convention." In his history of the SBC published in 1994, Jesse Fletcher concurred that I "was able to give some hope to the moderates that more even-handed days would come."

But I knew I couldn't please everybody. In September a group of men led by Cecil Sherman asked me if I would "voluntarily" agree to give up the power to appoint the committee on committees—which moderates had used for years to shape the ideology of all the boards and associations but the conservatives had just begun to do—and share it with the Convention vice presidents. I couldn't possibly agree to a rule change like that, and neither could the conservatives who made up a clear majority of the Convention. If the denomination wanted to reverse the ideological drift of its agencies back away from the conservative viewpoint, all it had to do was elect a moderate president. While I looked for points of harmony between the two sides and did all I could to nurture them, I couldn't allow the other side to change the rules as soon as things stopped going their way.

Grady Cothen gave me points for effort, though he still didn't like my refusal to give up the president's appointment power. "He seemed really to try," Grady wrote of me, " without dealing with the central issue. Whatever the rhetoric or efforts, the crux of the matter would be his appointments."

In this tense atmosphere people were more likely than usual to say things better left unsaid, and others were more likely to take offense at them. Dr. Criswell blasted Keith Parks, president of the Foreign Mission Board, and William Self, an Atlanta pastor who had recently warned against a "swamp of creedalism" in the denomination. I had to disassociate myself with Criswell's remarks, calling them hasty and inaccurate, although his concerns proved to be valid later.

In October I convened a small, dedicated group from both sides of the issue to see whether we could tone down the rhetoric and focus on healing the divisions among us. My convention vice presidents, John Sullivan and Gene Garrison, were there along with pastors' conference president Fred Wolfe, Southern Seminary president Roy Honeycutt, Southwestern Seminary president Russell Dilday, Shreveport pastor William Hull, Adrian Rogers, and Paige Patterson. As a group we saw room for accommodation and accord, though there were certainly differences. There was, however, no willingness on the part of the moderate attendees to engage in dialogue with our concerns.

A month later I hosted a meeting of forty men representing every point of view to look again for more points of commonality. We had a good, wide-ranging discussion, but we still made no progress in finding common ground on the all-important issue of inerrancy. Inerrancy to me means a belief that everything in the Bible is true. If we can't agree on that, we can't agree on anything. And yet one pastor left our meeting warning the press of a "judgmental spirit and exclusivistic posture of fundamentalism" that lurked menacingly in the shadows. I'm sure there were others who agreed with him.

I was reelected unopposed in Pittsburgh in 1983. Commenting on my peacemaking efforts, Professor Glenn Hinson of Wake Forest said he felt "cautious optimism" at the Convention's work and that the "Baptist idea of voluntariness in religion will survive." In my Convention address that year, I tried to paint a picture of a denomination that was pulling together for a common goal, which I sincerely believed it was doing, rather than one shaken with dissention: "From every section of our Southern Baptist Convention recently . . . we have heard affirmations of our commitment to the Bible as the final authority for Southern Baptists. In this conviction . . . we must stand united. Our only hope for strength and vitality in our denomination is our renewed and continued commitment to this divinely inspired, uniquely transmitted, carefully preserved and totally reliable book."

The next year, as my term as Convention president was coming to an end, I finished a book titled *Authority: The Critical Issue for Southern Baptists*. I wanted to lay out the whole conservative-moderate debate in a complete, organized, rational way. Both sides had spent way too much time lobbing accusations, charges, and countercharges at each other. I did my best to take them one by one and explain what conservatives did and did not believe: there was no "take-over agenda"; no effort to take away academic freedom; no threat to the priesthood of the believer (which means each of us has a direct relationship with God, not that we can believe anything we want).

I also suggested a blue ribbon panel or committee to draw up a set of parameters for discussion at a Convention or recommend another forum for talking things out. "Unless Southern Baptists continue to stand for something other than simply cooperation with a program, in some political or social sense, there is no question that Southern Baptists will go down the same road that once-great denominations have taken. It will not be long before we will simply be a shadow, a caricature of what we once were."

Though he and I continued to have our differences, Grady Cothen was gracious in his final assessment of my two years as Convention president, which coincided with his last two years as president of the Sunday School Board:

"In evaluating Draper's efforts at peace, he appears to have been the most conciliatory of the presidents elected by the fundamentalist movement. He actually reached out to both sides in an effort to find that common ground he spoke about." (He did, however, also say that I "could not control either side" and didn't appoint people who "represented the broad spectrum of the convention.")

A year later a committee was appointed, as I had suggested, to try to resolve these denominational matters, but peace continued to elude us. Charles Stanley, pastor of First Baptist Church in Atlanta, was nominated in Kansas City to succeed me as Convention president. His opponent was Grady Cothen, who had nominated my chief opponent two years previously, and who had just taken medical retirement from the Sunday School Board. Cothen's account of his candidacy opens a historic window on those troubled times:

> There were serious problems for the moderates
> as convention time approached. They had difficulties
> finding a presidential candidate who had a chance of
> getting elected. This was a continuing problem. On
> two occasions, I had been approached by a group of
> behind-the-scenes denominationalists asking me to
> stand for president. I could not while I was president
> of the Sunday School Board. By the time I had retired
> early in 1984, the issues were so firmly fixed and the
> resistance to a denominational leader so firm that

there was little chance any one of us could succeed. We had been put in the category [Judge Pressler] called "liberals," and of course no review of sermons, addresses, and writings would convince the unconvincable. The need for another sacrificial lamb was so great, however, that I was persuaded to let my name be submitted. Health was a genuine problem, and I had great reluctance to risk what was left. . . . The fundamentalists told the press before the election that "Grady Cothen is a representative of the radical left." . . . [I] got beat on the first ballot by a man who was virtually uninvolved in Southern Baptist life— Charles Stanley.

So in 1984 I relinquished the president's chair, and all the meetings and travel it involved, and gratefully turned my full attention back to my family and my church in Euless. Meanwhile, the Sunday School Board had a new president to carry it across the continuing rough seas both it and the Convention were sailing through. And the fog was closing in.

CHAPTER 25

Into Rough Waters

In August 1982 Grady Cothen had requested medical retire-ment. Though he was only sixty-two that year, his con-tinuing health problems and long hospital stays made it hard for him to do the job he wanted to do. John Bryant headed a search committee of trustees that sifted through a list of prospects and recommendations. One candidate they were interested in was the executive vice president of Southwestern Seminary, Lloyd Elder. Near Christmas that year Bryant called Elder's office to say the committee wanted to interview him. A staff member explained that Elder and his wife were vaca-tioning in Hawaii and gave him the phone number there.

Bryant reached Elder and explained the situation on the nominating committee. "We've received your name as a candidate for president of the Sunday School Board. We've gone through your résumé and are interested in interviewing you for the job."

"Thanks very much," Elder answered, "but I don't think I'm interested."

"Please think about it overnight," Bryant replied, "and I'll call you back tomorrow."

Elder agreed to sleep on it. It was a question whether to stay in a position where he was satisfied and appreciated or make another one of the moves he had felt God calling him to consider over the years.

Prentice Lloyd Elder was born in Dallas in 1933, the fourteenth of Joseph and Dorris Elder's fifteen children. Supporting his large family as an independent merchant during the Depression, Joseph Elder moved them through twenty-four different states by the time Lloyd was eight. During World War II the Elders settled back in Dallas, where both parents worked in defense plants and Lloyd had the unaccustomed pleasure of going to the same school and church for three solid years. After the war, when Lloyd was in high school, the family moved to a farm in East Texas. They lived in two log cabins on the property; one had a wooden floor, and the other was packed earth.

In his book *Blueprints*, Elder recalls the life-changing summer of 1951 between his junior and senior years: "I went with my older brother, Carl, to Fairbanks, Alaska, to 'make a lot of money in construction.' And I did. But something far better happened. In a rented attic room I knelt beside my bed and received Christ as my Savior and Lord. The following night that confession was made public, and I was baptized into the fellowship of the First Southern Baptist Church, Fairbanks." After Robin Guess, a summer missionary from Howard Payne College in Texas, performed the baptism, "deep, abiding joy settled in."

When Carl felt called to preach, Lloyd decided he'd go to college and become a history teacher rather than follow his brother into the ministry. But he had a change of heart during a revival at Field City Baptist Church in Dallas and made a public commitment to special service. After attending Decatur Baptist College and earning a diploma from Howard Payne, Elder began graduate studies at Southwestern Seminary. He already had a taste of the pulpit. While he was working in Alaska, a little mission there needed a pastor and he was a "preacher boy"; his first flock was a seven-member mission at Big Delta, southeast of Fairbanks along the Tanana River.

He later served several Texas congregations before settling in at Gambrell Street Baptist in Fort Worth with his wife, Sue, for the longest of his pastorates. There, as he put it, the pastor and his family were "pastored" by the people during a time of great sorrow. In 1970 Sue and the children, Donna Sue, Janet Lynne, and Philip Lloyd, were in a tragic auto accident. Eleven-year-old Janet was killed and the others seriously injured. In the aftermath of his daughter's death and the long months of recovery for the rest of the family, "those great Baptist people" gave their minister priceless words of comfort, healing, and encouragement.

While he preached at Gambrell Street, Elder also became a director of the Home Mission Board of the Southern Baptist Convention. It was his first experience with a national SBC entity after many years in local and state denominational organizations. Also while at Gambrell Street, he served as chairman of the executive board of the Baptist General Convention of Texas.

In 1975 the executive director of the Texas Convention, Dr. James Landis, invited Elder to become his assistant. After preaching twenty-two years altogether, first as a student and then as an ordained minister, Elder moved into an administrative role in a large and complex state convention. Three years later he accepted an invitation to return to his alma mater, Southwestern Seminary, as executive vice president under Russell Dilday. He had been at Southwestern five years when the call came from the SSB nominating committee during his Hawaiian vacation.

The night after his phone conversation with committee chairman John Bryant, Elder called his brother Carl, "a very godly man and a good friend," to ask his advice; he also spoke with one or two other trusted confidantes. They all advised him to go for an interview even if he wasn't interested. When

Bryant called back the next day, Elder said he would come meet with the nominating committee.

"Fine," Bryant exclaimed. "I've already made a plane reservation for you. I found out from your secretary when you'd be back and we've already called our meeting." Elder described his visit with the committee as a "mutual interview." He told them he was happy where he was. When people asked him why he wanted to come to the SSB, he said he didn't necessarily want to come but rather was there at the invitation of the committee. "We went back and forth," Elder recalled in an interview years later. "It was all very cordial and very affirming."

The committee, Elder added, liked his "cross training" in pastoring, administration, and seminary leadership. They voted on the spot to offer him the job, but the chairman insisted they all think and pray about it for three days. And so three days later they voted again via conference call and made the offer official.

The Elder family moved to Nashville in April 1983, and Lloyd began a lengthy period as president elect. Grady Cothen remained president until February 1984. During those intervening months Elder met regularly with Cothen and the executive staff. As Elder observed, it was "not unlike a person becoming president of a company before he becomes CEO. He's drawn in but at a learning rate." When a policy or personnel decision came up that would have consequences for Elder down the line, Cothen invited him to participate in the meeting.

During his months of shadowing Cothen, Elder refined his management style and wrote a book presenting his views on leadership, *Blueprints: 10 Challenges for a Great People*. "I hammered out my leadership style," he explained. "I kind of knew what it was, but I did some extra study on leadership models."

"Cothen was an excellent mentor and a good friend," Elder said. Cothen systematically went over the Board's responsibilities and relationships with other Southern Baptist boards and organizations. He briefed his younger colleague confidentially on the SSB executives one at a time. Cothen had great confidence in his team. Based on Cothen's assessment, Elder believed "they could run General Motors."

Late in the transition period Elder began representing Cothen at board meetings when Cothen wasn't well enough to attend though he didn't make any decisions on behalf of the president. Jim Clark still did that as necessary. Elder also stood in for the outgoing president at state convention meetings and speaking or preaching at churches.

When he took over as president in 1984, one of the first things he did was to set up individual lunch meetings with the more than forty senior staffers who were appointed by the trustees. He had two or three of these meetings per week, explaining, "I decided I needed to get to know the people who were doing that leadership work in my behalf and in behalf of Southern Baptists face to face."

He described his second step as attending or scheduling a series of staff meetings where he got the chance to meet Board

workers and share with them his testimony, conversion experience, and sense of calling. He asked the people to tell him
in two or three pages about their passion for their work, what
they were doing now, and what they'd like to see done.

Elder also believed it was important to build relationships
with the state conventions. He knew from the legacy of J. M.
Frost and James Sullivan that the state conventions are SSB
partners. What were their needs? Their gripes? Their aches
and pains? It was important to know these things, especially
considering how unsettled the political landscape was.

At the 1984 SBC Convention in Kansas City, the conservatives nominated Charles Stanley to succeed me as convention president. I had appointed Charles chairman of the key
Committee on Boards the year before, where he had done an
outstanding job appointing Bible-believing Baptists to the
various Southern Baptist boards and commissions. I believe
the moderates thought this was the time when they could
turn the Convention back around. They still felt that the
rise of forces insisting on inerrancy was a fluke, a temporary situation that would settle back to normal after a few
years.

To oppose Stanley, the moderates got behind Elder's just-
retired predecessor, Grady Cothen. Stanley won a three-way
contest on the first ballot with 52 percent of the vote. Another
of Elder's past colleagues also garnered plenty of attention in Kansas City that week. Russell Dilday, president of
Southwestern Seminary, delivered a convention sermon that

strongly criticized the "misty flats of forced uniformity" and "muddy swamps of political coercion" he felt the conservatives were forcing on the denomination. I was saddened to see Dr. Dilday pound away at things that were dividing us rather than looking for ways to bring us together.

As I told a reporter for the *Fort Worth Star Telegram*, "I think [Dilday has] gotten into an area of controversy and polarization that we don't need. I'm not critical of his courage or right to speak out. I just regret the inclusion of his voice to be a polarizing factor. I'd like him to speak out and invite all the people to come to the Southern Baptist Convention in Dallas next year instead of saying 'these are bad guys and let's get rid of them.'" Later that year I was elected to the board of trustees at Southwestern, where I would be seeing more of Dr. Dilday.

Lloyd Elder had predicted troubled times as he began his service to the SSB. In an interview years later he recalled that the search committee had been attracted to him in part because of what they considered to be conservative credentials. "They knew we were headed into rough waters. So they chose a candidate that was a noted conservative Southern Baptist-trained pastor. And it was intentional on their part. They accepted me for what I was, that I was a confessional conservative of the old stripe. That is, I was not siding with the reactionaries, or the ones out of power who were wanting in, or the other side that didn't want to get out."

By the time Lloyd became president of the Sunday School Board in 1984, the opposition to the conservative movement in the SBC had pulled out all the stops and the rhetoric was getting more and more heated. Roy Honeycutt, president of Southern Seminary, described a "holy war" on "unholy forces which, if left unchecked, will destroy essential qualities" of the Convention and his seminary. These comments are in a Baptist Press report dated August 29. Honeycutt claimed that conservatives "now propose fidelity to their particular and restrictive theory about biblical origin as a test of both faith and fellowship . . . damaging local churches, risking the destruction of our denominational heritage and compromising our Christian witness to the world."

During a speech celebrating the 125th anniversary of Southern Seminary, Honeycutt accused "fundamentalists" of "seeking to legalize life by eviscerating freedom from the gospel." He concluded, "If you meet one of these Southern Baptist Judaizers, tell him those of us who are free by the grace of God in Jesus Christ shall not submit again to slavery's yoke. For us there is no turning back to a limited legalism, no turning back." The faculty and students gave him a standing ovation.

Early the next year, in my capacity as a Southwestern trustee, I was pulled another level into the controversy when Dr. Dilday demanded one of his faculty members resign. Dr. Farrar Patterson, a tenured associate professor of preaching who had been on the faculty sixteen years, opposed Dilday's outspoken support of the moderate cause. Dilday accused him of falsely reporting that a faculty vote to support Dilday had been less than unanimous. Two-thirds of the trustees had to agree with Dilday for Dr. Patterson to be dismissed. Under the circumstances it was a straw poll on Dilday too. Nineteen trustees sided with Dr. Dilday, and twelve opposed him, fewer than the two-thirds required, so Patterson was not fired.

Though I was one of the twelve who opposed Dr. Dilday's motion to dismiss Dr. Patterson, I still supported Dilday's administration and said so to the press. Ken Chafin, former chairman of trustees, went on record insisting that the trustees' ultimate aim was to fire Dr. Dilday. Some time later the trustees considered doing exactly that, but I thought it was a bad idea because it would only have made Dilday a martyr for the moderate cause, and I lobbied against it. Dilday was eventually fired by his trustees, but it was after this point of the crisis was past and after I was no longer a trustee.

At the Sunday School Board in Nashville, Lloyd Elder kept an eye on the changes and controversy swirling around the denomination as he assembled his team of leaders and gave them their marching orders.

CHAPTER 26

Seeking Resolution

Lloyd Elder's style was to form a big management team and keep a close watch on it. Some would call him a micromanager, but it was one way to get a handle on the growing and far-flung components of the SSB. According to historian Leon McBeth, who worked with him later in his presidency, Elder assembled a Board Management Group. The core of this group was the Executive Officers Team of five vice presidents and one assistant vice president. The Executive Staff included that team plus division directors and others, which were in turn part of the Program Leadership. Program Leadership comprised about half of the fifty-member Administrative Management Group, the lead component of Board Management.

During his time serving with Dr. Cothen in 1983, Elder initiated the position of associate to the president, the leader who would coordinate the Executive Officers Team, and named James D. Williams to the post. Williams had spent more than twenty years as a professor at Southwestern Seminary, where he headed the doctoral studies program in religious education. He and Dr. Elder had been friends since they served together at Gambrell Street Baptist in Fort Worth as pastor and minister of education.

Another senior figure at the Sunday School Board during the transition was Jim Clark, who had been Cothen's executive vice president. When Williams was promoted to executive vice president in 1987, Clark moved over to lead the office of publishing and distribution as a senior vice president until his retirement in 1989 after more than thirty years of service to the Board.

The members of the Executive Officers Team divided responsibility for the Board's wide-ranging operation. James Williams was in charge of planning and coordination. Jimmy D. Edwards headed the office of church programs and services: family ministry, student ministry, telecommunications, Ridgecrest and Glorieta, church recreation, and more. E. V. King led the business and finance office: accounting, personnel, security, financial and legal services, procurement, and similar duties. Gary W. Cook was in charge of church program organizations: Sunday school, church music, discipleship training, church administration, and related services. Senior vice president Clark oversaw Baptist Book Stores, Broadman Press, Holman Publishers, and the Genevox music publishing business. Assistant vice president Lloyd Householder managed the office of communications.

During the search that ultimately led them to Dr. Elder, the SSB presidential search committee noted that they believed the Board was the most important entity in the SBC and therefore its presidency was the "single most strategic position in the SBC." The Board had to provide high quality materials to all Southern Baptist churches even as they were becoming more diverse. "We have got problems in the Southern Baptist Convention," the committee observed. "Increasingly, the Sunday School Board and its president must act as a major reconciling force in the SBC to constantly emphasize the all important things that unite us."

In *Blueprints*, Elder advanced ten challenges he saw for Southern Baptists as he began his presidency:

1. Spiritual and organizational renewal of the denomination
2. Rediscovering the central purpose and rich heritage of Southern Baptists
3. Recognizing the importance of a central core of biblically based beliefs freely confessed under the lordship of Christ
4. Spiritual awakening dependent on the providence and work of God

5. Nurturing servant leadership, after the example
of Christ, in local churches and throughout the
denomination

6. Open communication that promotes understanding
and trust

7. Shaping inevitable changes in the denomination in
ways that enhance its ability to participate in God's
creative and redemptive work

8. Acknowledging differences, resolving conflicts, and
living together in trust and strength

9. Taking concerted action, both as believers and as a
denomination, to bring others to salvation in Christ
and fellowship in His church

10. Building our lives, churches, and denomination on
the firm foundation of Jesus Christ and His Word at
all times under all circumstances

The year after Elder took office, 1985, was surely a challenging one in many ways for the SBC. The Convention met
in Dallas where Charles Stanley, my successor as president,
was running for reelection. The year before in Kansas City,
just over thirteen thousand messengers had elected Stanley
to his first term. That was three thousand more attendees
than we had when I ran for reelection unopposed at
Pittsburgh in 1983. Now more than forty-five thousand
Southern Baptists, an all-time record, had come to town to
decide whether the conservative Dr. Stanley would continue

leading the denomination or be unseated by a moderate challenger.

Along with fellow Texans Russell Dilday of Southwestern and Herbert Reynolds, president of Baylor University, Lloyd Elder supported Winfred Moore in his bid to oust Stanley. Moore was pastor of First Baptist Church in Amarillo and president of the Baptist General Convention of Texas, where Elder had served before joining Dr. Dilday at Southwestern. Stanley defeated Moore with more than 55 percent of the vote. In a gesture of reconciliation, Moore was elected first vice president.

A motion was made to replace the nominees for the Committee on Boards with a slate appointed by state convention presidents and Women's Missionary Union organizations. This would short-circuit the work being done by conservative Convention presidents to appoint conservative members to boards in various Southern Baptist entities. Dr. Stanley ruled from the platform that the fifty-two candidates had to be replaced one at a time. A participant moved that the messengers take a vote. They did, and for the first time in SBC history a ruling of the chair was overturned. But the professional parliamentarian serving at the meeting ruled the vote out of order. There was quite a commotion as people insisted on honoring the vote on one hand or accepting the ruling of the chair on the other. In the end the nominees to the Committee on Boards stood as they had originally.

One hopeful result of all this discord was the Peace Committee, just the kind of group I had recommended in *Authority: The Critical Issue for Southern Baptists* to discuss what it means to be Southern Baptist and how to embrace diversity among believers without compromising the distinctives of our denomination. H. Franklin Paschall, who had been president of the Convention in 1967–1968 during a quieter era, proposed the idea to the Convention and twenty men and two women were appointed to the task along with Stanley and Moore as *ex officio* members. In its report two years later, this committee upheld the conservative view that the Bible is inerrant though it didn't bring the peace so many of us hoped it would. Seminary faculty members thought their presidents had sold out to the "creedal" opposition, and at least one moderate member of the committee resigned in protest over the committee's findings.

With this continued tension in the denomination, it should be no surprise that there were more doctrinal struggles at the Sunday School Board. For several years *The Baptist Student*, a magazine published by the SSB for college students, had raised some eyebrows at the Board and incited minor dustups with its progressive stance on contemporary cultural issues. After a 1982 article criticizing the political right, the Board required the editor to publish an article on the other side of the issue, which he did.

In February 1985, with ordination of women and other women's issues a hot topic in some Southern Baptist circles,

The Baptist Student published an issue on the role and function of women in Baptist life. Its editorial position drew a storm of protest from Baptists who challenged it as unbiblical and contrary to Southern Baptist beliefs. The trustees had just adopted guidelines for its publications on the ordination of women, and Elder felt *The Baptist Student* had not followed them. He issued a statement expressing his "displeasure to those involved" and affirming that the magazine "does not comply with current publishing guidelines." He added, "Changes are already under way that will insure that future issues of the magazine will be balanced and fair in its treatment of issues in Southern Baptist life."

Unfortunately, six months later *The Baptist Student* again took a strong stand against right-wing politics, blasting the Moral Majority founded by independent Baptist Jerry Falwell and sounding off on everything from tuition tax credits to appointing a US ambassador to the Vatican. Historian Leon McBeth reported "a hornet's nest of criticism among Southern Baptists and especially among some of the trustees."

The editor, Howard Bramlette, resigned, but instead of resolving the conflict, it made matters worse as the editor's supporters and critics squared off against each other. To some, this incident put SSB editors on notice that our publications would promote traditional, biblically based Southern Baptist views. To others, it meant that the Board was "caving in to a small pressure group." Editors with a traditionally conservative point of view no doubt saw it as an endorsement of their work, while, according to McBeth, "it sent a chill through other editors of the Board's many publications who wondered if something similar could happen to them."

The same month *The Baptist Student* took on the Moral Majority, an even more serious lapse appeared in the Life and Work Sunday school lesson. The study for July 7, 1985, was on Job. In an incredible series of statements, the lesson taught that the Satan who had a conversation with the Lord in Job 2 was not the devil of the New Testament; that Satan "was God's servant, not his enemy"; and that the Old Testament has "no concept of an empire of evil opposed to God." Furthermore, the lesson challenged the characterization of Job as a patient man of faith who never doubted God, and raised questions about Job's historical identity. The lesson claimed it was correcting "mistaken impressions" about Job.

The uproar that followed was probably the most widespread reaction to an SSB publication since James Baldwin appeared in a Training Union publication in 1964. And like the Baldwin flap, the Job lesson got through the system undetected because new or temporary people were serving in key positions and everybody thought somebody else would take care of it.

Elder summed up his report to the trustees on July 17 this way:

> Human error, human judgment, and the
> time crunch became factors. We had an editorial

supervisor at the point of retirement; the editor of
Adult Bible Study had taken a new position within
the Sunday School Board; a temporary editor was
secured in order to keep that particular issue on
schedule; that temporary editor also is an approved
appraisal reader and, therefore, inadvertently was
assigned the responsibility of reading that which he
had edited (that is not our policy or system but was
an error in the process for which we take accountability and apologize); the temporary editor approved
the manuscript for publication. These problems were
compounded one by the other.

Southern Baptists with questions about the Board's commitment to traditional biblical interpretation were doubly
concerned when the Board issued an explanation and then
changed it. At first the Board said the offensive statements
weren't in the original manuscript but added later by the
temporary editor (who was also the outside reader and should
have declined that assignment). Later the Board changed
their story to say that "the manuscript . . . is not unlike what
appeared in print."

McBeth described the incident this way:

A considerable debate erupted among the trustees when the Bible Teaching Committee, in whose
jurisdiction the Job incident fell, made its report.
That committee recommended no basic changes in

editorial procedures, but urged that "special care be exercised in determining the doctrinal and biblical commitment of writers by carefully reviewing their published works, their public statements, and their personal testimony." However, a substitute motion asked that "the administration be instructed by the trustees to take the necessary steps to implement a more discriminating policy for the employment of lesson writers for our curriculum materials." Some felt that existing policies and safeguards were adequate; others felt the Job incident itself demonstrated that safeguards were not adequate. After lengthy discussion, the substitute motion failed. However, an amendment to the original motion added the phrase "make needed changes" to avoid the impression that the Board would simply go about business as usual.

Different views about the role of women in Southern Baptist churches continued to flare up during this period. In Pittsburgh during my time as Convention president, the SBC had passed a resolution saying, "We encourage all Southern Baptists to explore further opportunities of service for Baptist women." Almost two-thirds of the eighteen-hundred-plus employees of the Sunday School Board were women, including more than fifty in management. The trustees in turn officially supported "the role of women in the home, in society, and in our churches" and resolved to continue publishing "curriculum and leisure-reading support for women who fulfill their calling in the marketplace, and in vocational service in our churches and denominational agencies."

The next year in Kansas City the Convention took a stronger line, adopting a resolution against ordination of women, which upset a lot of people and led to the controversial issue of *The Baptist Student* in February 1985. However, Elder said the Sunday School Board would "neither advocate nor disparage the ordination of women." Though the Convention had come out against it, Elder's position was that the resolution had no binding force. The Board was owned and operated by the Convention, but its operational decisions were made by its own trustees based on their interpretation of The Baptist Faith and Message.

The trustees looked for the middle ground, upholding guidelines that material published on the role of women in the denomination give clear support to basic Christian and Baptist beliefs and deal factually and fairly with differing views among Southern Baptists. They pointed out that ordination is a question decided individually by each church, not the denomination, and that it shouldn't become a distraction or a litmus test for Baptist believers.

The trustees further instructed that church literature and Convention Press books, written specifically for Southern Baptists, strictly follow these directives. Books from Broadman Press could express the authors' own viewpoints as long as it was clear that they didn't represent the official Southern Baptist position.

Even as the theological battle raged in the Convention, the Sunday School Board saw a steady demand for its products. By 1988 the Board was filling more than 460,000 orders and shipping nearly 70 million pieces of church literature a year. Nevertheless, the history of the Board in the years ahead reflected the tension in the denomination as the conservatives and moderates continued their struggle.

CHAPTER 27

Reaching Out

For all the turmoil in the Southern Baptist world, the Sunday School Board appeared to be moving reasonably well toward its hundredth year, its relationships with churches and state conventions relatively stable. Historically the Sunday School Board has had a direct financial relationship with a long list of Southern Baptist organizations. The Board generated an operating surplus at the end of its first year and remains the only SBC entity that doesn't depend on contributions for its income. It has a long history of assisting in the support of seminaries and other boards and institutions.

It's a credit both to J. M. Frost and his successors that the relations between the Board and other Southern Baptist groups remained strong through the tumultuous 1980s. Frost had established a system of returning some of the SSB proceeds back to state conventions; the more the states bought from the Board, the more money the conventions received in return. By 1987 the Board contributed $2.2 million per year to the salaries of state workers, and more than $3 million in "code 29 funds," money to help support large-scale projects sponsored by departments of the Board. The Board gave another $241,000 in "code 30 funds" appropriated to state conventions for special projects related to Board programs.

All along, some churches had not used SSB materials, either because they didn't use prepared materials, bought them from somewhere else, or produced their own. Over a ten-year period starting in the late 1970s when the conservative-moderate conflict began, the percentage of nonuser Southern Baptist churches grew from about 5 percent to about 10 percent. Another 37 percent used SSB materials for only part of their teaching and training. By 1988 more than seventeen thousand of the thirty-seven thousand Southern Baptist congregations used something less than the full range of SSB children and adult materials. Revenues at the Board grew during this period only because of price increases.

Detractors complained that the material was too expensive, though some said it had a cheap feel and appearance compared with other available publications. Others said competitive products had more for children to do and took less time for teachers to prepare. One of the most consistent complaints was that Board literature was dull, boring, and outdated. Lesson materials were, and remain, one of the most profitable areas of Board operations; losing customers is a blow to operating margins. But moreover, churches that didn't use SSB materials tended to be less involved in Convention activities in general. Of the congregations that didn't use Board publications, 47 percent of them also declined to contribute to the Cooperative Program and tended to be nominal or absent in state convention affairs. Using Board lessons gave congregations a connection with the SBC that bore other spiritual and cooperational fruit. Without that connection, churches were much more likely to drift away from the Convention.

Attracted by the healthy margins, many secular and religious publishers alike entered the field, especially after World War II when Sunday school attendance grew dramatically. Some of them had a limited range of lessons, targeting the most profitable market segments.

To its credit, the Board assigned a person full-time to the task of strengthening ties to existing customers and building bridges to churches critical of Board materials. Linda Thompson crisscrossed the country giving churches updated information about SSB publications and listening to their criticisms. Some churches still didn't know about the Life and Work lesson series begun in 1978. Their lack of Southern Baptist teaching materials left gaps in denominational knowledge. There were Southern Baptist children who had never heard of Annie Armstrong; others thought Lottie Moon founded the Moonies. Over the course of her first year or so in the field, Thompson prompted more than one hundred Southern Baptist congregations that hadn't used SSB products in the past to start using them.

The Board also worked to strengthen its historic ties with black Baptist churches. During its first five years the Board provided literature to black congregations throughout the South, usually at no cost. In 1895 black Baptists formed the National Baptist Convention and the next year set up the National Baptist Publishing Board. J. M. Frost gladly gave this new publishing venture permission to publish SSB materials under its own imprint. This practice of sending out materials written and prepared by the SSB under two separate imprints for two distinct audiences continued until the early 1970s.

By about 1972, the civil rights movement underscored a need for lesson material and other products specifically written for black churches. Blacks were joining Southern Baptist congregations in significant numbers, and more black churches were affiliating with the SBC. The Board began hiring more black writers to serve these groups and more black professionals to help lead various SSB program areas. In 1978 the Board set up the ethnic liaison unit to better communicate with black Southern Baptist churches, other black Baptist organizations, and multiracial churches.

In 1985 the special ministries department of the Board added a black church development section. Its immediate responsibility was to develop relationships and product lines for black Baptists in the Sunday school, discipleship training, church administration, and church music departments. Its ultimate goal was to strengthen black congregations by developing the best training and support materials for them possible. Partly as a result of this targeted effort, many black congregations set up dual affiliations both with the SBC and National Baptists.

During the 1980s the Sunday School Board also reached out to non-English-speaking congregations with another special ministries department section called Language Church Development/New Work. Its first focus was on Spanish-speaking Baptists. For many years Spanish congregations throughout the Americas used materials from the Casa Bautista de Publicationes in El Paso. But more and more Hispanic churches in the United States felt their needs were different from Casa Bautista's main market of Latin American Baptists and they should have their own distinctive literature. The SBC Foreign Mission Board agreed that the Sunday School Board ought to take on the task of supplying Spanish church materials for congregations in the US and Puerto Rico.

The Board's first Spanish publication was *La Fe Bautista* *(The Baptist Faith)*, an adult quarterly begun in 1964. By the late 1970s the Board produced Spanish translations of the Convention Uniform Series of Sunday school quarterlies and a series for adult teachers designed to supplement Casa Bautista materials. By 1986 the Board was filling orders for seventy thousand copies of Spanish material each month. Later the Board hired writers to produce lessons in Spanish, rather than translating the English, and added more original Spanish material and new translations from English to the catalog.

After surveying the demand for SSB products in other languages, the Board over the next few years added Korean, Vietnamese, Laotian, Chinese, French, Thai, Arabic, Japanese, and basic English for American Indians, internationals, and the deaf. This foreign language material has become one of the fastest-growing components of the Board's work.

Another major project launched during the mid-1980s was the New American Commentary series. Though it didn't grab headlines at the 1985 Dallas Convention the way Charles Stanley's controversial parliamentary rulings and other conservative-moderate issues did, the decision to produce a new Bible commentary was an important one. All of the participants there were doubtless aware that the existing *Broadman Bible Commentary* helped spark the whole ideological debate that had so consumed Southern Baptists for the previous several years. A new commentary could overcome the disappointment and discord many Baptists associated with the earlier one. However, the Convention's official position was that the new commentary wouldn't replace the old one; the two would be available side by side. The motion named the past five Convention presidents as advisors with final approval over the choice of editors and authors and charged the Sunday School Board with planning and publishing the new work.

The Sunday School Board began researching the need and market demand for a new commentary, studying other commentaries already on the market, and surveying Bible professors at Baptist and non-Baptist schools. The Board also polled hundreds of Baptist pastors, seminary students, and local church teachers, plus messengers at the 1986 Convention in Atlanta (more than thirty-seven thousand attended that year).

Based on their findings, a study committee of SSB trustees recommended they and the SBC abandon the idea. They saw insufficient need or demand for a new commentary and were afraid the project would further polarize the denomination. But the full board of trustees rejected the committee's recommendation and moved to go forward.

The motion, passed February 4, 1987, declared that the SSB would

notify the Convention that we are planning to proceed with the new commentary and that we instruct our administration to do so with haste. The commentary is to reflect a strong scholarly defense of the traditional authorship of the biblical books, Mosaic authorship of the Pentateuch, and a presentation of an apologetic for creationism in the introduction to Genesis. All authors involved in the writing of this commentary should hold to the position of inerrancy.

Here was a preemptive strike against any biblical inter-pretation that could produce the kind of uproar the earlier *Broadman Bible Commentary* did with its pronouncements on Genesis.

Adrian Rogers, whose election as Convention president in 1979 marked the beginning of the conservative resurgence, was elected once again in 1986. Meeting with the Sunday School Board as the commentary project began, he and they agreed that the approach should be true both to the Baptist Faith and Message and the Chicago Statement on Biblical Inerrancy. The Chicago Statement came from a 1978 meet-ing of about 250 Bible scholars from various denominations hosted by James M. Boice and James I. Packer, which issued its conclusion that the Bible was infallible and inerrant. Leon McBeth wrote, "Thus before the commentary was named it was commonly referred to as the 'inerrancy commentary,' and it was understood from the first that only biblical iner-rantists would be approved to write for it."

The SSB trustees set a timetable allowing only four years from the approval vote to release of the first volume in a proposed forty-volume set, by far the most ambitious publishing project in Board history. Michael A. Smith, a Southern Seminary PhD graduate who had been chief editor at Broadman Press since 1985, was named general editor. An advisory panel of Broadman people and the past SBC presidents then chose six consulting editors and two alternates: Russ Bush, Ken Mathews, and Larry Walker for the Old Testament, with Duane Garrett as alternate; and Paige Patterson, Robert Sloan, and Curtis Vaughan for the New Testament, with Richard Melick as alternate. Broadman and the consulting editors then chose forty-four authors for the commentaries.

Editors decided to use the New International Version of Bible text. While it was an uncomfortable departure for traditionalists who preferred the King James, it reflected the fact that the NIV had become the most popular English translation. They also settled on a title for the new project. Market research showed strong public resistance to any name that included the word "Baptist." The first recommendation, The New Evangelical Commentary, was rejected by the SSB trustees. In February 1989, with work well under way, the board approved the series The New American Commentary: An Exegetical and Theological Exposition of Holy Scripture.

The Sunday School Board hadn't added any office space since the operations building was dedicated under Dr. Sullivan in 1959. The whole Baptist Telecommunication Network operation had come into being since then. Holman Bible Publishers had become part of the Board after that time.

The new commitment to black churches and foreign-language literature had dramatically expanded the special ministries department. Once again in its history, the Board thought it would have room to spare for the foreseeable future, only to have every nook and cranny filled and more staff coming all the time.

With four office buildings totaling more than 360,000 square feet, another 300,000-plus square feet in the operations building, and a 100,000-square-foot garage, the Board owned buildings with a replacement value of more than $57 million dollars. The land was worth another $13.5 million. As the Board considered how to find room for more employees, it looked, as it had in Dr. Sullivan's day, at options outside of Nashville. In 1985 the executive committee of trustees approved the purchase of 51.3 acres on Elm Hill Pike for future warehouse and distribution center expansion but decided ultimately to keep the offices in downtown Nashville. Four years later the trustees approved a plan similar to the process that placed the Sullivan Tower on top of an existing two-story building in the 1950s: a new office tower on top of the Operations Building. The projected cost was $16 million, which the Board had in reserve. This new building was eventually christened the Centennial Tower; in 2006 the Board did me the high honor of renaming it after me.

Another building project in the 1980s, just across the street from the Sullivan Tower, was a new $20 million head- quarters for the Southern Baptist Convention to replace the building on James Robertson Parkway the SSB had given the SBC years before. The Board donated the land for the new building too—partly, Grady Cothen insisted, to keep the Convention from asking the Board to foot the bill for the whole thing. In fact the Convention did end up with a short-fall, and the Board took steps to help pay it. But along the way the process shined a spotlight on the conflict that still ran through the fabric of Baptist life and set in motion an unlikely chain of events that brought me to the Sunday School Board.

CHAPTER 28

Glorieta 1989

In 1984 the Southern Baptist Convention built its new five-story brick headquarters at 901 Commerce Street, a block from the Frost Building, for $20 million. While the expense had seemed responsible and manageable when the project began, a nationwide recession in the mid-1980s caused an unexpected drop later in the decade in the cooperative program revenues the Convention was counting on to help foot the bill. The Executive Committee voted to allot more of its own budget to pay down the $2 million building debt, but to do so they would have to make big cuts in foreign and home missions support and reduce their planned contributions to other agencies as well.

At the SSB trustees meeting in February 1989, Dr. Elder proposed making a gift of $400,000 to the Executive Committee from Board reserve funds to help them through the shortfall. This seemingly generous and unsolicited gift soon led to a firestorm over Lloyd's leadership and became yet another polarizing situation among Southern Baptist brethren.

The first problem, as trustee chairman Bill Anderson later explained, was that Elder promised the gift without discussing it ahead of time with the trustees. They were taken completely by surprise. Then, after the $400,000 was offered, the Executive Committee allocated $340,000 to start a new religious liberty organization in Washington. Several observers believed the committee acted because they thought the long-standing Baptist Joint Committee on Public Affairs had become too liberal and the committee was going to pull funding from the BJC and give it to a new, more conservative Baptist voice.

Elder explained that the Board was giving the money because they thought there was a financial crisis at the Executive Committee. If the committee could afford $340,000 to start a new agency, the thinking went, was their financial situation really that dire? When Elder questioned the Executive Committee's action, the committee reversed itself and left BJC funding in place. According to trustee minutes, a controversy arose over whether Dr. Elder indicated or implied that the Board might withdraw its contribution if the Executive Committee defunded the BJC. Elder immediately and consistently affirmed that he had not tied the SSB gift to continued funding for the Baptist Joint Committee. Even so, some trustees accused their president of pulling strings to keep a "liberal" Baptist agency afloat. Trustee chairman Anderson felt a "pervasive sense" that Elder was "upset at the executive committee for funding a conservative cause."

The questions continued for months, with further meetings, amendments to the February minutes, and charges and countercharges flying back and forth. The truth was that even though the Board had a reserve fund to dip into on behalf of the Executive Committee, the last few years had not been robust for the SSB either. In the final year or two of Grady Cothen's presidency, the recession had reduced investment income, receipts from Baptist Book Stores and the conference centers, and a few other areas. The Board kept growing overall but at a much lower rate than projected. (One bit of good news: the Board had decided to stay in downtown Nashville for the long term and sold their property on Elm Hill Pike for a 100 percent profit.)

A major reorganization in 1987 did not revive performance as hoped; a second reorganization in 1990 was designed to further fine-tune plans for a leaner, more productive operation. The SSB pared down its number of employees, instituted a salary freeze, and took other cost-saving steps.

They also began making more modest sales projections and operating on 95 percent of their budget figures.

Adding to the financial challenges was the Baptist Telecommunication Network. The biggest drain from BTN was a satellite transponder that the Board leased for $65,000 per month but used only six hours a day to transmit to about fifteen hundred or so subscribers. While they could control production and personnel cost, they were bound by contract to pay for the satellite access. There was also a noncancelable contract for a fiber optic cable line at $40,000 a year. Finally in 1990 the trustees decided to shut down BTN when their vendor contracts expired the next year.

By then there was another controversy on the table. It began innocently enough with a commission to write the centennial history of the Sunday School Board. At various times over the years, Southern Baptists had written about the history of the Board. Dr. Frost authored the first one in 1916. Though not much more than a pamphlet, *The Sunday School Board of the Southern Baptist Convention: Its History and Work* is the most complete account of the Board's earliest days. Even written in the reserved and formal style of the time, Frost's passion for and dedication to the Board come through clearly.

There was talk of having a more comprehensive and wider-ranging history commissioned, but it seems that everybody at the Board during those early days was too busy making history to stop and write about it. No one took on the task until the fiftieth anniversary year, when P. E. Burroughs wrote *Fifty Fruitful Years: The Story of the Sunday School Board of the Southern Baptist Convention* in 1941. A quarter century later Robert A. Baker marked the Board's seventy-fifth birthday with *The Story of the Sunday School Board* in 1966. After that came *The Sunday School Board: Ninety Years of Service* in 1981 by Walter B. Shurden.

The centennial of the Board in 1991 was an obvious time to commission a new history. To do the job, the trustees engaged Dr. Leon McBeth, professor of church history at Southwestern Seminary and an old friend of mine. He and the trustees agreed that he would write what they called an "interpretive history," meaning it would be a factual account with some measure of interpretation or guiding of the reader. The author would also sometimes take the liberty of drawing conclusions from the facts presented rather than leaving the reader to interpret and apply the information entirely on his own.

Up through the chapters on the Grady Cothen years, McBeth's manuscript was well regarded. I have quoted liberally from it throughout this book. The scholarship and writing, as expected, were first-rate. But when the author waded into the denominational controversy of 1979 and afterward, he unwittingly became a part of the controversy himself.

Particularly in the chapters on Lloyd Elder, some readers detected a strong editorial bias favoring the moderate cause and shortchanging the conservatives. His editor at

Broadman Press noted that McBeth's narrative went "quite often . . . beyond the facts to make interpretations about causes, underlying motives, possible consequences, and so on." Other interoffice correspondence described it as "heavily slanted in the anti-conservative way" and suggested that the "history written about living people was highly selective history . . . criticism could be raised that some of the living historical figures were allowed to interpret their own historical involvement." McBeth, the trustees, and editors at Broadman Press went back and forth for months discussing and revising the manuscript. Critics blamed McBeth for painting an overly rosy picture of Elder and his presidency. Dr. Elder explained that McBeth wrote what he saw and what he wanted to write and that Elder had no control over his interpretation of the facts and didn't want any. Ultimately the trustees accepted the manuscript, then shelved it. And so the much-anticipated centennial history of the Sunday School Board, *Celebrating Heritage and Hope*, was never published.

It was, however, cited by Lloyd Elder's critics as one of the reasons he should vacate his post as president of the Baptist Sunday School Board.

Along with the controversy over the $400,000 gift to the Executive Committee and several other points of contention, the editorial perspective of the *Celebrating Heritage and Hope* manuscript was front and center during a trustee meeting when a motion was made to dismiss the president and declare the office vacant. In advance of the meeting of

August 7–9, 1989, at Glorieta, trustees had cleared Elder of any wrongdoing over the cash gift while "regretting" his "judgment and timing," and had also begun steps to evaluate the president's performance formally and regularly. But during that August gathering, charges surged to the surface again in a heated debate.

The motion was made and seconded to remove Dr. Elder from office; after more discussion the motion was withdrawn without a vote.

Back in Nashville on August 11, Elder spoke to the Sunday School Board staff and responded to all the publicity and rumors about the trustee meeting head-on. He spoke frankly about how painful it was to listen to the motion to fire him in the presence of his wife and other visitors present; it was the most pain he'd experienced, he said, since his daughter died. To his credit, Elder responded to the charges against him in an evenhanded and civilized way. While denying most of the accusations against him, he never publicly attacked anyone personally and was circumspect in his remarks. In his comments to the staff, he promised to abide by the trustees' wishes and called upon everyone at the Board to redouble their effort to improve for the future. The staff gave him a standing ovation.

On August 31 Elder sent a written response to the trustees affirming his desire "to clarify and strengthen trusting relationships, focus on the great mission of the Board, and get on effectively with the work we have been given by the

Convention." Admitting he had been "humbled and corrected" by his experience, he promised he would attack his
work with new vigor and enthusiasm. "I live in the land of
awakened reality," he said.

In his history manuscript, Leon McBeth wrapped up his
discussion of the 1989 trustee meeting and its aftermath this
way:

> At various meetings since Glorieta, Elder has
> received sustained applause. This groundswell of
> support encouraged Elder and Board leaders to
> hope that they might be able to put Glorieta behind
> them and get on with their work. Clearly we are
> too close to Glorieta for historical interpretation.
> However, this much is clear: the response among
> Southern Baptists shows that they do not want their
> denominational leaders treated as Elder was treated
> at Glorieta, and they will express their feelings about
> such matters.

Bill Anderson, who chaired the Glorieta meeting,
reflected on those tumultuous days in a letter to me in 2006.
McBeth's report of a "groudswell of support" was, he said,
"pure hagiography." McBeth was an acquaintance and ex-
professor of Anderson's. "I felt sorry that he was fed, in my
studied view, misinformation as to what was actually happening in the SSB trustee meetings," Anderson wrote, "par-

ticularly the Glorieta one. When I read his account, I felt he was reporting on a meeting I had missed."

After the Glorieta meeting, the general administration committee of the trustees established the president's performance work group to assess the president's record and his fitness to continue in his position. On January 4, 1991, the committee called a special meeting to review the president's performance. The report was critical in four areas: management of the centennial history manuscript; business ventures including BTN that had been expensive failures; continuing declines in the sale and circulation of Board literature; and controversy about the president taping telephone calls. While several writers, including Jesse Fletcher, have said the centennial history was the last straw, I believe it was the conflicting accounts of the phone calls being taped that finally spurred the board to take drastic action.

Bill Anderson concurs with this conclusion. Elder had taped conversations with him twice. Then, when he "quizzed him about them in the presence of the trustee performance workgroup, Lloyd denied, twice, that they had occurred. . . . He was caught in a lie when telling the simple truth would have removed that issue from the table." One of the most curious aspects of the situation, Bill added, was that the phone calls were neither confidental nor particualy important.

Though Anderson spoke against firing Elder at the Glorieta meeting, he recalled in his recent letter to me other trustee criticisms of Elder, including his inability to deal

with the Board's "general administrative malaise," and the
"persistent tendency . . . for SSB leaders to withhold from the
trustees all the facts about the serious financial slippage."

A called meeting of the full board of trustees was set for
January 17 to hear the committee's recommendation that the
president be relieved of his duties. The day before, the committee met privately with Dr. Elder to share their findings.
Through his attorney, the committee then received word that
Elder would like to request early retirement. By the time the
trustee meeting convened at seven o'clock on the evening of
January 17, Elder's lawyer and the Board's legal department
had already negotiated a retirement package.

To prevent a repeat of the parliamentary free-for-all that
had taken place during the 1989 Glorieta meeting, Daniel
Collins, chairman of the general administration committee,
had brought a professional parliamentarian from New York
to assist with procedural matters if needed. But there were no
fireworks.

Chairman Anderson called the meeting to order and
announced that the president's performance work group had
concluded there were problems with the president's work.
He told the trustees that Dr. Elder had decided to take early
retirement as "the most viable alternative." Then he invited
Elder to speak.

Dr. Elder talked of his desire to effect an orderly transition of leadership and that he had decided on early retirement
based on the answers to three questions: What was best for

the mission of the Board? What was best for the Southern Baptist Convention and its missionary work? What was best for his effective leadership as president? Above all else, he said, he was seeking the will of the Lord.

Collins passed around copies of the proposed agreement between Elder and the Board, which stated that he would remain as president for a year or until thirty days after his successor had been appointed, whichever was earlier, then become a consultant to the Board for a period, followed by retirement. There was a lengthy discussion during which Elder responded to the charges, much of which was spent on the issue of tape-recorded telephone conversations, Elder affirming he had taped them only under specific, reasonable conditions, and other speakers remembering the facts differently.

At last the trustees voted on the motion to accept the general administration committee recommendation to grant early retirement that was "not a result of, or based upon, political or theological differences between the board and the president, but honest differences of opinion with regard to management style, philosophy, and performance." Vote was by a show of hands; only two trustees voted against the motion. The meeting concluded with the trustees in a season of prayer on their knees.

In August Dr. Elder assumed the H. Franklin Paschall Chair of Biblical Studies and Preaching at Belmont University, which is affiliated with the Tennessee Baptist Convention. In

1996 he founded the Moench Center for Church Leadership at Belmont and, ten years later, was still leading that program, developing curriculum, training support, and seminar materials.

He looks ahead, not back. As he recently remarked, "One of these days we're not going to be here. But when the day is done and when we're gone, the question that will test how well we did our work is the question: How are the churches doing? That's pastoring, and that's also good administration."

Meanwhile, while Lloyd was preparing to change careers, a Baptist preacher from Texas was about to get the surprise of his life.

CHAPTER 29

From Preacher to President

I watched with a mixed sense of sadness and excitement as all this went on at the Sunday School Board. It was unfortunate that the theological debate distracted so many people and led to broken fellowship among Christian brothers. But I also believed it was essential that Southern Baptist leaders and organizations stand unwavering in defense of scriptural inerrancy, and the result of all the discord was that the denomination was reaffirming its position.

Though I had never been involved directly in the SSB, I recognized it as one of the oldest and strongest components of the Southern Baptist Convention and deeply admired and appreciated all it had done over a hundred years for the kingdom of God and for the spiritual health of millions of Baptists. For most of that time it had been not only a source of inspiring Bible Study curriculum and training, books, music, and other materials but also a source of revenue that supported Southern Baptist work across the country and around the world.

Since 1975 I had served as pastor of First Baptist Church in Euless, Texas, between Dallas and Fort Worth. Euless was a small town on the prairie until construction started on the Dallas-Fort Worth Airport in the late 1960s. In only a few years after that, the population increased 500 percent. The churches there were growing, and it was a great place to be serving the Lord and encouraging His people.

The people there welcomed Carol Ann, our three children, my mother, and me with open arms (my mother had lived with us since my father died in 1966). I preached my first sermon as their new pastor the week before Thanksgiving 1975. This was a church that wanted to be a spiritual light in a growing community, and everyone enthusiastically pitched in to get the job done. Early the next year the church set its budget goal above half a million dollars for the first time and then oversubscribed it. There was a wonderful spirit there that indicated great things for the future.

In 1978 I was nominated as president of the SBC pastors' conference held annually before the SBC Convention. I didn't win that year, but I was elected in 1979, the year Adrian Rogers was elected president of the Convention and the conservative movement went into high gear. As a member of the SBC Annuity Board and a trustee of my alma mater, Baylor University, I already had some notion of the state of Baptist affairs on a national level, especially the tension between the seminaries and other Baptist institutions (such as Baylor) versus the inerrancy stance affirmed by the Baptist Faith and Message statement and literally centuries of Baptist theological interpretation.

One memorable lesson on the conservative-moderate issue came when I was chairman of the Baylor trustees' academic affairs committee. In 1978 the president of Baylor, Abner McCall, and executive vice president, Herb Reynolds, recommended a professor named Jack Flanders to be the new chairman of the religion department. The committee approved Flanders's nomination based on the recommendation of McCall and Reynolds.

It was only later that I read two of Flanders's books, *The People of the Covenant* and *Introduction to the Bible*, and realized this man's views were completely at odds with mainstream biblical interpretation, much less a commitment to inerrancy. *The People of the Covenant* literally made me nauseous. I wrote Dr. Flanders what I hoped was a friendly and conciliatory note saying I wanted to talk to him about his evident position that the Bible was man's record of his understanding and concept of God rather than God's inerrant revelation to man.

I made a trip soon to meet with Dr. Flanders and other interested parties. I tried to be as honest and frank as I could in my letter inviting him to the meeting: "The position of *The People of the Covenant* is not in keeping with historic Baptist belief and teaching. I personally will not be satisfied until the book is removed from the curriculum and every effort is made by the teacher in the classroom to present the full picture of the Bible in its various academic approaches."

I had invited Flanders and the trustees who were also pastors to the meeting and was surprised when I got there to see Dr. McCall, Dr. Reynolds, and the Baylor legal counsel there too. I had discussed my concerns with each pastor individually before the meeting, and each of them agreed that Flanders's position was incompatible with biblically accurate, intellectually honest teaching. When the time came, they were behind me—*way* behind me. Not one of them took a stand in support of my position.

But the faculty surely took a stand for one of their own. A written response to my criticism said in part, "These demands raise grave questions concerning the academic freedom of the faculty and students of Baylor University and concerning the cherished Baptist beliefs in the priesthood of the believer, involving competency of every believer, the absolute soul liberty of every believer, and the individual responsibility before God of every believer in matters of religion."

The SBC was starting to get involved in the same sort of argument over Southern Baptist polity and personal faith. I believe the conflict was strongest at the seminaries, where liberal viewpoints had a big following, but the issue was something every Southern Baptist had to consider prayerfully and carefully.

An important step in understanding the debate is realizing what "priesthood of the believer" actually means. Southern Baptists—and most Protestant denominations to one degree or another—believe the Bible teaches that each Christian has a direct line to God, a personal relationship with Him. Each believer, in other words, is his own "priest," confessing his sins, asking forgiveness, giving thanks, and making every other kind of communication with God one-on-one. We don't believe in having a priestly bureaucracy act as the go-between between us and God: confession to a priest, penance, and so forth are completely counter to biblical teaching.

Defending the priesthood of the believer isn't the same as saying a Southern Baptist can believe anything he wants to believe. Opposing heretical teaching is not opposing the priesthood of the believer. They are two different things. One has to do with the relationship between God and man, and the other has to do with being true to the Bible. Challenging nonbiblical teaching is not challenging a Southern Baptist's right and duty to pray directly to God. It *is* challenging him to accept the authority of the Word of God. Every man and woman is free to doubt the inerrancy of Scripture; but if they do, they should not expect Southern Baptists to pay their salaries. And they should not be teaching in Southern Baptist seminaries or writing Southern Baptist literature.

The final disposition of the Flanders matter came in the summer of 1980. In short, the trustees as a group chose not to support my position. While encouraging the administration to hire professors who "believe the divine inspiration of the whole Bible, and that the Bible is the infallible Word of God and truth without any mixture of error," it also allowed *The People of the Covenant* to remain a Baylor textbook and Jack Flanders to remain chairman of the religion department.

Only one other trustee stood with me in this matter and most of them changed their attitude toward me. I became the butt of jokes on the board and in classrooms, and Jack Flanders threatened to sue me (though he never did). When my daughter, Terri, graduated from Baylor, the trustees chose not to even invite me to lead a prayer at graduation, despite the fact that I was the only SBC president since George W. Truett to be elected while serving as a Baylor trustee. In fact, I haven't been invited back to campus since. I've never thought theological disagreement ought to keep people from being friends with each other, and I regret that sticking to my principles cost me those relationships. But I don't regret the decision for one second.

While the theological battle raged on in the denomination, First Church Euless was one place where everybody was pulling together. We had revived Wednesday night suppers, started a women's ministry and weekday Bible studies, begun an around-the-clock intercessory prayer ministry, hired our first ever director of evangelism, and added a thousand members to our roll. The youth started meeting in the high school across the street to ease the overcrowding.

We began construction on two new buildings. But when the thirteen acres next to us became available, we put the second building on hold and purchased that property, which gave us freeway frontage. One of the buildings was nothing but a big hole in the ground for a couple of years, but we eventually got everything finished.

One reason the church in Euless didn't strain its resources to complete their buildings on schedule was that the people there had a real heart for ministry. My wife, Carol Ann, and I went on several mission trips to Brazil during those years, witnessing door-to-door and sharing our testimonies. We witnessed to everybody who'd stand still long enough: taxi drivers, people on the sidewalk, it didn't matter. I also preached revivals. Later our church helped a congregation in the Brazilian state of Minas Gerias build a new church building, which they graciously named after me.

Back home, the Euless church enthusiastically supported my election as president of the SBC in 1982. When we got back from New Orleans at the airport in Dallas, church members were waiting for us there with a big black limousine to take us home in style! Though it wasn't always that visible, we felt the love of those church members in one way or another every day.

Writers and commentators on both sides of the ideological divide agreed that during my two terms as president of the Convention, I did everything possible to soften the discord and bring the two sides together to look for common ground. I always thought the opposing forces agreed on a lot more than they disagreed on. But my lesson with Jack Flanders taught me to be realistic about changing people's minds and hearts. Only God can do that.

My years as SBC president were two of the most incredible, wonderful years of my ministry. They were the best years of growth our church ever had. Certainly they played a big part in preparing me for the future, though I didn't suspect it at the time. The deacons at First Church Euless delighted in giving me the freedom to help lead the Convention and look for ways to heal the hurts it had experienced.

I like to meet people and talk to them face-to-face. I think it's possible to communicate a lot more clearly that way. During my SBC presidency I traveled more than 300,000 miles on behalf of Southern Baptists. That included leading a group of Southern Baptists and Jews to Israel, speaking to the Southern Baptist Directors of Evangelism in Puerto Rico, an address to the European Baptist Convention in Germany, and three trips to the White House.

After handing the president's gavel over to Charles Stanley at the end of the 1984 Convention, I had the opportunity to spend more time on the mission field and more time serving the church. In ten years our annual budget at Euless had grown from $500,000 to $4.5 million, and weekly attendance from about nine hundred to about twenty-five hundred. God was doing great things in Euless; and the staff, lay leadership, and members gave sacrificially of their time and resources to help in His work.

One Sunday night in 1986, a missionary from Kenya who was back in the US for surgery on his leg came to speak to our congregation. He told us he was looking for forty people to come share the gospel in Mombasa, Kenya, on August 1, less than four months away. God impressed upon me that this was His special invitation to our church, and I said so to the people that night. Then I added, "We'll have forty people there August 1." Believe it or not, when the time came, we had forty-seven.

I preached at the First Baptist Church of Mombasa, Kenya. After that I preached in the street with a bullhorn that played "The Eyes of Texas" when you pushed a button on the handle. Later I went to the ferry landing (Mombasa is on an island just off the coast) and preached to people waiting for the boat. In a week our group recorded more than six thousand professions of faith.

I returned to Africa three more times while I served at Euless. The last time, in 1990, I joined more than five hundred Christians from sixteen states to participate in the Mombasa Kenya Coast Crusade. In a month we had almost seventy thousand professions of faith. The last Sunday we were there, we processed from the church to the Indian Ocean where eleven other preachers and I baptized people for three hours. That day we baptized more than a thousand new Christians.

Back in Texas, the church was growing like never before. Also in 1990, I was elected chairman of the trustees of Southwestern Seminary in Fort Worth. I was busy, fulfilled, challenged, and absolutely content with my life. That's when I got invited to a meeting that turned everything topsy-turvy.

Early in 1991, trustees of the Sunday School Board of the Southern Baptist Convention announced they were looking for a new president. A search committee was appointed in February and began the long, difficult but important job of identifying candidates for the position. Someone recommended me to the committee. Grateful as I was to be considered, I had no interest in the job. I had been preaching since I was fourteen and pastoring since I was twenty. I felt sure it was what God had planned for my life. I loved what I did and had no desire to do anything else.

The search committee called regularly for three months. Each time I declined to meet with them. Finally they asked if I would meet them at the DFW airport to advise them. I said I'd be glad to help. I arrived for the meeting, sat down at the table, and someone passed out briefing folders to everyone. Then I realized they were there to talk to me about the position. I'd been tricked! I pushed away the leather notebook they had prepared for me—not an unfriendly gesture, I hope, but just a reaction of surprise—and repeated my earlier statement that I wasn't a prospect for the position. We met for nearly two hours.

The meeting got me to thinking about what God really wanted for me, rather than what I really wanted. When they called again, I said I was open to the idea. By then, though, they had already offered the job to another applicant. When he turned it down, the committee called one more time. As I always did when considering any big change, I thought and prayed about it with Carol Ann over several days. After a while we decided the Lord was calling us to labor in a new vineyard. And so with tears and heartfelt wishes of thanks for sixteen wonderful years in Euless, we pulled up stakes and headed to Nashville. This would be a very new experience for me. I'd been a preacher my whole life, not an administrator or corporate officer. I'd only been in the SSB building in Nashville once in my life, and now I was the new guy in charge.

CHAPTER 30

Centennial Snapshot

On July 18, 1991, just about one hundred years exactly after the Sunday School Board was founded, the trustees of the Sunday School Board in Nashville passed a resolution calling me as their eighth president. The vote was seventy-six for, none against, and one abstention. It was heartening to have that kind of support; I knew I would need everybody's help, hard work, and sincere prayers to do the job the Lord had in mind.

There were great traditions at the Sunday School Board and many dedicated people. There were also things that needed changing—some of them had needed it for a long time—and employees were shell-shocked and worn out by the tension and troubles of the last several years. Both people and programs needed attention. A reorganization like the Board had gone through twice already in the recent past was not what I had in mind but something very different. I had never run a corporation, much less a multimillion-dollar one with more than sixteen hundred full-time employees, so I had a lot of homework to do.

The first step was to gain a working knowledge of Board operations as fast as possible. In completing his controversial history of the SSB, Leon McBeth had taken a good snapshot of the Board's work on the threshold of its centennial year. These were the active programs the Board had in place:

Church Programs and Services. This umbrella organization was responsible for seeing that all the Board's products and services were generally acceptable to Southern Baptist churches, campus organizations, families, associations, and state conventions. It handled research, curriculum design and evaluation, long-range planning, and marketing consulting.

Sunday School. One of the largest and most visible components of the Board, this section had also undergone some of the biggest changes over the years as the SSB and the denomination grew and developed. Originally the Board and Sunday school development were one and the same, as Sunday school development was the Board's original task.

I. J. Van Ness was the first to departmentalize Sunday school work, separating adult, youth, intermediate, and other categories into their own separate departments. Later they were gathered, along with Vacation Bible School, back into one department. James Sullivan had made that department part of the Education Division; later it reverted to an independent Sunday School Division.

Since it produced so many of the Board's products, the Sunday School Division had absorbed a lot of criticism for materials that were perceived to be outdated, inconvenient, and out of touch with Southern Baptist issues. Over the last several years the division had done some detailed self-assessments and instituted a number of changes in response: requiring teachers to collect fewer outside resources, larger type for some adult publications, a strong lesson each January on the biblical view of abortion, and other modifications.

The Board produced three separate lines of Sunday school literature: the venerable Convention Uniform Series and the Bible Book Series, both based on the King James translation, and the newer Life and Work Series based originally on the New American Standard translation and converted to the New International Version in 1991.

Discipleship Training. This was the modern version of what started out as the Baptist Young People's Union in the 1890s, became the Baptist Training Union in 1934, Church Training in 1972, and Discipleship Training in 1989. By any name, the training ministry was having a rough time. Whereas church members were looking for ways to spend time together in generations past, by the 1990s there were many more choices, especially on Sunday night (the traditional training class night) when families tended more toward football games and television shows than going back to church.

To halt or at least slow the downward trend in discipleship training attendance, the department developed a series of modules that could be used any time of year, any time during the week, at church, in homes, and even by people studying alone, and offered them alongside the traditional weekly training curriculum. It also introduced the Lay Institute for Equipping (LIFE) series preparing laity for discipleship, leadership, and ministry.

Family Ministry. The Family Life Department started in 1946 and produced *Home Life*, a monthly magazine that became one of the Board's all-time best-selling products. Though building strong families through home Bible study had always been an objective of the Board, Grady Cothen made it a primary focus, adding numerous other publications such as *Christian Single*, *Mature Living*, *Living with Teenagers*, and others. This department also led in observing Christian Home Week every year and conducted family life seminars at Ridgecrest and Glorieta, state conventions, and other gatherings.

Student Ministry. What began as an effort to bring Baptist Young People's Union to college campuses eventually grew into a comprehensive Bible study for students there, plus an invitation to mission work and guidance on maintaining a Christian lifestyle on campus. As the SSB centennial appeared on the horizon, there were Baptist Student Unions on more than a thousand college campuses reaching almost 150,000 students. This ministry program of the Board also published *The Student*.

Church Music. Begun in 1941 under the legendary hymn writer and song leader B. B. McKinney, the Church Music Department had seen early success with the *Broadman Hymnal*. Millions of copies were sold. Later hymnbooks, the *Baptist Hymnal* of 1956 and another by the same name in 1975, fell short of the old *Broadman Hymnal*'s success. These song collections didn't reflect the changes in Southern Baptist worship practice over the years. With congregations clamoring for a more versatile combination of favorite standards, traditional gospel music, choruses, and contemporary praise songs, more and more Southern Baptist churches were buying hymnals from other publishers.

Overall real sales growth at the Board had declined during the past few years to the point where the SSB was struggling to meet operating budget. Historically hymnals had been a strong source of revenue. The Church Music Department had high hopes for a new hymnal scheduled for release in 1991. The team there had worked to make this centennial year hymnal more attractive to Southern Baptists and more suitable for modern worship in all its forms. Church choirs and music groups were the fastest growing components of many Southern Baptist churches in the late 1980s. The Sunday School Board had to improve its books and other publications dramatically to earn their support.

Church Administration. This department advised Southern Baptist church leaders on ways to lead more effectively. Its publications and seminars focused on helping churches operate more smoothly, their staffs work together more effectively, and their services be more meaningful and inspiring. Church Administration conducted seminars and workshops on a variety of topics from stress management and pastor burnout to conflict resolution and staff relations. Their publications included *Church Administration* and *The Deacon.*

Church Media Library. This area of service to Southern Baptist churches had seen its ups and downs. Early in the twentieth century many churches collected books and study materials to use as their Bible study curriculums. After World War II people generally had a lot more leisure time than they had before, and church libraries grew in response to the demand for more reading material. Churches collected large numbers of children's and youth books and publications for young readers to enjoy while their parents attended church meetings of one sort or another.

Television and other new diversions caused a decline in church library use. The Sunday School Board and other publishers met this challenge with new products: records and filmstrips at first, then cassettes and videotapes. Many churches changed the name of the library to "media center." The Board was developing new audio and video products for this market. The Church Media Library Department provided training and operational assistance to church libraries and media centers and operated the libraries at Ridgecrest and Glorieta.

Church Recreation. As we saw earlier, there was some controversy in the beginning over whether it was appropriate for churches to be in the recreation business. Fortunately Southern Baptists eventually realized that directing leisure activities was a legitimate ministry. Church softball leagues, church gyms, activities for retired adults, and many other recreation-oriented outreach programs have become an indispensable part of congregational life for many churches.

This department offered recreational leadership training and leisure activity programs to churches. One of the most successful organized programs of all is Centrifuge, which began as a way to keep bored teenagers occupied while their parents attended seminars and workshops at Glorieta. By the late 1980s the program had expanded beyond the conference centers to other areas and welcomed more than thirty thousand participants per year, hundreds of whom made decisions for Christ. A newer recreation program, Crosspoint, revolved around sports.

Church Architecture. Founded to help SBC churches design and construct buildings best suited to their worship needs, this department published various books, surveys, and even blueprints to assist congregations of every size. The department also consulted on site selection, furnishings, financing, and other related topics. Though it worked mostly behind the scenes, this group provided a valuable service especially to smaller churches without wide experience in dealing with architects and other building professionals.

Conference Center Operation. Ridgecrest and Glorieta had become major centers of Southern Baptist life, and this department was formed specifically to run them. These large facilities were in almost constant use and needed continual maintenance, repair, expansion, and modernizing. Though the various groups using these conference centers paid their own program costs, the Board had to arrange for house-keeping, food service, security, and other services. The goal was to have the centers break even. Some years they did, and some they didn't.

Bookstores. I. J. Van Ness was the first Board leader to see the value in bookstores. Dr. Frost had been wary of them as a money-losing operation. Originally the Board sold its wares by mail order, then opened a store on the ground floor of the Frost Building in Nashville. Under Van Ness and his successor, Dr. Luther Holcomb, the board bought up bookstores operated by various state conventions and other groups. By the end of the 1980s, the Board owned a chain of sixty-three stores.

Unfortunately, like some of the Sunday School literature, hymnals, and other products, the Baptist Book Stores had become tired and dated. In spite of gradual price increases over the years, store revenues fell below projections year after year.

Broadman Publishing. Formed in 1934, Broadman Publishing had its roots in *Yates the Missionary*, a book produced in spite of the Southern Baptist Convention's concern that it was too much of a financial risk. By the end of the 1980s, Broadman had hundreds of titles in print and issued about seventy-five new releases every year on Christian theology, ethics, church history, music, collections of children's stories, devotional guides, sermons, and more.

Though all Broadman books upheld the revised Baptist Faith and Message statement of 1963, many non-Baptists also bought them; Broadman positioned itself as a general trade publisher. A second publishing imprint, Convention Press, was established in 1956 to publish study guides and other materials targeted at an exclusively Southern Baptist audience.

Broadman had also ventured into audiovisual products and developed computer software. The publisher set up Church Information Systems to market and service computer programming that congregations could use to maintain membership and class rolls, keep financial records, organize the media library, and do other jobs. CIS ran a significant loss at first. Its struggles, plus a change in bookkeeping that moved some Broadman revenue to another department, helped account in part for the fact that Broadman Press was not in healthy shape. But it was also true that both in content and appearance, Broadman books had some ground to make up compared with the competition.

Bible Publishing. In a little more than ten years since the Sunday School Board bought Holman Bible Publishing, Bibles had grown into a significant ministry and a steady source of revenue. Holman produced a large variety of Bibles including the popular UltraThin line. There were a variety of study Bibles in several translations, pew Bibles, and two different Spanish translations. The division also published hundreds of thousands of low-cost New Testaments for evangelical outreach around the world.

State Convention Support. Based on the pattern established by J. M. Frost, the Board gave back to the state conventions every year a portion of the money churches in that state spent on SSB products and services. We worked hard to nurture ties with state Southern Baptist conventions and encourage them to buy materials from the Board.

Southern Baptist Convention Support. The Financial and Business Services division promoted relations between the SSB and the Convention and managed the Board's annual direct contribution to the SBC. In addition to the millions of dollars funneled back into state conventions every year, the Board also traditionally made a substantial contribution to the budget of the SBC Executive Committee, which freed up Cooperative Program funds to be used by other SBC entities.

General Management. This internal division also coordinated strategic planning, budgeting, operational control, communication, and other functions among the various divisions and departments of the Board. In 1978 the division added a Systems Information Department that began using computers to support these internal activities. By the Board's centennial year, the Southern Baptist Convention Network allowed SBC churches, state associations, agencies, and other groups direct access to the Sunday School Board computer databank. With that resource they could do everything from read a Baptist Press release to register for a conference at Glorieta.

Those were the programs and products of the Sunday School Board as it approached the end of its first century. As I stepped through the door, the Board had annual revenues of $196 million, a new nine-story Centennial Tower under construction, and a faithful core of customers and partners in ministry. My task was to learn, by God's grace, what we were doing well and what we could do better.

CHAPTER 31

———

A New Course

To appreciate how far the Board has progressed in the last few years, it's helpful to look briefly and generally at where we were then.

There was a feeling of being in a "caretaker" mode. Two reorganizations in the last few years hadn't produced the results everybody wanted. Employees in general didn't seem engaged or challenged or inspired by what they were doing. Lunches and coffee breaks tended to be long and leisurely. One of the most important ways I thought I could help the Board early on was to encourage a sense of urgency, purpose, and mission.

When I arrived, the president's office was on the eleventh floor of the Sullivan Tower. Up there I felt insulated and isolated. I wanted to know what was going on and wanted people to know where I was and have access to me personally. I had the office moved to the ground floor between the main entrance and the employee cafeteria, right in the middle of the action.

I knew that if any progress was going to be made on my watch, it would be because I had the advice of some good, strong leaders and together we were able to set a vision for the Sunday School Board and get everyone else to share that vision. To do that, I formed a senior executive team that consisted of four skilled and godly vice presidents.

First was Mike Arrington, a great friend of mine from First Baptist Euless, a deacon there who had been an executive with Texas Utilities. Anything that needed doing at the church, he did. What made him especially valuable is that he was the consummate consensus builder. He spent a lot of his time at Texas Utilities working with groups like the arts council, the Heart Fund, the Rotary, and other community organizations, listening to their needs and looking for mutual goals to work toward together.

Before I even moved to Nashville, I asked Mike if he would come to the Board as my strong right arm, and I also talked to the trustees about it. Mike was talented, extremely loyal, extremely capable, and I knew he'd watch out for my backside. His wife, Paula, and Carol Ann were dear friends, which added to the blessing of having him join me in my new position.

Gene Mims and Chuck Wilson, both SSB trustees, joined me as vice president of church growth and programs and vice president of trade and retail markets. The final executive team member was E. V. King, vice president of finance and administration. Some people were comfortable with the old way of doing things, and we faced considerable resistance at first. But the five of us forged ahead.

Mike, Gene, and Chuck all felt the Board should have a mission statement in order to focus our effort and set a direction for the future. The SSB had never had a mission statement. I'd never had a mission statement before and didn't much see the point of one at first. But they were insistent. Finally I agreed to go along with it, and it turned out to be an absolutely wonderful idea. I'll always be indebted to them for seeing it through. As Proverbs 29:18 says, "Without vision the people perish."

The original mission statement was: "We will assist local churches and believers to evangelize the world to Christ, develop believers, and grow churches by being the best world-wide provider of relevant, high-quality, high-value Christian products and services."

Now that we had a statement of our mission and direction, we had to figure out how to fulfill it. As the senior executive team considered what to do, I was glad I'd had contact with several of my predecessors who offered their help. I particularly appreciated the time James Sullivan put into welcoming me to the presidency of the Board. He was theologically conservative but had never thought the Board should take a stand that left anybody out if at all possible. In that way we disagreed: I believed the Board should take a strongly conservative position. But that didn't keep us from being friends, and it didn't keep me from admiring his leadership. He was a great supporter for me. Though he himself had retired sixteen years before, he sent me in September six handwritten pages of his administration philosophy.

I still have that list. Of the forty-four points, he put stars beside nine of them:

> 2. A person who steps out of the pastorate into a denominational job steps down, it matters not how high or big the position.

> 10. Good organization is like good digestion. When it is working, you are not aware of its existence. When it is not working, you will find it hard to think of anything else.

> 14. The Sunday School Board is different from any other existing institution on earth, so you cannot learn by someone else's trials and errors. You must

learn from your own, leaning heavily on the Lord to see you through troubled waters.

15. Always be truthful. This will not only keep you with a clear conscience but with a consistent leadership which will not be questioned by people who doubt your integrity. No one has a good enough memory to survive dishonesty.

26. Hopefully, you will wish to avoid conflict. But if it is unavoidable, follow the example of the old mariners who, when storms were sure and impending, would nail down the hatches and ride out the storm, however furious. This is better than to compromise your principles or violate your conscience.

27. Take your work seriously, but never yourself.

29. As aggravating as they are, you can be blessed by morons and gadflies if you will respect them as people and possible blessings. A moron's questions make you examine the merits or weaknesses of your decisions and actions. A gadfly makes you furiously angry, but in turn that will help you from going to sleep on your job.

30. Do not give up your sense of humor regardless of the intensity of the emotional high voltage of the moment. Criticism or even silence itself may speak volumes and let off excess steam when the atmosphere is super charged. This will help you preserve your sanity and effectiveness.

33. Patience is especially helpful in controversy or crisis times. Did you ever get mushy mud on your clothes? If you tried to brush it off immediately, all it did was smear it. Give it a little time and it dries into dust. Then you can brush it off easily and move on.

And one more that I especially appreciated:

21. Don't try to answer criticisms made against you regardless of their viciousness and lack of truth. Your friends will know better and your enemies will not believe your response regardless of how true it is.

Dan Collins, chairman of the general administration committee of the trustees, recommended we work with the Delta Group, a management-consulting firm in New York, to take a look at our structure and consider how we might make it better. The Delta Group recommended a major restructuring of the Sunday School Board. To help us figure out specifically what to do, we set up a series of work groups consisting mostly of staff-level employees. They were the ones who best knew the nuts and bolts of how things worked in the past, and we'd be depending on them to carry out any changes for the future.

We formed four work groups totaling about one hundred employees: the external/customer group, organizational option group, people resources group, and communications strategy group. We excused them from their regular work for six weeks, set them up in offices in another building, and challenged them to answer the question, "How can the Sunday School Board move into the twenty-first century?"

We got back a lot of wonderful, creative ideas, but the one that shocked everybody most was the organizational option group's recommendation that the Board needed a radical downsizing and realignment. They basically said, "This is what we really think you ought to do, but we don't think you've got enough guts to do it."

Yet it was exactly the kind of bold, aggressive step the Board needed to make. There's no doubt in my mind that the senior executive team would have come to a similar conclusion, but the fact that the employees themselves recommended it would give it tremendous power and momentum.

We simply had too many people for the amount of revenue we generated. Each employee represented about $92,000 in income. While this allowed us to tread water, it wasn't ever going to allow us to grow in our business and in our ministry and do the things we wanted to do. To get bigger, we were going to have to get smaller first.

It was also true that there were people at the Board, including some vice presidents and some employees with long years of service, who had never been properly equipped to do what they were in charge of doing. We had a multi-million-dollar ministry with former preachers in key positions. Added to that was my own lack of experience as a corporate executive! I had to have strong business people in those key positions who were committed Christians and experienced in business.

There were certain people who simply had to move on to other opportunities. They were good people serving in positions where their God-given talents were not being used and required talents for the job were not apparent. Legally we could have had them clean out their desks and put them on the street. But morally we had an obligation to do better; as Christians we were called to treat them with respect, dignity, and compassion.

The senior executive team, along with counsel from others, put together what we called the Voluntary Retirement Incentive Program. We designed it to include everybody we knew we wouldn't have a place for going forward. To qualify, employees had to be at least fifty-two years old and the total of their age and years of service had to be at least seventy-seven. If they retired voluntarily, they would get a retirement benefit equal to what they would have earned based on years of service, without an early payment penalty. Employees under sixty-two would get an additional benefit equal to what their Social Security benefit would be at sixty-two, and be paid that amount monthly until they were that age. Employees sixty-two and over would get a payment equal to what their benefit would be at sixty-five until they turned sixty-five.

The only problem was that, to keep from running afoul of discrimination laws, we had to offer the package to everyone who qualified. This meant there was some risk of losing people we didn't want to lose and drastically raising the cost of the program (which would be a write-off, though funded by the retirement trust fund).

When we announced the plan, there was some loud grumbling from a number of employees who felt we didn't appreciate their years of service. Mike Arrington had the unenviable task of telling the vice presidents involved that it was time for them to move on to new fields of service. Some workers protested loudly, and we told them they didn't have to leave us but that in three months there might not be a job for them.

It was a wrenching experience. One of the vice presidents was a man I'd gone to Baylor with, an old and dear friend. But I couldn't allow our friendship to get in the way of what needed to be done for the good of the Board and the Convention. Billie Pate, the leader of the work group that developed the organizational plan, told me the only time she couldn't sleep at night was when, after taking the names out of the boxes in the organizational chart in order to restructure it, they had put names back in the boxes of the new chart and realized who would be gone.

We were told that about 30 percent of eligible employees on the average took advantage of an offer like this. One hundred ninety-one people qualified under our guidelines for the early retirement incentive, which meant we should expect about fifty-seven of them to go. But 159 employees accepted the package! There was some grumbling about early retirement, but nobody ever complained about the financial incentives. It was a generous, expensive way to let these people find a new place of service if they wanted to, or to retire early.

November 1, 1992, was the date the early retirees left us: 159 employees retiring the same day. There were signs in the elevators bemoaning Black Tuesday and pictures of me with a crown on my head and a caption that said "King Jimmy." Some in the denomination read a political message into the process that absolutely wasn't there. In his book *Soul Freedom*, Grady Cothen later wrote that "about 150 of the God-called and God-led employees were forced into retirement. There were no substantive explanations or discernible reasons. . . . They were simply employed when the former leadership was in office." I can only assume Grady didn't realize that the *employees* came up with the plan, not I. And these were employees that the "former leadership" had hired.

While it was a large number of employees to leave at the same time, the departing retirees roughly represented the number of people who left every year through regular turnover.

Other employees who didn't like the new direction we were headed left on their own before long. There was some tension and anxiety early on but never what I would call a great exodus. And the experience level remained high: before early retirement, our employees averaged just over ten years at the Board; afterward the average was 8.8. Throughout the process, I never felt any hostility directed at me personally. It was against the situation, and I was the most visible symbol of change at the time.

We did have to fire a few people outright, but in almost every case they were flagrant wrongdoers. Several people falsified expense reports or stole from one of the bookstores among other things. One lady posted credits to her credit card for nonexistent merchandise that she said she returned and got to us for about $50,000. One of the most outrageous cases was a man who created a dummy corporation and sent us invoices for work he had never done. Eventually he collected about $350,000 before we caught him.

Despite all the challenges and tensions of downsizing and reorganizing, there was good news for the Board that year, much of it thanks to projects and products that were initiated by my predecessor. The 1991 *Baptist Hymnal*, published on the heels of two hymn collections that had been less successful, had sold two million copies its first year—an incredible vote of approval by Southern Baptist congregations (and other denominations as well) across the country. The MasterLife discipleship course had spread to 115 countries around the world in fifty-two languages. Sixty thousand copies sold of The New American Commentary and fifty thousand of the *Family Worship Bible* showed that we had strong core products and a faithful customer base.

When the year was over, 1992 turned out to be our first ever $200 million year. That meant more money that we could return to the state conventions, to the Cooperative Program, and to winning souls for Christ around the world. Now the challenge was how to serve the Lord and our fellow Southern Baptists better every year in a changing and uncertain world.

CHAPTER 32

Catching Up, Moving Ahead

Over the next five years the Sunday School Board of the Southern Baptist Convention changed more than it had in the last fifty years combined. We had some catching up to do. And we also wanted to position the Board as an indispensable source of supplies, publications, and support materials for the future.

Reinvigorating the Sunday school materials was one of our main objectives. The need for children's Sunday school lessons brought the Board into being in the first place. There may have been congregations out there that had used SSB materials for a century, but our sales figures told us our publications weren't keeping up with the needs of Southern Baptists. Though they provided more than 30 percent of our income and were our largest single revenue source, sales of curriculum and training products had been more or less flat for a long time, and in recent years the number of items sold had been slowly but steadily declining.

We set up a Sunday school task force that surveyed thirteen thousand people asking what they needed and wanted in Sunday school lessons and how the Board could make its lessons better. We knew our lesson series were grounded in Scripture and that the teaching was solid and unambiguous. The survey revealed that people also wanted them to be easier to use, requiring less preparation and support materials, and more relevant to contemporary life and culture.

Over the next two years we took our three curriculum programs completely apart and reassembled them. We never wavered in our allegiance to biblical inerrancy and traditional Southern Baptist interpretations. And we preserved the distinctions among the various series. But we came up with lessons that speak to today's churchgoers about today's issues. The Bible Book Series became the Explore the Bible Series. The historic Convention Uniform Series became the Family Bible Series, and the Board relinquished its longstanding ties to the Uniform Series. (On top of improving the lessons, this made economic sense too. For years we had done the lion's share of lesson development for the consortium of denominations that produced the Uniform Series, then turned around and paid the group $25,000 a year for permission to use the material!)

We didn't change the Life and Work Series as much but freshened and redesigned it as we worked on the others. Even that relatively minor change produced major improvement: four consecutive quarters of increased sales, measured by number sold, after twelve years of decline.

Another move that helped reposition the Board for the future was combining Broadman Press, Broadman Supplies, and Holman Bible Publishers to form Broadman & Holman (now B&H Publishing Group) in August 1992. Broadman Press had a distinguished list of titles stretching back over almost sixty years. Broadman Supplies offered literally thousands of different items for Sunday schools and represented the Board's oldest, largest, and most profitable line of products. Holman Bibles, descended from the oldest Bible publisher in America, marked its 250th anniversary by joining forces with its two Broadman counterparts. Though our ultimate aim remained the same as always—supplying materials to churches for spreading the gospel and winning souls for Christ—forming Broadman & Holman marked a new commitment to publishing, modern marketing, branding, distribution, and publicity. Those in turn would generate more resources for Christian outreach.

In its first year Broadman & Holman was ranked ninth out of the top ten Christian publishers in America by *Christian*

Retailing magazine. To the *Experiencing God* study series produced by the discipleship and family development division, Broadman & Holman added a hardcover *Experiencing God* book by Henry Blackaby and Claude King, elaborating on Dr. Blackaby's teaching about how to grow personally closer to God. By 1995 the SSB warehouse was shipping thirteen hundred copies of *Experiencing God* every day. An online study course was added the next year, along with materials in Spanish and Korean. A youth edition, videotape series, and the *Experiencing God Study Bible* combined with 3.4 million study guides sold to make this a landmark series in the history of the Board.

In 1995 we introduced books by Beth Moore, whose energetic and inspiring presentations to women about their role in God's kingdom and the joy to be found in it attracted an ever-increasing audience. Bible studies for women were published by our Church Resources Division, and B&H followed those with trade books, putting the Bible study materials in a popular trade book style. Within three years her books sold half a million copies, and she and the SSB became strong partners together in her women's ministry.

Broadman & Holman also expanded into video production and distribution. They launched the *Secret Adventures* series for children and teens, built around the daily trials and triumphs of Drea Thomas and her family and friends. These shows were filmed in California by top professionals and included classic-style hand-drawn animation sequences.

Each show had a guest star: Michael W. Smith made his acting debut in one show; John Tesh of the popular TV show *Entertainment Tonight* was in another; pro basketball star A. C. Green appeared too, along with other personalities. *Secret Adventures* won a whole shelf full of awards for its high-quality, family-friendly entertainment value, including a Gold Camera Award from the US International Film and Video Festival, yet each show also had a biblical lesson for Drea to learn. Although widely acclaimed, the series did not sell enough for us to continue that effort.

Closer to home, B&H chose a Nashville studio to produce *Storybook Tree*, a fanciful series for young children featuring Henry Cory and a cast of puppet characters.

B&H gained exclusive religious distribution rights to the hit CBS television show *Christy*, based on the novel by Catherine Marshall. Through an arrangement with the Billy Graham Evangelistic Organization, Broadman & Holman Video agreed to distribute Dr. Graham's World Wide Film catalog of inspirational movies, crusades, and other topics. By 1995 the Sunday School Board was the largest distributor of Christian videos in the world. We also got into record retailing by introducing Genesis Records to complement our seven-year-old Genevox music publishing business.

The Board considered what to do about Ridgecrest and Glorieta conference centers. They needed remodeling and modernizing. Ridgecrest attendance was flat, and use of Glorieta was declining. As the twenty-first century approached, people were changing their ideas about what they wanted in church retreat facilities. The Spartan rooms and basic services that earlier generations had been satisfied with were no longer enough. The SBC centers were losing business to more modern, more comfortable competitors.

As a first step toward responding to the needs and expectations of contemporary visitors, the conference centers set up their first ever toll-free reservation line and began accepting reservations with credit cards. We knew that comprehensive overhauls of the centers were essential, but they would also be expensive. Ridgecrest and Glorieta broke even at best; they couldn't fund their own rehabilitation. We didn't want to siphon any money away from what Southern Baptists would give to their own churches or accept any funds from the Cooperative Program.

What we decided to do was identify donors willing to contribute beyond their usual gifts to fund renovations that would bring these historic retreats up to modern standards. The Rutland Family Foundation of Covington, Georgia, stepped up with a $1 million gift to build a three hundred-seat chapel at Ridgecrest. By setting that generous example, they played a major part in moving the funding process forward.

Centrifuge, the youth ministry that had developed almost by accident at Glorieta and become incredibly popular, was revised to use in inner-city ministry to children. The goal here and with numerous other programs was to respond to the fact that Southern Baptists had become a melting pot of more than one hundred ethnic or language groups. By the mid-1990s there were approximately thirty-eight thousand Southern Baptist churches, twelve hundred of which were African-American and twenty-six hundred Hispanic.

During these years we also started to turn the Baptist Book Stores around. We equipped the managers system-wide with advertising and promotional ideas and tools for helping them make some waves in their communities. We reconfigured the book ordering process, consolidating it in Nashville. At my first trustee meeting as president of the SSB, I had learned that some of our stores were selling books by a televangelist whose views were heretical and who claimed God healed people through him and "proved" it by highlighting these dramatic "cures" on his TV show. That sort of claim can really confuse people as to what Christianity is all about. We immediately withdrew all his books and others' whose theology was not compatible with the Baptist Faith and Message. We had to give the stores clear guidelines and then expect they would follow them. The bookstores also set up toll-free mail-order services in English and Spanish.

The Sunday School Board realigned its computer services and systems. Some of our computers were the first ones the Board bought and were now twenty years old. We had about twenty-five different mainframe systems throughout our operations. In 1995 the Board purchased a Vista Publishing System that replaced all of the old systems. It cost almost

$5 million but was projected to pay for itself in operational savings in only two years. The Board also handed off its last remaining Church Information Systems (CIS) customers to Automated Church Systems of Florence, Alabama, ending a service that had never come near reaching its potential.

In the first year or two of my administration, we were still fine-tuning some of our organizational changes and managing the business side of the wide-reaching alterations. Including write-offs that should have been made earlier, the board experienced an $8.2 million operating loss in the 1993–1994 fiscal year. The trustees wisely decided to absorb the loss and clean up the books for the new road ahead, taking steps to see that we didn't have a deficit again.

Forty-five more positions at the board were eliminated, and the senior executive team was revised, though some of their job responsibilities stayed essentially the same: Mike Arrington became vice president for corporate services; Gene Mims, vice president for church growth and programs; E. V. King, vice president for finance and administration; Chuck Wilson, vice president for trade and retail markets. In the larger management group, Doug Anderson became director of the marketing research department; Harry Piland, director of church growth and Sunday school division; Roy Edgemon, director of discipleship and family development division; and Jim Shull, director of production services department.

Once again, these changes came as a result of the employee-led task forces.

Retirements and changes led to some more fine-tuning in the mid-1990s: Ted Warren, a successful oil industry executive, became our chief operating officer; Jim Carter drew on his military and banking experience as vice president for finance and administration; Mark Scott brought his own financial experience to the position of vice president of retail; and Ken Stephens, a former missionary with wide experience in the Christian publishing industry, became director of Trade Publishing. Gene Mims, the only pastor on our leadership team besides me, and Mike Arrington continued with their previous responsibilities.

Between 1992 and 1995 overall retail sales for the Board grew by nearly 50 percent. This allowed us to make additional investments in the future. For example, the Board bought a new four-color printing press that saved $1 million a year by printing in-house jobs that had always gone to outside vendors.

As exciting as it was to see the Board infused with all this energy, and as encouraging as it was to see revenue grow from $202 million in 1992 to $284 million in 1997, it was even more rewarding to see how the SSB reached the world for Christ through its products and financial contributions. The message went out in books, periodicals, Bible study materials, music, the Internet, and the lives and witness of almost two thousand employees and their families.

Among that list, True Love Waits was and is a unique outreach tool. It was originally a program for teenage students encouraging young men and women to sign pledges that they would remain sexually pure in preparation for marriage. The movement commanded the international spotlight on July 19, 1993, when 211,000 signed pledge cards were displayed in the National Mall in Washington, DC, and covered the entire mall from the Washington Monument to the Capitol.

The Christian message of chastity until marriage runs counter to overwhelming pressure from today's culture to live in the moment and "do what comes naturally." What the culture doesn't say is that doing what comes naturally leads to venereal disease, AIDS, physical and psychological torment, broken marriages, broken families, single-parent households mired in poverty, and a long list of other practical disasters. Moreover, it's against biblical teaching, which shows us how to live healthy, happy, fulfilled lives if we follow God's plan.

True Love Waits has been a beacon for Christian morality in a culture that mocks and belittles our Christian worldview. Even more exciting, where it has been allowed, True Love Waits has made incredible strides in controlling the AIDS epidemic in Africa. As I write this, there is no cure for AIDS and no prospect of a cure on the horizon. True Love Waits can literally keep young men and women from contracting a 100 percent fatal disease by inspiring them to take a biblical approach to their relationship. This ministry is one of the most important evangelism tools that I've seen in my lifetime.

Another kind of outreach the Sunday School Board began that I believe helped transform the entire organization was in the summer of 1996, when the Board began partnering with the Foreign Mission Board (now the International Mission Board) to grant Board employees paid leave to go on short-term mission trips. This program has grown into a major focus of Board activity: now not only do we send money and supplies into the field; we send our own people, who are transformed by the experience for the rest of their lives. They come back to their jobs here with a new sense of purpose and calling that gives them a renewed sense of dedication. It has also transformed the churches they attend as they share their overseas experiences.

It was an exhilarating few years, and by the late 1990s the tide had turned unmistakably. Our products were better, our systems were more efficient, our management team and employees displayed a new sense of optimism and drive. My job was to keep building bridges between the Board and Southern Baptists across the country, to give employees the resources they needed to work, provide a clear direction, then get out of the way. During the 1996–1997 fiscal year I was on the road 144 days and visited twenty-nine states. The news was encouraging; our denomination noticed we were doing things differently. Now that we had everything pointed in the right direction and under way, the next big challenge was to keep it going.

CHAPTER 33

LifeWay

For years the number of Baptist Book Stores had been stalled at around sixty-two or sixty-three. One factor that contributed to this plateau in growth was that some retail centers resisted a store with Baptist in the name. I believe it was also true that some shoppers who would have liked the store if they had ever gone in, didn't go in because they weren't Baptist and figured there was nothing inside for them.

Though the stores' main objective was to make Southern Baptist materials easier for Southern Baptists and prospective Christians to buy, they had developed into modern retail bookstores. They carried a range of books besides SSB titles, music, videos, gift items, stationery, greeting cards, and more. They had become a lot more than their name implied.

The bookstores were in the process of changing their name to LifeWay Christian Stores when we decided to consider a name change for the SSB. At that time the bookstores put a hold on their plans until the decision was made regarding a new name for the SSB.

Since Sunday school materials represented only about 30 percent of what we did as a corporation, a biblical and more comprehensive name was in order. We were bigger, more competitive, with broader horizons than at any time in our history. A lengthy process ended with the decision to ask the SBC to allow us to officially change our name to LifeWay Christian Resources. On June 9, 1998, at the annual convention in Salt Lake City, the SBC agreed. After 107 years, looking ahead to the second hundred years, the Board traded its original name for LifeWay Christian Resources of the Southern Baptist Convention.

Of course there were those who questioned such a fundamental change after so long, but the new name was on solid theological ground. It comes from the familiar Bible passage in John 14:6 when Jesus says, "I am the way, the truth, and the life." We put *life* and *way* in the name, and a cross, the symbol for truth, in our new logo. Though in form it's modern, the very name is a witness for Christ. It also describes the extensive range of Christian resources we now carry, without implying our merchandise is specifically for Baptists. Although every resource we provide is consistent with the Baptist Faith and Message statement, thousands of non-Baptists are using our resources.

As we began implementing the change approved at the 1998 Convention, we surveyed more than six hundred ministers and laity across the country. The majority strongly supported the new name. Some added that LifeWay gave Southern Baptists a valuable and exciting new ministry tool. As quickly as practical, we changed all the signs and stationery, the imprints on all our products, and even the identification on our Nashville headquarters (though we did leave the historical "Baptist Sunday School Board" carved in limestone above the columns in front of the Frost Building).

So now we were LifeWay. With so much change in the air, this seemed like the right time to revisit our mission statement. It had served us well through years of dramatic growth and restructuring. But now our sights were higher. We could do more. Rather than limiting our mission statement to providing resources, it was time to raise the bar, to produce resources that could transform people who encountered them.

Our new mission statement became: "As God works through us, we will help people and churches know Jesus Christ and seek His kingdom by providing biblical solutions that spiritually transform individuals and cultures." In its shortened form on business cards and phone messages it became "Biblical solutions for life."

The number of new projects and resources grew as fast as we could develop the ability to start them. For example, in the spring of 1996 LifeWay introduced LeaderCare in response to a need that people are hesitant to discuss: pastor burnout. Because it's an uncomfortable issue, it tends to be ignored until a crisis develops, which can be devastating for a pastor in distress, his family, and his congregation. The stress on a pastor can be unremitting. Because he's seen as the strong, spiritually mature figure in a community, there's often nowhere he can turn when he himself is looking for counseling, a break from the pressure, or just needs to let off steam. LeaderCare established a pastor hotline, provided counseling, and hosted retreats for pastors who feel overwhelmed by their responsibilities. The result has been a significant drop in the number of forced terminations of Southern Baptist pastors.

LifeWay also partnered with churches and other SBC entities to develop promising ideas that they came up with. In January 1998 LifeWay joined forces with First Baptist Church of Daytona Beach, Florida, to make their FAITH Sunday school evangelism strategy available across the denomination. This Sunday school program (its acronym is based on the words Forgiveness, Available, Impossible, Trust, and Heaven) includes evangelism that shows members how to reach out to their own neighbors—the unsaved, former churchgoers, and members—with the gospel. Implemented on a large scale,

FAITH results were impressive for churches of every size, in every part of the country. By the year 2000 more than twenty-two thousand people representing five thousand churches had attended more than two hundred FAITH clinics, with the numbers growing every year.

Ministry-Fuge, or M-Fuge for short, was another cosponsored outreach. This was an evangelism program developed in cooperation with the International Mission Board. Begun in 1999, M-Fuge offered high school students the chance to travel overseas to share their faith.

Building on its success with Henry Blackaby, Beth Moore, and The New American Commentary, Broadman & Holman Publishers made its strongest push ever into secular stores. The publisher branched out into new literary worlds with books that weren't overtly religious but were built on a biblical worldview. They began publishing an exciting line of fiction titles, a range of children's books—always a popular category—along with value-priced paperbacks, and a collection of gift items.

LifeWay International was formed to make these and other tools—Sunday school and training materials, Bibles, periodicals, supplies, and much more—available to churches around the world. By the end of its first full year of operation in 1999, LifeWay International was serving churches and missions in sixty countries.

B&H marked a historic first in June 2000 when *Payne Stewart: The Authorized Autobiography* spent thirteen weeks on the *New York Times* bestseller list. Stewart was a top professional golfer known for his elegant retro-style plus-fours, snap-brim caps, and golf shoes tipped in sterling silver. He was also known for his bad temper and strong language. At the height of his success, Stewart had a Christian conversion experience that transformed his personality and reinvigorated his playing. After his death in a plane crash, his widow, Tracey, chose Broadman & Holman to publish his story. Writing with Tennessee author Ken Abraham, Tracey celebrated Payne's life and Christian faith; the book carried Payne's testimony to the *Today* show, *Sports Illustrated*, and other major secular media outlets.

On the retailing side, LifeWay Christian stores opened twenty-five stores in about three years, far and away the fastest growth in its history, and opened the one-hundredth LifeWay store in Knoxville, Tennessee, in 2001. The inventory, design, lighting, and displays were light-years ahead of where they had been only a few years earlier. LifeWay had caught up with the bookstore competition and was now preparing to pass it by.

Another important modernizing move was establishing the LifeWay E-business group. As more communication and commerce found its way to the Internet, LifeWay needed to respond. LifeWaystores.com allowed people anywhere in the world to order from LifeWay electronically. Soon we had customers in eighty countries.

In February 2001 LifeWayLINK came online. This is a service that assists churches in setting up and maintaining their own Web sites. Though there's a charge for some services, the basic Web hosting service is free. LifeWay also introduced family-friendly online filtered Internet access. As the Internet worked its way into the mainstream of American life, it became clear that some of the content would be blasphemous, pornographic, or just plain revolting. (It's like ordering a book and having the vendor send you an offensive magazine along with it saying, "But you don't *have* to look at it.") The LifeWay service electronically filtered out offensive material.

Of all the exciting changes taking place at LifeWay at the turn of the twenty-first century, nothing was more essential than the Holman Christian Standard Bible. The idea for it came about as a result of looking at what was happening in the world of Bible translation. For hundreds of years the dominant translation of the original Hebrew, Aramaic, and Greek into English was the King James Bible, published in 1611. In America, the Revised Standard Version of 1952 was one of the first popular alternatives. It let people read the Scriptures without struggling to understand the Shakespearian language of the King James.

Several other popular translations appeared, including the New International Version, which eventually became the most popular new translation overall. While it was a good thing to translate the Bible so more people could understand it more clearly, some modern translations changed the original biblical text to reflect the translators' modern cultural preferences and opinions. One widely discussed area was in the biblical use of gender. In the name of contemporary political correctness, translators changed "son" to "child," and "father" to "parent," and made many more changes that altered the meaning of the original text.

How could Christians be sure their Scripture translations would always be faithful to God's Word? How could they be certain cultural preferences, political pressure, or profit motive would not persuade a translator to bend the words a little here and there to make them more palatable, even if they were less true? If they held fast to the truth now, what would keep them from altering the translation in fifty years? Or in five years? One surefire way to keep a translation truthful was for Bible-believing Christians to own one themselves.

After looking at several options, Broadman & Holman reached an agreement with the Bible scholar Arthur Farstad to sponsor and publish a translation project he had been working on independently for several years already. But in a sad turn of events, the Lord called Dr. Farstad home only weeks after signing a contract with B&H.

Dr. Ed Blum, who had worked closely with Dr. Farstad, and B&H executive editor David Shepherd took over the project. Working in groups based around the world, ninety scholars retranslated every word of the Old and New Testaments directly from the original languages. Their aim was to produce a translation that was both accurate and relatively easy to read. By the time the whole Bible was completed in 2004, LifeWay had spent about $10 million on this work, by far the biggest investment ever in a single publishing project. But to me the result is priceless: a faithful translation that will remain faithful regardless of the cultural, social, or political winds swirling around it. Other Christians evidently agree. Comments all around have been positive, and sales are strong, with promising potential for the future.

By 2001, the end of my tenth full year as president, all of us at LifeWay could see that the Lord had showered His blessings on us and on our work. Revenues had more than doubled to $414 million. We had forty-four hundred employees, evenly divided between permanent and temporary workers, and productivity per permanent worker was up about 50 percent.

Credit for this ten-year trend goes to a strong management team of world-class businessmen and inspired leaders. Mike Arrington and Gene Mims continued in the roles they had filled so well from the beginning. Ted Warren, Mark Scott, Ken Stephens, and Jim Carter had joined us at various times along the way and added their shoulders to the wheel. On March 1, 2002, LifeWay added a technology division; because technology had become a vital part of our communication and outreach, we also added a leadership team position in technology. Tim Vineyard stepped up with his tremendous technological experience to assume that responsibility.

After ten years I also took time to reflect on the initiatives that drove us to do what we did and shared them with LifeWay employees, management, and friends:

1. *Building and strengthening relationships.* All my life

I've believed that having good relationships is the
key to successful leadership and a successful team.
LifeWay also has to take the initiative in partnering
with individuals and groups outside the Southern
Baptist Convention that share our commitment to
witness for Christ.

2. *Helping the churches.* One of our top priorities is
meeting the needs of Southern Baptist churches;
our church resources division must respond to those
needs, both expressed and unexpressed.

3. *Strengthening families.* LifeWay must take the lead in
strengthening families throughout the Convention.
We already offer a long list of resources and special
events, but we can do better.

4. *Positioning ourselves for even more effective ministry.*
We're doing that in many ways, most importantly
with the Holman Christian Standard Bible,
modernization and expansion of LifeWay Christian
Stores, and a new, more ambitious than ever ten-
year plan to completely revitalize the Ridgecrest and
Glorieta conference centers. (In addition to the new
Rutland Chapel, a new 120-room lodge at Ridgecrest
marked one of the first steps in this ambitious
project.)

5. *Expanding our global focus.* In recent years LifeWay
has trained 167 international volunteers to train
church leaders around the world; seen forty-two

thousand people commit their lives to Christ as a result of LifeWay mission trips; and made LifeWay resources available in eighty-one countries through local distributors.

6. *Becoming a kingdom enterprise.* LifeWay strongly supports the SBC Empowering Kingdom Growth initiative by dedicating our resources to prayer and the furthering of God's kingdom.

In 2002 LifeWay reached the *New York Times* bestseller list again, this time with *Mission Compromised*, a novel by controversial former National Security Council officer Oliver North. Under direction of his superiors, but in violation of US law and public policy, Lieutenant Colonel North had funneled money to US-backed rebels fighting to overthrow the Marxist government of Nicaragua in the mid-1980s. North had survived his public dismissal and prosecution—part of what became known as the Iran-Contra Affair (the money had come from secret weapon sales to Iran; the Nicaraguan rebels were called Contras)—to become a widely respected commentator and broadcaster. He also made his mark as a dynamic Christian and an outspoken supporter of a biblical worldview. *Mission Compromised*, his first fiction work, saw more than 300,000 copies in print during its first year.

Also in 2002 LifeWay completed another headquarters expansion, adding a new cafeteria, main entrance, more than eight hundred new parking spaces in a multi-level garage, and continuing a multiyear process of renovating existing space. We also built a prayer chapel honoring the late Harry Piland, longtime director of LifeWay Sunday school, whose friends helped finance its construction.

The LifeWay management team and employees continued coming up with creative new ways for us to deliver "biblical solutions for life." Beth Moore, consistently one of our most popular authors, hosted her first ever Internet-only Bible study, *Believing God,* that attracted fifty-four thousand participants. We jumped into the large and growing home-school market. We introduced the *TruthQuest Student Bible* based on our Holman® CSB translation. We launched the new LifeWay ¡Español! brand to more effectively reach the millions of Spanish-speaking Christians who could benefit from our materials. We partnered with a large Brazilian publisher to offer some of our products in Portuguese.

The good Lord had us rocking along on an exciting course, and that got me to thinking about next steps. I had always said that when it came time for me to retire, I wanted to leave when people were asking, "Why?" not when they were asking "When?" LifeWay was in good shape: business was up 250 percent overall since 1991; Broadman & Holman revenue had tripled; we doubled the number of bookstores and tripled their business. I was in excellent health and couldn't wait to get to work every morning.

It was the right time to think about passing the torch.

CHAPTER 34

From Here On Out

Nobody ever suggested to me that it was time to retire. But I had known for several years that I wanted to finish out my service at LifeWay differently than I'd seen other denominational leaders do. Having watched how difficult it was for Dr. Criswell to turn loose of things in Dallas when the time came, I promised myself then and there that I would pray sincerely for God to let me know when to retire. Financial necessity caused Dr. Frost to stay on for years after he should have; controversy and disagreement with the trustees brought Dr. Elder's presidency to a rocky conclusion. I believed that the real test of my ministry would be not what happened while I was president of LifeWay but what happened when

I left. That meant that it was critically important for me to leave the right way.

I believe there are people who build a great ministry over time and then sabotage their own legacy because they don't know when or how to relinquish their position. They don't know how to make the transition; they don't know how to get out of the way and hand the work off to somebody else. One of the challenges about retiring is that you only get one chance to do it right.

I thought about advice I'd received and my own experience coming to the Board in 1991. I remember Dr. Sullivan telling me he didn't even know where to park or where his office was on his first day. Badly needed reforms had been delayed, and he faced a daunting task in reinvigorating and restructuring the organization. He told me, "I had to come in here with a baseball bat and take over."

I learned exactly what he meant when I came to Nashville. Nobody was particularly glad I was there. It wasn't because they had anything against me personally; it was just that there was so much tension and change to deal with, and I was the symbol of a new and unknown state of affairs. I didn't want my successor to be in that situation. I wanted the next president of LifeWay to come in the door with flags waving and people cheering and everybody excited.

To help make sure that happened, I wanted to retire at the top of my game, not after I was clearly declining and everybody was wondering when the old codger was finally going to give it up. I wanted to retire in a way that would position the new president to succeed. More than anything else, his success would define my legacy.

I thought about retiring at sixty-five. But I felt great, the organization was doing well, and there were some things I really wanted to see through to their conclusion. The Holman Christian Standard Bible® translation was still unfinished. The conference center refurbishing was still not where I wanted it to be: at that point we hadn't dedicated enough energy and money to the task. So I kept on going.

About three years later Ted Warren, my chief operating officer, asked me when I thought I might retire. I said, "I don't know. As long as I feel good and feel like I'm up to the job, I'll probably go at least until I'm seventy, and perhaps longer."

He looked at me and said, "That's not very comforting to the people who work with you."

I said, "What do you mean?"

He explained, "It's so uncertain. People don't know what they can count on and what they can't."

He was right. I went home and talked with Carol Ann about it, and we agreed that Ted was right. We really needed to set a time and then just work toward that time. So I decided I'd work through my seventieth birthday in 2005 and retire early in 2006. That would give me fifteen years at LifeWay and fifty-five years of Christian service all together. (Plus I'd get to stay for all the Christmas parties!) I told the executive management team what I'd decided but waited until it was time to start the process of looking for a new president before I officially informed the trustees. If anybody asked me about it, I wasn't evasive. I'd said I would probably retire after I turned seventy. I never tried to keep it a secret.

Seventy was a good time for me to move on and for LifeWay to have a new, younger leader. When I came as president, not a single vice president was on the Internet; by 1996 they were all on the net, all had e-mail and had transitioned into the digital age. If the next fifteen years was going to bring as much change as the previous fifteen did, LifeWay needed someone who could see them through that period and chart a bold course for the years beyond. Technology was transforming the publishing business, transforming the retailing business, and transforming the methodology of Christian ministry and outreach around the world. I considered it an accomplishment when I could open my e-mail on the first try. A new leader at LifeWay would have a command of twenty-first-century capabilities that I could scarcely imagine.

I gave the trustees a year's notice that I wanted to retire, and they immediately formed a search committee. My plans were never a surprise; in fact, when it finally came, my retirement was almost a nonevent. Trustees kept employees abreast of everything that was going on. Ted Warren and I met with the search committee and gave them a big notebook we'd put together of information about LifeWay and the kind of leadership they needed to consider as they looked at various candidates. During our annual fall retreat in 2004, we spent the whole time on the presidential transition, discussing what traits and skills the new president would need and how to make the process as smooth as possible. (One fun exercise: what would make a bad president?)

That was the only time I met with the search committee. They gave me periodic updates, but I didn't even know whom they were considering until they got down to the last three. I was surprised at their final choice, not because he wasn't the best candidate for the job but that for such a high-profile position he was somebody most Southern Baptists did not know. He was a seminary professor, and everyone had assumed a large church pastor or denominational executive would be chosen.

Thom S. Rainer was founding dean of the Billy Graham School of Missions, Evangelism and Church Growth at Southern Baptist Theological Seminary in Louisville, Kentucky. Before coming to Southern Seminary in 1994, he had been a church pastor. He was perhaps best known as a consultant and researcher on church growth and cultural trends, and the author of numerous books on the subject. Before earning his master's and doctorate degrees from Southern, Thom had a successful career in the world of finance and was vice president of corporate lending for a major regional bank. His many gifts, his dedication, and his passion for ministry made him an ideal candidate for the job. His wife, Nellie Jo, and sons Sam, Art, and Jess have enthusiastically supported him in his new place of service.

He came to LifeWay in time to work alongside me for three and a half months, meeting the executive staff, attending meetings, and becoming familiar with all the issues and opportunities he would face as president. We took him across the street to meet with the leaders of the SBC Executive Committee and other key people in the SBC. We took him to meet the mayor. We did everything we could think of to help him feel comfortable and to equip him for the task. With a smile he says, "My spiritual gift is ignorance," but he learned fast. He and Nellie Jo did a wonderful thing to introduce themselves to the LifeWay community: they systematically went around the whole Nashville headquarters complex, meeting and shaking hands with every employee.

Thom wanted to have a hand in coordinating and managing his executive team. Also, as I had done fifteen years earlier, he brought a capable and trustworthy associate with him to assist him in his new role. Tom Hellams, who had been executive assistant to the president of Southern Seminary, was appointed vice president and executive associate to the president at LifeWay. This meant that my COO, Ted Warren, would not have a place in the new administration. Thom wanted Ted's departure to take place before I left. I told Thom at the time I thought that was an awkward and distracting step to take, but looking back I believe it was much better to have done it then than for him to try to do it early in his own presidency.

On February 6, 2006, in Van Ness Auditorium at the Nashville headquarters, Dr. Thom Rainer was installed as the ninth president of LifeWay Christian Resources. SBC president Bobby Welch was there to welcome and congratulate him; Albert Mohler, president of Southern Seminary, Morris Chapman, president of the SBC Executive Committee, Wayne Hamrick, chairman of the LifeWay trustees, and many other denominational leaders took part in the festivities as well.

By that time, Carol Ann and I had already built a new house west of Dallas in Colleyville, and made plans to join First Baptist Church in Euless where I last pastored. Our children and grandchildren were all in Texas, as were many of our friends from the days in Euless and First Baptist Dallas. Moving there was like a homecoming. And it gave me the chance to look back a little and to look ahead.

People have asked me over the years what my management philosophy was. I don't suppose I ever had a formal management policy. I don't ever remember not getting what I wanted, but I don't ever remember demanding it. That was the way I led LifeWay and the way I pastored a church. I believe the key to being an effective leader is getting people to think your ideas are theirs. If you let them take the credit, they'll buy into the idea and work all-out for it. Leaders have to give their people freedom to work, communicate clearly, and build good relationships.

By giving people freedom, I mean giving them real decision-making responsibility, removing the roadblocks to their doing what needs to be done, and letting them know that it's all right to fail. People who are too afraid of failure never try anything. They'll never implement new ideas or do something a new way because it might not work. You have to hold people accountable for their actions and decisions, but you can't make them afraid to make mistakes. Overbearing rules or leading by intimidation does nothing but run an operation into the ground.

When people make mistakes, I always ask, "Did you mean to do that? Did you do it on purpose?"

Of course they say, "No."

Then I say, "Well, don't do it again. Now let's get on with our work."

There's no shame in an honest mistake. But learn from your error and don't make the same mistake twice.

When I first came to LifeWay, we had one of the few satellite uplinks in Nashville. The others were owned by television stations that used them all the time. Since we used ours only six hours a day, we frequently subleased time on it to businesses, record companies, and other groups. One day we got word that country music star Hank Williams Jr. wanted to use our uplink for a live feed promoting his upcoming tour. The LifeWay people involved explained that there were certain rules he had to follow: no swearing, no promotion of alcohol, no lewd gestures, and so forth. He agreed and came to our TV studio for the broadcast.

During the telecast Hank got all excited about the tour, which was sponsored by Budweiser beer, and started referring to his "Budweiser Tour." It wasn't anything disrespectful on his part; he was just enthusiastic about his subject and forgot all about our "no alcohol" rule.

After Hank was finished, somebody came to me appalled at what had happened. Since the feed was live, there was nothing anybody could do about it now. I said, "Did you do it on purpose?" Of course they didn't. They had explained the rules, and Hank had agreed to them. The mistake wasn't their fault. "Then it's OK," I said. "If we get any flak about it, I'll take the hit."

A week went by, then two weeks, and I thought we'd slipped it through without anybody noticing. Then I got a call from George Kinchen, our trustee in West Virginia. There was an article in the Huntington, West Virginia, paper about Hank and his Budweiser Tour, with a photo taken from the TV screen. There was Hank in a TV studio with a television monitor in the background labeled Baptist Sunday School Board. I told George what happened, and he forgave me, and that was the last I ever heard of it. Some people said if it had happened under one of my predecessors, somebody would have gotten fired. But my letting it go went a long way toward winning credibility with the employees; the story got around the Board pretty fast.

I think a leader's job is to create an atmosphere where people can succeed. I'll give them the credit if things go well and take the blame if they don't. A leader has to be secure enough about who he is to let other people take credit for his good ideas. He should not see other people's ideas as a threat to his leadership. He learns to bring out the best in people and help them succeed. Jim Collins wrote a book called *Good to Great* where he proposes that the greatest leaders of the latter half of the twentieth century weren't the Lee Iacoccas and other high-profile people but were humble, self-assuming people who didn't seek the spotlight.

Those who are genuinely humble don't realize how humble they are. It's been one of the great blessings of my life to know Billy Graham personally. I agree with all the writers who say the same thing one way or another: he has no idea how important he is. He is genuinely astonished at what God has done in his life and doesn't consider himself important.

Humble people aren't afraid of looking bad, which means they're not afraid to take risks. The more worried you are about looking good, the less you're going to risk tarnishing your perfect public image. A few years ago at LifeWay, we revamped our Sunday school lessons series and ended up doing away with a series that represented something like $90 million in annual revenue. It was a huge risk. But it was a bigger risk not to look ahead to ways of using our resources to produce even better and more effective lessons in the future.

Risk taking is what has allowed LifeWay to support so many components of Southern Baptist outreach over the years. Milton Ferguson, president of Midwestern Seminary, told me that LifeWay saved Midwestern from bankruptcy in the 1960s with a gift of $250,000, though there's no record of it anywhere. Dr. Sullivan said more than once that the old Sunday School Board saved every entity in the Southern Baptist Convention from bankruptcy during the Great Depression.

When I was ending my term as president of the Southern Baptist Convention, I had lunch with Herschel Hobbs. He pointed at an exit sign above the door. "See that exit sign?" he asked. "That's what you are about to be: an ex-it." Now I'm an ex-it at LifeWay. But I don't think people in Christian service ever really retire. They simply shift from one area of service to another.

One thing I'll be doing in the future is rooting for LifeWay and cheering on Thom Rainer. There's so much going on there as they head further into their second century. I'll also continue preaching and have been invited to teach as well. I'm going to keep up with my mission work too. In fact, I've got to get finished with this book so I can go to Africa next month. For years I've kept a huge glass vase on the floor beside the desk in my study at home. Every time I get back from a trip, I put my boarding passes in the vase. I don't know how many hundreds of passes are in there already, but the pile seems to be growing as fast as ever.

One of the passions in my life now is a new ministry of LifeWay called "A Defining Moment." This is a philanthropic initiative I was able to start during my last year as president to raise money for Christian outreach programs around the world that LifeWay is well positioned to undertake but which they would never have the financial resources to accomplish.

One major objective of "A Defining Moment" is to help produce the first translation of the Bible into Mandarin Chinese from the original languages by Chinese scholars. The Gospel of John is already completed. The New Testament will be finished in time to distribute during the 2008 Olympic Games in Bejing—a once-in-a-lifetime opportunity to gain access to Chinese people on a broad scale; the Old Testament will follow in 2010, when the world's fair is held in Shanghai.

Another big project "A Defining Moment" will support is carrying the True Love Waits message of sexual abstinence to thirty African countries. In Uganda, where TLW has been in place since 1993 and the wife of Uganda's president has been its national spokesperson, the incidence of HIV/AIDS infection in the population has gone from 30 percent to 6 percent. That represents six million people and their families spared the tragedy of AIDS.

"A Defining Moment" will help Cuban Christians prepare for the inevitable upheaval that is coming when Fidel Castro passes from the scene and his Communist dictatorship crumbles. It will help Baptist churches in Kenya train teachers, Bible instructors, and other kingdom builders. It will nurture discipleship training in India, where people are hungry for Christian teaching and the thousands being saved need resources for growth to Christian maturity.

This giving initiative has the potential to achieve miraculous results in Christian outreach and is set up to be implemented by a relative handful of people who share the vision, have the means, and realize that all they have comes from God and that as good stewards it's up to them to use some of it to advance His kingdom. As volunteer ambassador-in-chief and head cheerleader, I will be spending a lot of time on "A Defining Moment" over the next few years and expect to add plenty more boarding passes to my collection.

Dad always said, "Be kind to everybody because everybody's having a hard time." If there's anything I've learned over fifty-five years of ministry, it's that kindness is indispensable in leadership, in ministry, and in life. God loves us all even though we're all sinners who can never atone for all our sins. I believe we should do all we can to love others as God loves us. Encourage people, love them unconditionally, communicate clearly and often, praise them when they do well, and forgive them when they fail.

In the 1970s when automated telephone services first came out, I decided to record a Christmas message to members of my congregation. A company in Dallas had a system that would play a recorded message and enable the listener to record a response. I drove down to the company's recording studio and sat in the little sound booth to read my message. In my remarks I wished everybody at church a Merry Christmas and said that God loved them, my family and I loved them and wished them the Lord's blessing in the year ahead, and asked if there was anything I could do for them that Christmas.

When I finished, I looked through the glass into the control room and saw the audio engineer bawling his eyes out.

"Jack!" I asked. "What's the matter with you?"

He looked up at me, tears running down his face, and said, "Preacher, do you realize how many people never hear anybody say 'I love you'?"

Whether it's an expression of Christian love, a Bible lesson for children, a commentary on Christlike living, or anything else stemming from the Word of God, a Christian's ability and willingness to share the gospel is at the heart of his faith. For 115 years now, LifeWay Christian Resources and its historical forbearers have worked diligently to communicate the truth of the Bible. In many forms and many languages, LifeWay is continuing that work into its second century.

George W. Truett once said, "Hats off to the past, coats off to the future." A look back at the LifeWay legacy gives us much to celebrate. A look at our world today reveals we have plenty left to do. It is my prayer that the men and women of LifeWay will be inspired by all who have gone before them to spend a diligent season of labor in the Lord's vineyard, and that they will enjoy the peace and fulfillment that comes only from serving Him.

Bibliography

Baker, Robert A. *The Story of the Sunday School Board.* Nashville: Convention Press, 1966.

Barnes, William Wright. *The Southern Baptist Convention 1845–1953.* Nashville: Broadman Press, 1954.

Burroughs, P. E. *Fifty Fruitful Years: The Story of the Sunday School Board of the Southern Baptist Convention.* Nashville: Broadman Press, 1941.

Clemmons, William Preston. *The Development of a Sunday School Strategy in the Southern Baptist Convention, 1896–1926.* Doctoral dissertation (1971) in the SBC Archives.

Cothen, Grady C., and James L. Dunn. *Soul Freedom: Baptist Battle Cry.* Atlanta: Smyth & Helwys, 2000.

———. *What Happened to the Southern Baptist Convention?: A Memoir of the Controversy.* Atlanta: Smyth & Helwys, 1993.

Criswell, W. A. *Why I Preach that the Bible is Literally True.* Nashville: Broadman & Holman, 1995 [1969].

Davies, G. Henton. Broadman Bible Commentary: *Genesis.* Nashville: Broadman Press, 1969.

Draper, James T., Jr. *Authority: The Critical Issue for Southern Baptists.* Old Tappan, NJ: Fleming H. Revell Company, 1984.

Elder, Lloyd. *Blueprints: 10 Challenges for a Great People.* Nashville: Broadman Press, 1984.

Elliott, Ralph H. *The Message of Genesis: A Theological Commentary.* Nashville: Broadman Press, 1961.

Fletcher, Jesse C. *The Southern Baptist Convention: A Sesquicentennial History.* Nashville: Broadman & Holman, 1994.

Frost, J. M. *The Sunday School Board of the Southern Baptist Convention: Its History and Work.* Nashville: Sunday School Board, 1916.

May, Lynn E., Jr. *A Brief History of Southern Baptist Sunday School Work.* Manuscript (1964) in the SBC Archives.

McBeth, Leon. *Celebrating Heritage and Hope.* Unpublished centennial history of the Sunday School Board, 1990.

Perry, John. *Walking God's Path: The Life and Ministry of Jimmy Draper.* Nashville: Broadman & Holman, 2005.

Pressler, Paul. *A Hill on Which to Die.* Nashville: Broadman & Holman, 1999.

Shurden, Walter B. *The Sunday School Board: Ninety Years of Service.* Nashville: Broadman Press, 1981.

Sullivan, James L. *Baptist Polity as I See It.* Nashville: Broadman & Holman, 1998.

————. *God Is My Record.* Nashville: Broadman Press, 1974.

Other sources include personal letters and interviews, LifeWay annual reports, trustee meeting minutes, and company correspondence as cited in the text.